After the Decolonial

For Maxine Molyneux
and
in memory of Guillermo O'Donnell

After the Decolonial
Ethnicity, Gender and Social Justice in Latin America

David Lehmann

polity

Copyright © David Lehmann 2022

The right of David Lehmann to be identified as Author of this Work has been asserted in accordance with the UK Copyright, Designs and Patents Act 1988.

First published in 2022 by Polity Press

Polity Press
65 Bridge Street
Cambridge CB2 1UR, UK

Polity Press
101 Station Landing
Suite 300
Medford, MA 02155, USA

All rights reserved. Except for the quotation of short passages for the purpose of criticism and review, no part of this publication may be reproduced, stored in a retrieval system or transmitted, in any form or by any means, electronic, mechanical, photocopying, recording or otherwise, without the prior permission of the publisher.

ISBN-13: 978-1-5095-3752-5
ISBN-13: 978-1-5095-3753-2 (pb)

A catalogue record for this book is available from the British Library.

Library of Congress Cataloging-in-Publication Data

Names: Lehmann, David, author.
Title: After the decolonial : ethnicity, gender and social justice in Latin America / David Lehmann.
Identifiers: LCCN 2021016748 (print) | LCCN 2021016749 (ebook) | ISBN 9781509537525 (hardback) | ISBN 9781509537532 (paperback) | ISBN 9781509537549 (epub)
Subjects: LCSH: Latin America--Social conditions--21st century. | Latin America--Economic conditions--21st century. | Equality--Latin America. | Latin America--Race relations. | Multiculturalism--Latin America. | Sex role--Latin America.
Classification: LCC HN110.5.A8 L424 2022 (print) | LCC HN110.5.A8 (ebook) | DDC 306.098--dc23
LC record available at https://lccn.loc.gov/2021016748
LC ebook record available at https://lccn.loc.gov/2021016749

Typeset in 10.5 on 12 pt Sabon by
Cheshire Typesetting Ltd, Cuddington, Cheshire
Printed and bound in by Great Britain by CPI Group (UK) Ltd, Croydon

The publisher has used its best endeavours to ensure that the URLs for external websites referred to in this book are correct and active at the time of going to press. However, the publisher has no responsibility for the websites and can make no guarantee that a site will remain live or that the content is or will remain appropriate.

Every effort has been made to trace all copyright holders, but if any have been overlooked the publisher will be pleased to include any necessary credits in any subsequent reprint or edition.

For further information on Polity, visit our website:
politybooks.com

Contents

Preface: In the Time of COVID	vi
Acknowledgements	x
List of Abbreviations	xi
Glossary	xiv

Introduction		1
1	The Latin American Decolonial	19
2	Indigeneity, Gender and Law	72
3	Religion and Culture: Popular, Indigenous and Hegemonic	121
4	From Popular Culture to the Cultures of the People: Evangelical Christianity as a Challenge to the Decolonial	152
Conclusion: Democratizing Democracy		171

Notes	187
References	202
Index	223

Preface: In the time of COVID

Being a Latin Americanist is an emotional involvement. Over fifty years, my life has been enhanced immeasurably, and sometimes dominated, by the irresistible embrace of friendships, partnerships and solidarities. It is like a force field, a vortex, not infrequently tied to utopian imaginaries and the political crises in which they lie buried – crises which in these fatal, murderous years of 2020 and 2021 (as so often, everywhere but Uruguay and Costa Rica) have tested the frontiers of credibility.

It has been an intellectual, professional and personal roller-coaster rising and falling between ephemeral victories of progress and justice and long periods of despondency – the pain of Chile's September 1973, of Argentina's dirty war, of Peru's Sendero Luminoso . . . Few of us do not have friends and colleagues who have suffered exile, imprisonment, torture and death, and that was before the unspeakable, indescribable cruelty of the current occupant of the Brazilian presidency and the irresponsibility of his Mexican counterpart, together presiding over the deaths of hundreds of thousands from disease and organized violence – a multiple of all the dictatorships together.

In the 1970s, Latin American Studies were a festival of ideas and conviviality shrouded in the hope that eventually times would improve and that we would contribute to that improvement. Debates and disputes among the theoretical-political factions raged – in the days when we used to speak to each other. Ours is the luckiest generation ever – something for which future, less fortunate generations may not forgive us. We have been blessed with an abundance of research and travel funding, and the internationalization of postgraduate education which has opened the way to enduring intellectual partnerships and personal friendships.

If I write a book which is quite critical of some of the most influential progressive ideas of our time in Latin America and beyond, it is because

vi

of those experiences and those tragedies. The record of left wing and progressive governments in the region is deeply disappointing: the only truly successful ones were the two terms of Lula's presidency in Brazil, and Mujica in Uruguay. But even Lula's time in office was tarnished by corruption, and then retrospectively by the trials (literally) and tribulations of his successor Dilma Roussef. The impeachment of Dilma, in her second term, was ruthlessly unfair, subjecting her to cruel, shameless, misogynistic vilification. The only other truly left-wing governments were Chile's Unidad Popular, the first period of the Peruvian military regime inaugurated in 1968, and the early Sandinistas, but they all crashed out in military overthrow, economic crisis or armed insurrection openly supported by US intervention. In the light of subsequent prevailing orthodoxies, even the Christian Democrat government that preceded Unidad Popular, could be regarded as left wing. I do not regard post-1973 Peronism as a left-wing, let alone socialist, force, nor will I confer that title on Chavez-Maduro or Correa. They used control of the state to perpetuate themselves in power and neuter opposition, without undertaking sustainable universalist programmes to eliminate poverty or reduce inequality: instead they have distributed benefits to their followers and prebends to their associates and sought to suffocate the media. Evo Morales, like Lula-Dilma, did undertake consistent left-wing reforms only to fall victim to his own abuse of power. Cuba belongs in another category: while Castro's road to power has been imitated, without success save, briefly, in Nicaragua, no political force has ever proclaimed Cuba as a model of government or development.

The leading figures of the decolonial have assembled in a single category the highly diverse group of Chavez-Maduro, Correa, Morales, Mujica and Lula-Dilma, and adopt a dismissive attitude to Marxism; their interpretations privilege culture and colonialism, race and ethnicity over economics, capitalism and class. I ask whether they offer a convincing diagnosis of the current situation and its origins and whether it offers a basis for a historical project to pursue social justice.

I use the words social justice in a universalist sense: sustainable redistribution of income and wealth that extends into the future and is not undone by coups d'état or economic crisis. It is a demanding criterion, for sustainability means that reforms are not undone even in the event of electoral defeat. If they are not politically sustainable, what is the point?

The decolonial is likely to label such universalism 'neoliberal' and 'Eurocentric'. Yet, when I look beyond the grand schema to the research it inspires and the movements it applauds, I find, despite explicit or implicit protestations to the contrary, that the aspirations of legal and feminist anthropologists and indigenist movements like the Zapatistas,

vii

especially indigenous women leaders, are universalist. They are sceptical of projects of cultural regeneration unless they go together with commitments to gender equality, to a reduction of class inequality and to an end to the organized violence which is more pervasive in Latin America than in almost any other part of the world.

The leading figures of the decolonial (its 'gurus') – Aníbal Quijano, Boaventura de Souza Santos, and Water Mignolo – give a 'Latin-style' voice to the social science 'cultural turn'. Rejecting Marxism and, implicitly, its cousin *dependencia*, as Eurocentric, they replace demonization of US imperialism with demonization of European colonialism, and they have shifted the stakes in the global confrontation between the peoples of the Global South and the predatory forces of world capitalism onto the cultural terrain. Colonialism still refers back to the sixteenth century, but the ethnocidal culture and the epistemicide of that period is projected forward to the present and the word is applied to almost any structural power relationship. Latin America's social polarization is conceived in binary racialized terms, perpetuated by cultural inauthenticity and a colonialist modernity inspired by 'Europe'.

It cannot be denied that the decolonial has captured the spirit of the times. Their disinterest in economics mirrors the abandonment of the 'neoliberal' free market ideas by white nationalists in the United States and illiberal democrats in Europe, and the science-denying, COVID-negating 'anti-globalists' surrounding the current Brazilian president. But the decolonial, lacking the radio and TV stations and the billionaire funders to confront those machines, shies away from the politics of the street or the ballot box and confines itself to the podiums of academia.

COVID has arrived as if sent by the merchants of culture war to provide the most dangerous of battlefields the region has known since the Conquest itself, which brought an epidemic that killed 90 per cent of the indigenous population. More murderous than all the twentieth century revolutions, and counter-revolutions, the pandemic has not only revealed cruel inequalities of class and race in the light of day. It has also revealed intractable cultural rifts and has shown that these do not follow ethnic, let alone racial, frontiers. Rather they divide different concepts of religion (those who claim to know God and his will from those for whom religion is tradition and an ethos) and different epistemologies (those who trust science from those who trust only what they themselves are able or willing to see and hear). Today's denialists are as guilty as the colonial invaders and, in response to those who think that adherence to indigenous knowledge and belief systems stands in contradiction to modern science, I have yet to hear that any are to be found among indigenous peoples, their leaders, their shamans or their healers. Denialists

viii

doubt the authority of modernity in the form of science, yet in the name of a perverted notion of modernity disguised as predatory development, they attack indigenous physical and cultural survival. The decolonial denounces modernity for its destruction of indigenous knowledge and the imposition of Eurocentric science, yet today's 'Eurocentrics' seek to destroy indigenous societies in the name of science-scepticism while leaders of indigenous peoples look to the science of climate change and biodiversity, and of course to vaccination, to defend themselves.

As we have known ever since the founding of development economics in the post-war period, Latin America desperately needs a redistribution of income and wealth. By now, it is widely recognized that racial exclusion and gender inequality were missing from the reformisms of that time. But gender and race are neither precisely comparable nor stable categories, as Rogers Brubaker found in his sharply insightful *Trans* (Brubaker 2016). Brubaker was surprised to find that the two words have, so to speak, changed places, notably in the United States: whereas it was for a long time thought that race is a 'construct' while gender was taken to be a stable objective category, it was increasingly being claimed that race was neither a construct nor a matter of self-assignment, whereas gender had become much more fluid and a matter to some extent of personal choice. This controversy will come to the fore when we discuss the role of judges and committees in deciding whether Brazilian university applicants qualify for quota places reserved for blacks.

My argument in the coming pages is that women are a force in indigenous and Afro-descendant movements, and the advance of their feminism should continue to spearhead the undoing of structures of racial exclusion. Movements in defence of indigenous groups and Afro-descendant populations and of women's movements ultimately look to universal values of citizenship and human rights and thus do not offer arguments in support of the decolonial denigration of human rights or citizenship as 'Eurocentric' or, worse, 'neoliberal'. Gender cuts across – *intersects* – the most extensive range of social cleavages and, as the more universal category, it should lead the way in conjunction with classic measures of redistribution and with vigorous punishment of racial and sexual discrimination.

London
April 2021

Acknowledgements

My thanks go first and foremost to Maxine Molyneux whose unfailing encouragement has guided this project from its ragged beginnings as a short polemic to its present incarnation. I dedicate this book to her, and also to the memory of Guillermo O'Donnell whose unique combination of imagination and good sense inspired me and many others, and whose loss I still feel acutely.

I am extremely grateful to Fiona Wilson who read an early draft and, apart from encouraging me to continue, has also given some very sage and welcome advice.

Jean Khalfa generously gave precious time, enabling me to draw on his unparalleled command of the life and work of Frantz Fanon. Mónica Moreno and Rachel Sieder also gave generously of their time, and their detailed comments saved me from several errors of fact and judgement.

Julie Coimbra, moving spirit of the Cambridge Centre for Latin American Studies, has been willing to help in so many ways, especially during the COVID months.

Many other people have helped me, sometimes without even realizing it, by pointing to ideas or sources or stories that found their way into the narrative. Among them I thank especially Antoinette Molinié, Carlos Bolomey, Christian Gros, Claudia Dary, Dawn Ades, Fabiola Bazo, Fernando Calderón, Joanne Rappaport, Libia Tattay, Luis Vazquez[†], Mara Polgovsky, Marjo de Theije, Mónica Moreno, Raphael Lehmann, Richard Chase-Smith, Sarah Radcliffe, Sian Lazar, Simon Susen and Véronique Boyer.

At Polity Press I want to thank John Thompson and Neil de Cort for their sustained encouragement and patience.

List of Abbreviations

CDI – Comisión para el Desarrollo de los Pueblos Indígenas (National Indigenous Peoples' Development Commission – Mexico; formerly INI, later INPI)

CGEIB – Coordinación General de Educación Intercultural y Bilingüe (General Coordinating Body for Intercultural and Bilingual Education – Mexico)

CIDOB – Confederación de Pueblos Indígenas del Oriente, Chaco y Amazonía de Bolivia (Confederation of Indigenous Peoples of the Oriente, Chaco and Amazon Regions of Bolivia)

CIESAS – Centro de Investigación y Estudios Superiores en Antropología Social (Advanced Research and Teaching Centre in Social Anthropology – Mexico)

CIS–INAH – Centro de Investigaciones Superiores del Instituto Nacional de Antropología e Historia (Advanced Research Centre of the National Institute for Anthropology and History – Mexico)

CLACSO – Consejo Latinoamericano de Ciencias Sociales (Latin American Social Science Council)

CONACAMI – Confederación Nacional de Comunidades del Perú Afectadas por la Minería (National Confederation of Peruvian Communities Affected by Mining)

CONADI – Comisión Nacional de Desarrollo Indígena (National Indigenous Development Commission – Chile)

CONAMAQ – Consejo Nacional de Ayllus y Markas de Qullasuyu (National Council of the Ayllus and Markas of Qullasuyu, that is, of the land and territorial councils

LIST OF ABBREVIATIONS

of the Qullasuyu, or southern region of the former Inca Empire)

CRIC – Consejo Regional Indígena del Cauca (Cauca Valley Regional Indigenous Council – Colombia)

CSUTCB – Confederación Sindical Única de Trabajadores Campesinos de Bolivia (United Confederation of Unions of Rural Workers of Bolivia)

EIB – Educación Intercultural Bilingüe (Intercultural and Bilingual Education)

ENAH – Escuela Nacional de Antropología e Historia (National Anthropology and History School – Mexico)

EZLN – Ejercito Zapatista de Liberación Nacional (Zapatista National Liberation Army)

FLICA – Festival Literário Internacional de Cachoeira (Cachoeira International Literary Festival)

FLN – Front de Libération National (National Liberation Front – Algeria)

ICMBio – Instituto Chico Mendes de Conservação da Biodiversidade (Chico Mendes Conservation and Biodiversity Institute – Brazil)

INAH – Instituto Nacional de Antropología e Historia (National Anthropology and History Institute – Mexico)

INALI – Instituto Nacional de Lenguas Indígenas (National Indigenous Languages Institute – Mexico)

INCORA – Instituto Colombiano de Reforma Agraria (Colombian Agrarian Reform Institute)

INCRA – Instituto Nacional de Colonização e Reforma Agraria (National Colonization and Agrarian Reform Institute – Brazil)

INI – Instituto Nacional Indigenista (National Indigenous Institute – Mexico – later CDI-Brazil)

INPI – Instituto Nacional de los Pueblos Indígenas – (National Institute for Indigenous Peoples – Mexico; successor to CDI)

ISER – Instituto Superior de Estudos da Religião (Institute of Advanced Religious Studies – Brazil)

IURD – Igreja Universal do Reino de Deus (Universal Church of the Kingdom of God)

MAS – Movimiento al Socialismo (Movement Towards Socialism – Bolivia)

MERCOSUR – Mercado Común del Sur (Southern Common Market)

MPB – Música Popular Brasileira (Brazilian Popular Music)

xii

LIST OF ABBREVIATIONS

MST – Movimento dos Trabalhadores Rurais Sem Terra – (Landless Rural Workers' Movement – Brazil)

NAFTA – North American Free Trade Agreement (later USCMA)

PRI – Partido Revolucionario Institucional (Mexico)

PT – Partido dos Trabalhadores (Workers' Party – Brazil)

SERVEL – Servicio Electoral de Chile (Chilean Electoral Service)

THOA – Taller de Historia Oral Andino (Andean Oral History Workshop)

TIPNIS – Territorio Indígena y Parque Nacional Isiboro Secure (Isiboro Secure Indigenous Territory and National Park)

UAIIN – Universidad Autónoma Indígena e Intercultural (Autonomous Indigenous and Intercultural University – Colombia)

UFMG – Universidade Federal de Minas Gerais (Federal University of Minas Gerais – Brazil)

UNICH – Universidad Intercultural de Chiapas (Intercultural University of Chiapas – Mexico)

USCMA – US–Canada–Mexico Agreement

UVI – Universidad Veracruzana Intercultural (Veracruz Intercultural University – Mexico)

Glossary

ayllu – autonomous communal authority overseeing land allocation among households in highland Bolivian communities

cabildo – council of a community or locality

caboclos – people of mixed race (Indian, black, white) in Amazonia; also spirits that assume innumerable forms as their presence is detected or summoned by a medium

calidad indígena – legally recognized indigenous status

campesino – peasant or small farmer

Candomblé – type of possession cult in the Yoruba tradition

capilaridade – capacity of asocial movement to penetrate deep among the interstices of a social milieu

cholas, cholos – persons of mixed race or intermediate social status in the Andean socio-racial hierarchy

cimarronaje – having features in common with escaped slaves (cimarrones)

cocaleros – coca growers

colonos – colonists who come from outside and bring 'uncultivated' land under the plough or who occupy territory where the state is virtually absent. Usually, these lands and territories are used and occupied by indigenous peoples

compadre – co-godparent

criollo – of mixed white and indigenous race; also means native to or bred in the Americas (but not indigenous)

despatriarcalización – process of removing patriarchal features from society

ejido – form of quasi-collective land tenure under the Mexican Agrarian Reform

estética negra – a politically nuanced style of dress and hair fashionable among young black people in Brazil, especially Bahia

GLOSSARY

interculturalidad – an approach to education and institutional arrangements that recognizes indigenous heritage and encourages indigenous participation and the learning of indigenous languages and culture

ladinos – elite predominantly white people constituting a quasi-caste in Guatemala

machis – Mapuche shamans (mostly women)

malandragem – roguishness

mandar obedeciendo – 'to lead while obeying' (said to be a Tojolabal motto)

media luna – 'crescent moon': the lowland region of Bolivia comprising the departments of Tarija, Pando, Beni and Santa Cruz

mestizo – light-skinned

moreno – brown-skinned

movimento negro – black movement

originario – founding, as in *nación originaria*, referring to indigenous ethno-linguistic groups

paramilitares – 'paramilitaries', organized groups who engage in violent action against Indians and social and indigenous activists, and nominally against guerrillas, in Colombia

pardo – brown; used in official statistics and classification in Brazil

preto – literally 'black', denoting the deepest black skin colour; a term mostly used in Brazil in official statistics and classifications, which do not use *negro*

quilombo, quilombola – settlements of escaped slaves and the people who live in them

regiones de refugio – literally refuge zones, referring to isolated regions with predominantly Indian populations living outside the market economy

resguardos – the institutional form of indigenous ownership of land in Colombia

saudade – a distinctively Brazilian nostalgic sadness or sense of loss, and associated musical styles

sindicatos campesinos – peasant unions (Bolivia)

tercermundista – supporter of a nationalist, anti-imperialist worldview which opposes the countries of the global South (formerly 'Third World ') to Europe and the United States

terreiros – sites of *Candomblé* ceremonies

usos y costumbres – customs and traditions of indigenous people

Introduction

In recent decades the most academically influential intelligentsia of the Latin American left have retreated behind the walls of the university, even while they denounce the social order more comprehensively than any previous Latin American ideology. In their diagnosis, Latin American society is characterized by a polarized and polarizing colonial apparatus of racialized domination that has existed unchanged for 500 years and infuses all relations of unequal power and status as well as the mindset of its populations. This diagnosis functions as an indictment of institutions, socio-economic structures and ideologies – like Marxism and liberalism – as well as of the subconscious mechanism where racial prejudice is implanted. There results a cast of mind in which ethnic identities not only have their place, as they must do, but also take precedence over other themes like class, gender, violence, institutional stagnation and collapse, public health, organized crime, corruption . . . the list is very long.

This reductionism discourages political activity by creating a climate of despair and negativity, and indeed this philosophy of the decolonial, or *lo decolonial*, as I call the Latin American branch of postcolonialism, constitutes a hemisphere-wide network whose activism is directed at the internal life of academia rather than at politics on the street, in the media, in election campaigns or in institutions of the state. It denounces the Marxist nebula, which over generations guided even the moderate Latin American left, for its denial of the racial basis of domination, and disqualifies liberalism for its complicity with colonialism and slavery. Paradoxically, then, the world of the decolonial is characterized by quietism in the public sphere of politics and shrill rhetoric within the halls and Twittersphere of academe. In this it can be contrasted with feminist tendencies that also call themselves decolonial, and in addition autonomous, and are more involved in extra-mural politics by virtue of

INTRODUCTION

their activist field research and their participation in women's and LGBT movements.

This distinctively Latin American tendency is a largely self-sufficient subculture, so I will restrict myself to the output of Latin Americans and Latin Americanists – many operating out of the United States – and of particular authors whom they quote. I also take care to refer to particular writings, and readily admit that it is impossible to cover the entire output of a very prolific group of authorities. My plea is for the restoration of the pursuit of universalist social justice to its rightful place in the thought of the region's left, and I conclude by according the pursuit of gender equality at least parity with the politics of racial and ethnic identity and racial empowerment.

By universalist social justice, I mean a primary focus on the redistribution of income and wealth based on socio-economic criteria and an understanding of social class and gender as drivers of inequality. Universalist justice also means the investigation and punishment of acts of racial discrimination. This is particularly important because whereas indigenous populations can mobilize along identity lines in support of claims to intercultural education, to restitution of usurped lands and to the re-establishment of their own institutions in the form of laws and self-government, Afro-descendant populations rarely are in a position to make such claims, yet they are also victims of racial exclusion and acts of discrimination. To free those populations of these burdens, policies must focus on universal justice and universalist equality, as must policies to change gender inequalities, and they can also include affirmative action. This distinction between identity politics and universalist justice, which are far from mutually exclusive, remains important.

The other reason for foregrounding universalism is largely practical and has little to do with the frequently drawn contrast between universalism and relativism. It is based on the observation that the frontiers of racial and ethnic populations, and thus the basis on which resources will be allocated under affirmative action or multicultural policies, are impossible to draw independently of political judgements about where those frontiers lie, or even personal judgements about whether a particular person is black, brown or white, or *indio, cholo, mestizo* or *blanco*. Distribution on the basis of socio-economic status, gender, age or region, in contrast, is in principle less likely to be challenged for its subjective character. Of course, the criteria of class belonging are subject to debate, but at least they can be established on the basis of agreed rational discussion. I have set much store by the merits of gender as a universalist basis on which to pursue equality, even though self-assignation is an ever more prominent element in gender classification, simply because the

2

scale of the phenomenon is still small compared to the exclusive use of self-assignation in racial and ethnic classification. Although the ground is shifting under both regimes of classification, I still would maintain that for some time to come classification by gender will remain less open to politicization. I therefore advocate the restoration of a degree of balance between gender and race in discussions about inequality and rights, even while allowing plenty of room for intersectionality between them.

On this basis, universal rights are rights that belong to all human beings and should be adjudicated according to features that can be assigned to all human beings. This is the case for differentiating features such as age, gender and social class, whereas indigenous laws can apply only to people of particular indigenous groups. Indigenous rights, however – as distinct from indigenous laws – are universal in the sense that anyone claiming indigenous status should be treated in accordance with universal rights, not least the right to non-discrimination. My argument in the chapters that follow is that the systems of indigenous law advocated in decolonial debates are for the most part perfectly compatible with universal rights and should not be considered different in kind from positive law, even if they apply only within a certain population or region.

The institutional and social setting

Since about 1992 race, ethnicity and gender have become the leading topics shaping the scholarly interpretation of two of Latin America's most distressing problems: inequality and the abuse of human rights by both state and private actors. This is the case among Latin Americanists throughout the western hemisphere and also in Europe: those subjects have set the agenda in publication, in conferences and in university teaching. The broadly left-wing or simply dissident political sensibility which has long dominated the humanities and social science departments of public universities remains, but the content has shifted from Marxism towards identity politics. By identity politics in the university context, I mean recourse to racial, ethno-linguistic, religious and gender ascription or belonging for explanations of advantage and disadvantage in society as a whole, but also in internal matters affecting the university, such as the curriculum, the profile of the student body and the professoriat. The *bodies* of those involved are also at stake in the less visible and less audible shaping of scholarly and pedagogical discourse and exchange. The academic business of teaching, of the exchange of research and of management, is influenced (not necessarily in a negative sense) by

INTRODUCTION

the physical and online presence, or absence, of people who recognize themselves and are recognized by ascription to a population defined by skin colour, by religion, by gender or by ethnic or ethno-linguistic background.

Identity politics occurs when such belonging, in and of itself, confers authority or legitimacy on a speaker or author. It comes in many shapes and forms, sometimes to include and sometimes to exclude, sometimes to break down barriers and sometimes to erect them, sometimes to facilitate exchange and sometimes to interrupt it.

The visibility and audibility of identity politics comes at a time of growth in the number and presence of students from Afro-descendant and indigenous backgrounds in Latin American universities and research institutions, but the presence of professors from those backgrounds lags far behind. Nonetheless, universities have been pioneering spaces where those groups have found a voice ahead of other institutions such as professional bodies or the judiciary.

There has also been a change in the class composition of the professoriat, which is now drawn less from the upper-middle classes than was once the case. University salaries may guarantee security to those with tenure, but they no longer guarantee an upper-middle class existence, and an ever-increasing number of highly qualified people with Masters degrees and doctorates, finding difficulty getting a full-time academic job, are making a living on short-term or hourly contracts. The proliferation of private and public universities and the concomitant growth of student numbers have also expanded the profession, contributing to refined gradations of prestige, status, income and locational differences. This structural change may have added an edge to the traditional dissident posture of academics.

The expression 'ivory tower' is anachronistic in a world where there are millions of undergraduates, hundreds of thousands of graduate students and tens of thousands of professors. Academia today constitutes a political arena and a market all of its own where interest groups compete for resources, for departments and centres, for publication outlets, for research funds and for the power of patronage.

A similar scenario exists in the United States where identity politics has been a standard feature of university life for longer than in Latin America and where significant numbers of students and professors teaching and following courses on Latin America are immigrants or people from immigrant families. This US-based contingent can be said to form a single constituency with Latin American humanities and social science: the distinction between a Latin American scholar and an 'American' scholar is blurred. They conduct their exchanges equally in English, Spanish and

Portuguese, are riven by similar disagreements and are fired by similar enthusiasms. Until 2020, the more prominent figures among them have been fixtures on the same hemisphere-wide lecture, workshop and conference circuits. Decolonial scholarship is a mutation of identity politics adapted to the arena of the university and of scholarship.

Identity politics brought the question of representation into the university and now contests the content of teaching. In its Latin Americanist strand, decolonialism's theme is not inequality of access to science but the biases and prejudices that lie at the heart of science itself and the instrumentalization of science to fashion weapons used against indigenous peoples and Afro-descendants.

Much as it may challenge the institutions of science and academia and all they stand for, decolonial advocacy depends on those institutions. This marks a difference from the radical autonomist wings like Black Power that broke away from anti-racist movements such as civil rights. Decolonials express little interest in those breakaways, or in the Latin American guerrilla forces that broke with the 'Moscow line' after the Cuban Revolution and went into action across the region over three decades. Yet the decolonial theoretical onslaught on today's social order is even more radical: those Marxist revolutionaries had no issues with science or with modernity, and for the most part assumed that in a socialist society the problems of indigenous peoples and people of colour would be overcome, as would inequality between the sexes (to use the language of the time). They sought a different modernity, but a modernity nonetheless, in which the class structure and economic system would be replaced. Decolonials contest the entire culture of modernity and are dismissive of the universal values embodied, in their very different ways, in Marxism and liberalism. Yet professionally they remain within the 'system', and although they do profess admiration for the questionably democratic practices of Chavez-Maduro, Christina Kirschner, Evo Morales and Rafael Correa, they certainly do not advocate violence.

So much is background. I have depicted it in summary form because scholarly writing tends to sidestep the institutional context of its production, but to offer a full analysis would require another research project. We have much to learn from ethnographies and a macro sociology of academia that would test these generalizations.

Critique of the decolonial

Chapter 1 offers a genealogy of the decolonial, beginning with three precursors – Said, Fanon and Emmanuel Levinas. I show Said to be a

INTRODUCTION

universalist occasionally co-opted by over-binarized anti-western versions of identity politics. Fanon's universalist values are ignored by the decolonial and his outlook on the world vulgarized by making him into an enemy of European culture and a supporter of nationalism, neither of which describes his values. Fanon's eloquence is directed against racism, pure and simple: he fiercely opposed *négritude* and blackness as an identity to be valued in and of itself, and his ideal was a world without race. When he sympathizes with violence, it is in the context of the response of the peasant masses to the unspeakable violence inflicted by French colonial forces, but he does not provide a blanket endorsement of violence, as even Hannah Arendt, often quoted for her hostility to Fanon, eventually recognized. Their invocation of the notoriously impenetrable but widely admired Levinas as a precursor is the most puzzling, and setting him besides Fanon equally so, making for a very odd couple. In what I call an instance of 'forced politicization', they have even co-opted his *Leçons Talmudiques* in support of an effort to make Levinas into a *tercermundista* or Third World nationalist.

The decolonial in its Latin American version is further criticized for several reasons:

- its trivialization of the universal in human rights, in feminism and in science;
- its confection of a binary opposition of the indigenous and the European, or western, as if almost nothing has changed in 500 years and with no consideration of the heterogeneity of hundreds of ethnolinguistic groups;
- the relativization of human rights in contention with collective rights;
- its obliviousness in the face of the mixtures and exchanges which pervade race, religion, culture and class relations in Latin America;
- the confusion of differences of culture with different 'epistemologies';
- its obliviousness to women, to inequalities of gender and to violence against women (excluding the feminist variant of the decolonial)
- its oversimplified use of the word 'neo-liberalism'.

The leading philosopher of the decolonial, Enrique Dussel, is a difficult figure to summarize: formed in theology and an adept of liberation theology, during the 1970s he oversaw the multi-volume *Historia de la Iglesia en América Latina*. The 600-page first volume, despite its unorthodox organization, interspersing transcribed documents and narrative, bears witness to the depth of his Catholic learning and to his vast knowledge of the history not only of the Catholic Church but of religion in the entire region, going back to pre-conquest times (Dussel 1974, 1983–1994). Yet

INTRODUCTION

after that his writings bifurcate: on the one hand highly politicized and polemical interventions; and on the other complex philosophical works which he places in a phenomenological lineage quite different from his early involvement in liberation theology. Other leading decolonials (principally Boaventura de Sousa Santos, Walter Mignolo and Nelson Maldonado-Torres) write in a macho style that disqualifies all that stands in their way, proclaiming a set of 'truths universally acknowledged' without offering evidence when they refer to history and, when they are philosophical, name-dropping in the place of a reasoned genealogy. Their attack on western science is unsupported by an account of science itself, and their interpretations of colonialism are based on superficial generalizations or, when they do use historical sources, on misinterpretation. They write as if today's colonial order is no different from that of the sixteenth century and do not explain why they sidestep the influence of the United States – once the whipping boy of choice for Latin American nationalist and marxisant thought. Decolonial 'gurus' even single out Descartes as responsible for reducing non-European peoples to the status of non-humans and describe his *cogito* as a banner for colonial conquest. The result is a polarization of the field between their fans and their critics or, better, between their fans and those who ignore them and are ignored by them. The field of Latin American Studies has become divided: fans and non-fans attend separate conferences, organize separate panels, publish in separate journals and thus avoid the clash of ideas – a refusal of exchange that is a common feature of contemporary scholarly life in general. I do not venture a view on whether this is to be blamed on the decolonials or on their opponents.

I do not claim that the decolonial has been built on false problems. Some decolonial writing is based on an important theme, which Boaventura de Souza Santos calls the 'abyss'. The abyss divides society into two spaces: that which is governed by law and inhabited by people who receive the protection of the law and the state, and a vast periphery where government is in the hands of unofficial bodies (like drug traffickers and militia), where official bodies only enter to inflict repression or exactions, where business is conducted with neither regulation nor certification nor taxation, where citizens, having no effective rights, are reduced to the condition of supplicants. Although the model is simplified beyond measure, it does convey vividly the failure of many Latin American states. It also should highlight the interdependence of the two 'worlds', especially the dependence of politicians on traffickers and militia, and their penetration of police forces. And then, in the penultimate chapter, there is a surprise as we find evangelical churches poised on the edges of the abyss, and sometimes straddling it.

7

INTRODUCTION

The colonial in anthropology

The next chapter approaches the decolonial in anthropology via the usages of the influential term 'internal colonialism' in mid-twentieth-century Mexican scholarship, and the feminist and legal anthropology which has been a salient feature of recent Mexican social science.

A close reading of this very rewarding literature shows that, despite their occasional protestations to the contrary, Mexican feminist anthropologists are universalists because, while by no means dismissing the value of cultural recognition, they prioritize the question of violence against women and effective equal opportunities for them over the cultural rights of indigenous peoples.

Those anthropologists were the first to extract a feminist message from the Zapatista phenomenon, which hit the headlines on January 1994 as an uprising more strategic in its theatrical performance than in its political effectiveness, and continues as a quasi-independent enclave in the Southern Mexican state of Chiapas. The original Zapatistas and associated organizations said little about activist women or gender, although they demonstrated their feminism by the presence of women in leading positions, including as military commanders, but in their subsequent research the anthropologists found women who infused the movement's message with a defence of their rights and their bodies. The Zapatista leaders were the product of a Marxist and Maoist stream going back to the 1960s, and only discovered their indigenous vocation after they had found glamour in the world's media. By returning to the literature on the background to the uprising and its setting in the Lacandonian jungle of Chiapas I have been able to recognize its originality and the context in which its ideals were forged.

The feminist anthropologists force open the issues of class and ethnicity (Hernández Castillo 2003; Sieder 2017). The most original figure among them, the Bolivian Silvia Rivera Cusicanqui, defies categorization in one or another camp of identity or left-wing politics and rejects identification with one or another racial or ethnic group in a society at once predominantly *indio* and also marked by pervasive *métissage*. These feminist-ethnic intersections draw our attention to important tools in the understanding of Latin American society, and in later chapters I describe those in detail with examples, mostly from Bolivia, whose intelligentsia have generated some of the most compelling debates about race and gender.

8

INTRODUCTION

Popular religion, culture and ethnicity

To begin to see beyond the decolonial, I explore the conceptualization and application of everyday words like *indio* or *mestizo* and the frontiers they convey in the interpretation of the region's acute inequality. This means taking account of blurred social and racial frontiers and the frequent ambiguity of relationships across those frontiers, and avoiding assumptions about the homogeneity and uniformity of ethno-linguistic and racial populations and frontiers. I then move on to the subject of popular culture, which in Latin American is a crossroads, a meeting point and sometimes a flashpoint for socially stratified and racially differentiated streams, to show how the interpretation of cultural practices in terms of race, ethnicity, gender and religion can both take account of intersectionality and avoid binarization.

I begin with the supernatural (religion) and the pervasive presence of mixture and of borrowing, both self-conscious ('reflexive') and filtered through decades and centuries of the collective unconscious. Decolonial writing on indigenous knowledge or science misses out on the place of ritual and the difference between rituals of healing and the efficacy of healing. It tends to assimilate the efficacy of folk remedies and folk wisdom (for example, as applied to agricultural practices) to scientific knowledge: because it is the fruit of generations of experimentation and observation in societies based on agriculture and animal husbandry, such wisdom may well provide reliable guidance for growing plants, raising animals and treating minor ailments, but as knowledge it should not be described as scientific in the usual (Anglo-Saxon) sense[1] because it is not conducted in the impersonal institutions of science. Conversely, every day there is abundant evidence of indigenous support for modern science: indigenous organizations throughout the Amazon and the Andes are constantly campaigning on climate change which is devastating their livelihoods, and during the current pandemic, when Amazon Indian groups are suffering from a higher death rate than the population as a whole, leaders have told that, although people have tried their folk medicine, they are painfully and tragically aware that they need the almost inaccessible resources of modern medicine.

The decolonial concept of indigeneity sets aside the multi-directional influences whereby, in the field of religion, popular Catholicism incorporates indigenous ritual and ceremony and indigenous ceremonies incorporate Catholic practices shaped by centuries of mixture. Outsiders are alert to the colonial or indigenous origins of the practices and symbols they observe, but those who perform them – whether they think

9

INTRODUCTION

of themselves as *indios, cholos* or *mestizos*[2] – seem uninterested in such questions of authenticity. The discussion becomes even more convoluted when ethno-historians tell us that urban intellectuals in Bolivia are misinterpreting indigenous concepts like the now globalized Pachamama, or when we learn that indigenous healers in Chile, practising out of dedicated spaces in public hospitals and travelling the globe to administer their herbal remedies, are sought out by people who make no claim to an indigenous heritage at all.[3]

As with religion, so with race and ethnicity. The field is riven with markers of inequality, yet the frontiers are porous. Using a Bolivian case, I describe the perpetual exchanges of ethnic symbols and markers and the ways in which they serve nevertheless to solidify social inequalities and racial exclusion, something that cannot be said of art, music, dance and civic commemorations. Evo Morales solved the problem by inventing a pan-ethnic indigenism which gathered all the country's indigenous peoples, indeed the entire population (except the lowland rancher elite) under its wing. Like the country's nationalist 1952 revolution, which gave birth to a *mestizo* middle class, the new ideology disregarded the internal inequalities and fractures of the coalition, especially the lowland Amazonian Indians, and oversaw the continued development of a *burguesía criolla* – imperfectly translated as a 'Creole bourgeoisie'.[4] Morales made his political career as leader of the tightly organized and hierarchical coca growers' association (the *cocaleros*) fighting for freedom to grow their crops. The coca leaf was a useful cultural symbol – the first of many deployed by Evo – but their demands were not cultural – they wanted freedom to grow and sell their crop and the cancellation of the government's agreement with the United States to destroy their plantations.

Exchanges of ritual practices and ethnic markers across boundaries that have evolved over centuries can be conceptualized as a dialectic of the erudite, or elite, and the popular, in which the awareness and definition of what is one and what is the other are subjective and fluctuating. This formula sets aside issues of ethnic authenticity and heritage and subsumes fields such as religion and civic celebrations into a broader framework, which is provided by Nestor García Canclini. Canclini's writing revolves around hybridity, stimulated by a Mexican art world at once conscious of the country's popular heritage and attuned to global trends and fashions. The dialectic is compounded by agonizing over the artistic status of folk art and crafts such as the artefacts one buys in provincial markets, but then migrates into postmodern register when he considers the 'kitsch' architecture in the Americanized cities of the country's northern border. The dominant theme is of porous frontiers.

INTRODUCTION

Race, ethnicity and gender: in search of social justice

How can one think of social justice on the basis of the experience of indigenous movements? Taking as examples the Zapatistas and the less well-known but more institutionalized Colombian Consejo Regional Indígena del Cauca (Cauca Valley Indigenous Regional Council – CRIC – which celebrated its fiftieth anniversary in 2021), I emphasize institution building and the advancement of women. As noted earlier, the women who have been active in the Zapatista areas of Chiapas have had to work hard to challenge generations of subordination. In the CRIC, we observe women advancing to positions of responsibility thanks especially to its initiatives in the field of intercultural education. Both movements have had to build organizations able to deal with economic necessities, with land tenure and with governance, requiring traditional institutions to be reformed substantially. The CRIC is founded on two colonial institutions – the *resguardo* and the *cabildo*; the *resguardo* is a territorial concept denoting land assigned to *indios*, in a regime of collective entitlement, and the *cabildos* are the institutions governing their internal affairs. Judicial procedures have had to adapt to the requirements of the national judicial system which has recognized and incorporated them. We know little of how the Zapatistas have dealt with issues of law, especially as compared to the openness of the CRIC, but sympathetic observers have received explanations of their painstaking system of consultation and feedback between local and regional decision-making bodies. We have to take their word for it, but it would appear that they are establishing procedures that are more in keeping with modern ideas of participatory democracy than indigenous concepts of authority, despite the constant reiteration of the formula *mandar obedeciendo* ('taking command while obeying'), drawn from Chiapas indigenous culture.

There is an emerging pattern of judicialization of the indigenous and race questions, perhaps on the pattern of the judicialization of politics which has been much remarked upon in the region. In Colombia, the judicial system can intervene to rule on the correctness of indigenous proceedings. In Mexico, land tenure disputes involving indigenous title have long fallen within the purview of the state's judicial system, not of indigenous customary proceedings (*usos y costumbres*).

The Brazilian affirmative action system for entry to universities has brought about what many would regard as a strange, even unacceptable, situation in which it is not unusual for judges to decide a person's racial assignment, and for formally established university committees to review applications for entry via the race quota to check for 'fraudulent'

11

self-assignments of skin colour. The quotas are in effect a positive discrimination system that reserves places for black, brown and indigenous people in a country whose chromatic race relations regime renders racial classification essentially contestable, so it is not surprising that disputes – even denunciations – may arise, leading to judicialization.

These examples are not evidence that universalist concepts of *social justice* are being implemented via the courts, but they do show that as a result of indigenous mobilizations in Colombia and of the adoption of affirmative action policies in Brazil, universalist criteria of law are being applied to the causes of indigenous or Afro-descendant justice. The road, however, can be rather rocky: judicial involvement in land tenure in Mexico and the implementation of local government in accordance with *usos y costumbres* in Colombia have not been immune to the influence of organized crime, guerrillas or paramilitaries. The most complete case of confluence of an indigenist rationale and the judicial system that I have found is in the Mexican state of Oaxaca, where the entire electoral system was reformed in the 1990s to allow institutional recognition of *usos y costumbres*. Yet this has also brought the national and state electoral authorities into an oversight role in which they have intervened to enforce legislation concerning women's participation and gender parity in elections in the face of persistent chicanery.

Indigenous movements press governments to pass legislation and to make resources available, but it is noticeable that in order to survive and evolve over time – like the CRIC and the Zapatistas – they have to build institutions of their own, and we see how in those processes women come to the fore.

We can see contrasts by comparing the weakness or absence of indigenous movements in Mexico outside Chiapas and in Chile where indigenous claims are mobilized in fragmented ways and have not developed institutionally. The difference arises from a lack of depth which would enable them to extend their activities, in Chile, beyond the ceremonial role of shamans to, for example, governance, education, the law and land tenure. Yet the Chilean Mapuche struggles and the repression inflicted in their region by the government have made their cause emblematic for the nationwide movement to democratize the country's democracy: in Santiago's Plaza Dignidad (as it has been popularly re-baptized) the only flag to be seen at regular demonstrations is the Mapuche flag – no party emblems, no national flag – and a Mapuche woman was elected president of the country's Constitutional Convention in 2021.

The goals of indigenous movements are very often the same as those of other movements, such as those fighting for housing in cities and not least those fighting for human rights. They are in the forefront of

INTRODUCTION

causes of universal concern, for example, contesting mining licences in vulnerable environments like the Amazon and the Andean highlands and Guatemala, and resisting illegal mining especially in the Amazon. Conflicts over mining and indigenous rights claims to territorial autonomy and over environmental defence are often one and the same.

This universalism was particular evident in the early days of the Zapatistas. In conjunction with catechists trained by the Archdiocese of San Cristobal de las Casas, they were defending people from different ethno-linguistic groups who had been forced to migrate as a result of the shift to cattle rearing in highland estates where for generations they worked in semi-feudal conditions. Those people were *indios* but had been living in conditions of servitude rather than in corporate communities, and their leaders were steeped in the rhetoric of liberation theology and secular revolution. They were most certainly victims of racial oppression, and the banner of indigenism served as a rallying cry, as a source of solidarity and importantly as a magnet attracting the sympathy of a certain current of international opinion, but the restoration or protection of indigenous culture formed but one part of their demands. Their movement was inspired principally by a demand for land, for the confirmation of their tenure of land they were already occupying, for socio-economic improvement, and for freedom from repression by the state and landlords. Even before the armed uprising in 1994, they were building institutions, forming cooperatives to manage land they had occupied in the Lacandón forest – but these were not indigenous community institutions.

Evo Morales played this counterpoint between indigenist and other themes like a virtuoso. He cleverly proclaimed the country's indigenous vocation in terms which made the word 'indigenous' itself an ethnic category while downplaying the recognition of numerous ethno-linguistic groups within it. The Constitution drawn up under his auspices recognized formally a long list of nations with their own languages and legal systems, but the recognition remained on paper. He may well have feared the divisive effects of such multiple recognitions, and those whose livelihoods depended on the fragile ecological equilibrium in the Amazonian lowlands were an obstacle to his hydrocarbon-driven neo-developmentalist strategy.

Evangelical Christianity

Although this popular-erudite dialectic offers a neat framework, spanning the supernatural and also the world of art, music and culture in general, the epidemiological – indeed pandemic – spread of evangelical

INTRODUCTION

Christianity has produced a large and noisy culture area where it does not apply. The same goes for the decolonial, whose reification and exaltation of indigenous culture and knowledge loses some of its credibility in the face of the success of evangelicals among indigenous peoples. For a century, the churches have built cultural worlds where indigenous religious practices, but not indigenous identities or languages, have lost their resonance (save as channels of demonic possession), and where political demands for indigenous rights receive little encouragement. The evangelical, or Pentecostal, faithful, with their rituals of healing and baptism, consummate a rupture with both the Catholic popular culture of fiestas and commemorative processions and the affirmation of class and ethnic difference in carnivals, dance and music, while also rejecting the permissive society and, more recently, departures from traditional forms of marriage and gender roles. The ideal evangelical life requires withdrawal from civic and religious fiestas, at least in principle, renunciation of alcohol and tobacco, and embodies an aspiration to middle-class respectability. In a pattern that invites comparison with social movements, with education and with the professions, women are a driving force in their ranks, though rarely in the leadership. Participation in church life also encourages women to bring about change in their families and to strive for entrepreneurial success.

Evangelical culture seems to stand at the antipodes of what the decolonial might conceive as a politics in its image. Why have a following who could be expected to pursue liberation from colonial oppression, being predominantly drawn from low-income groups and from excluded racial and ethnic populations, joined the churches in such great numbers? How could they have placed their trust in preachers who show no interest in the structures that oppress them or in the racism that excludes them? How can they accept a doctrine that invokes divine authority in teaching self-reliance and legitimizes the neo-liberalism responsible for their oppression? How could it be that Pentecostal churches persuade not only indigenous people who live in the market economy and under the direct authority of modern state apparatuses but also others (in remote highland and lowland tropical environments), who have had but limited contact with states or with the hegemonic languages, to engage in practices that appear to glorify a divinity utterly foreign to their own traditions? How could they retain a predominantly female following while for the most part excluding women from positions of leadership? These questions become even more urgent when we come to neo-Pentecostal churches, with their highly centralized global organizations, their proclamation of material well-being as an end in itself and their disruptive intervention in electoral politics.

14

INTRODUCTION

Pentecostalism is not a comfortable sort of dissidence, but it is a dissidence in several senses: it is a religious dissidence which stands apart from a still hegemonic Catholicism; it is a cultural dissidence that stands against the permissive society and against intellectual elites, and against those elements of popular culture that draw on tradition, on indigeneity, on African heritage and on rituals of 'the world turned upside down' like carnival. It cannot be dismissed merely as false consciousness, as an artefact of neo-liberalism or as a money-making machine.

Interpreting Pentecostalism requires a compromise between the evidence of many shared characteristics within and between countries and cultures across the globe, especially the style of meetings and the ethical content of preaching, and innumerable local variations in scale and in class and ethnic composition. Explanations in terms of the power of neo-liberalism and its mediatic allies to intoxicate the minds of the illiterate masses may be criticized as expressions of patronizing intellectual arrogance, but there is plenty of evidence that certain sorts of churches – mainly neo-Pentecostals – are collecting incalculable amounts of money from followers in response to promises of health and wealth and a life free from demonic powers. Is this evidence of a partnership between the churches and neo-liberalism? And how do we interpret some pastors' collusion with the drug traffic as well as supposed addiction recovery? Evangelical politics have veered sharply to the right in Colombia and Brazil, while church leaders have successfully pursued political careers on the back of appeals to family values and a fierce denunciation of permissiveness and non-traditional sexualities, paving the way for the (very narrow) defeat of the consultative peace referendum in Colombia in 2017 and the large second-round majority of a fiercely illiberal president in Brazil in 2018. And yet Pentecostalism also retains many features of religion as we conventionally conceive of it: many local church leaders (the ones who do not pursue wealth and power) regard such extravagances with contempt, and there are also innumerable churches where prayer is an act performed for its own sake, rather than as a plea for a windfall or for help in finding a suitable life partner.

Pentecostalism has for long raised many questions for ready-made models in the interpretation of Latin American culture, and the recent aggressive political turn associated with neo-Pentecostalism has been an additional shock, both practical and intellectual, to those models, whether modernist, postmodernist or decolonial.

INTRODUCTION

Indigenous movements and democracy

The focus of academic and political debate about indigenous movements on what they have done for their followers and their ethnic constituencies, and on what external forces have done or should do for them, has distracted from what they do for society as a whole. By fighting discrimination, they also fight for civil and human rights. By demanding recognition, they raise awareness of a nation's history and of the neglect of their social exclusion and maltreatment in dominant as well as dissenting (Marxist and marxisant) narratives of a nation's history. This is most glaringly visible in the standard phrase voiced when Argentina's indigenous people are mentioned: 'there are no longer any Indians in this country: they were all massacred in the nineteenth century.' The phrase manages to recognize yet also to relativize the appalling violence unleashed against the Araucanian Indians by the Campaña del Desierto in the 1870s. It is also untrue: Argentina has in recent years 'discovered' or rediscovered a significant and vocal indigenous population. The recognition of these populations and of their right to full citizenship is a contribution to the democratization of a society – in Bolivia, it has gone together with an incorporation of a mass of the population whose previous political participation had been extra-institutional. In Chile, growing awareness of the Mapuche demands has contributed to the atmosphere of dissent and disillusion underlying the 2020 referendum and opening the way to a new Constitution. In Brazil, what began in the 1990s as a demand for quotas in universities for black students has extended into many walks of life, for example into the fashion world, into the allocation of funds for political campaigns, and into the appointment of public servants. Meanwhile, more and more Brazilians were declaring themselves black or brown so that by now there is a consensus that more than half the population count themselves as *negro* or *moreno* (brown) and thus as part of the quota-eligible class formally described in censuses as *pretos*, *pardos* and *indígenas* (black, brown and indigenous). The effect can be called democratizing in two senses: increasing awareness of racial discrimination and inequality in society; and an ever-broadening access to affirmative action. Unfortunately, as of 2021, the country's president has no interest in democracy, yet despite expressing hostility to quota systems, he has not attempted to reverse them.

If these movements have indeed contributed to a democratization of some kind in society, we must at the same time recognize that Latin American political institutions, that is, Latin American democracy, broadly speaking, has entered a retrogressive phase since 2010:

16

INTRODUCTION

authoritarianism and abuse of power are on the increase under governments of the right as well as others thought to be of the left.

Indigenous and anti-racist movements are openings. Assembled under a broad banner of identity, they are able to absorb, or shelter, a range of ideas and ideals and varied racial and ethno-linguistic groups. Indigenous movements represent indigenous people and are carried forward by their leaders, but the restoration or protection of indigenous culture is but one part of their demands and activities. Their most notable other achievements are in the spheres of institution building and the position of women. Because of the weakness or absence of the state, or to avoid co-optation, they build institutions of land tenure and collective self-management, and sometimes they construct development agencies with the help of international NGOs. Women are becoming more and more prominent in their ranks and among their leaders, often challenging deeply embedded practices. The democratic impetus embodied in movements of ethnic and excluded racial populations can eventually nurture embryonic forces that join with others to democratize society as a whole.

That impetus has also provoked a reaction. The abrasive conservatism that led to the election of Bolsonaro was justified by hostility to race quotas, to the reservation of land for Indians in the Amazon, and to liberal openings in the field of sexuality and gender. Repressive and patriarchal notions of family and male dominion have bolstered resistance to women's reproductive rights in many countries. The backlash is sometimes frightening.

But is there a choice? We have seen in Europe the consequences of different countries' ways of dealing with their Nazi past – compare Germany with Austria, Poland or Hungary. We see the never-ending rifts in the United States.

Some Latin American countries, through truth commissions and judicial processes, recognized human rights violations by recent authoritarian regimes, punished a few of those politically responsible and a few leading perpetrators and instituted reparation schemes. But the ghosts have not always been laid to rest – defenders of those regimes are sometimes elected even as presidents (in Brazil and Guatemala), and impunity and denial continue under elected governments. In Guatemala, Bishop Juan Gerardi, author of the Recovery of Historical Memory Report (REMHI, Recuperación de la Memoria Histórica) documenting responsibilities for human rights violations on an unimaginable scale, was murdered the day after its publication in April 1998.

Behind these recent traumas lie deeper and more ancient historical wounds: in England, the legacies of slavery, of imperialism and of Ireland underlie the separation from Europe and the possible dismemberment of

17

INTRODUCTION

the United Kingdom. In Latin America, the legacies of colonialism, of slavery and of Republican assaults on indigenous land and institutions weigh on contemporary resistance to recognizing injustice and discrimination: the weariness and the resentment will not go away . . . nor will the suppressed guilt that haunts the generations of beneficiaries.

To remember, to restore, to repair . . . and then to forestall and control the backlash. That, translated as a compromise between identity politics and social justice, could stand as the motivation for the chapters that follow.

1

The Latin American Decolonial

The 'decolonial' in universalist mode: Said and Fanon

This chapter discusses the decolonial as it is propagated and debated by Latin Americans and Latin Americanists. It begins with a consideration of precursors in order to show that, in contrast to the leading figures and texts of the Latin American tendency, their writings do not advocate a comprehensive rejection of the traditions of thought flowing from the Enlightenment, nor do they believe that those traditions are comprehensively discredited by association with colonialism. I start with Edward Said because of his unique role as the person who implanted within the humanities and social sciences an awareness of the depth to which imperialism and colonialism have shaped our – i.e. Europeans' – outlook. But his name and his book *Orientalism* have been quoted in support of things which are not in the book and which he did not say. Said does not provide the grounds on which to base the hostility to liberalism which marks Latin American decolonial writing, Said does not offer a basis for placing race at the forefront as the only explanation of human suffering, and his writings do not justify the primacy of ethnic or national identity as a basis for democratic demands.

I then discuss Frantz Fanon. It is particularly important to demonstrate his universalist commitment because he is so often invoked in support of a sort of racial reductionism.

Thereafter, I discuss the complicated question of Emmanuel Levinas and his influence, frequently invoked by decolonials sometimes together with Fanon. One could hardly think of two more different thinkers, and I argue that the attempt to recruit Levinas for the decolonial cause involves a distortion of his thought – though it has to be said that his thought is uniquely difficult to understand.

The decolonial has brought indigenous people and Afro-Americans out of the shadows to which they were consigned by standard science and the humanities. I will focus principally on Boaventura de Sousa Santos, Walter Mignolo, Nelson Maldonado-Torres and Enrique Dussel and offer an analysis of their thinking, their style and the coherence of their arguments.

Finally, I will arrive at decolonial feminism, which brings to the fore a dimension of contemporary and historic oppression overlooked by the thinkers just mentioned, yet more disruptive than the leading (male) voices of the decolonial. Feminism links up with ethnicity through arguments about the fate of women in contemporary indigenous society but also even before the irruption of colonialism. As a result, largely through Silvia Rivera Cusicanqui's writings and pronouncements against the current, I arrive at an interpretation of intersectionality which disentangles the frontiers of ethnicity, race, culture, religion, class and gender. In conclusion, I question the causal efficacy attributed to culture in explaining differences in outlook, in belief and in attitudes to science.

A cautionary word is in order in case my scepticism on the causal efficacy of cultural differences in explanations is misinterpreted: I do not disagree with those who would support the recognition of indigenous religious practices, who would encourage and fund bilingual and inter-cultural education, or who would fight to replace the hegemony of one or another set of cultural practices with a recognition of all the streams present in society. My criticisms are rather directed against those who would assimilate cultural difference to differences in 'epistemology', implying that people who follow different cultural practices (like religion or beliefs about disease and agricultural production) have a different sort of mind, a different notion of cause and effect. My claim is that differences about science, notably, are not cultural because they occur between people who share many cultural practices like religion and language. This is why I believe the use of the word 'knowledges' in the plural is misleading. We do not need to believe that non-scientific beliefs deserve our respect because they come from different cultural sources, because they don't. Respecting different religious practices does not commit us to recognizing their practical truth.

I also contest the over-racialization, or over-ethnicization, of accounts of many features of Latin American societies: their extreme inequality, the appalling violence perpetrated against poor people especially in big cities, the deficiencies of their public education systems, the disadvantages of women as well as their successes in overcoming them. Race and ethnicity have contributed much to these differences, but they are far from the whole story, and excessive emphasis on them has undesirable effects. One of these, which I have written about elsewhere, is the temptation offered to politicians to direct resources to particularistic multicultural policies and programmes instead of paying attention to the structural policies and reforms that affect all social groups – a practice that encourages clientelism and corporatism (Lehmann 2016a, 2018).

The other reason to avoid privileging race-based explanations is that all Latin American populations are the fruit of and the testimony to centuries of race mixture, or *mestizaje*. It is common to denounce *mestizaje* as a cruel trick to deceive people into thinking there is no serious racial divide and 'blame' those 'in the middle' (*mestizos*) for their inclination to distance themselves from the black population and leave them isolated in their struggle against racial exclusion. This is a sensitive issue because so much evidence shows that, in spite of their chromatic character in the region's racial hierarchies, differences in skin colour are highly correlated with indicators of socio-economic status (Telles 2004, 2014). Yet, at least in the Brazilian case, there is also some reason to believe that race *explains* inequality principally at the upper end of the social hierarchy (Biderman and Guimarães 2004; Henriques 2001). There is also evidence, again for Brazil, that women suffer more from racial exclusion than men (Telles 2004).

Apart from these pragmatic doubts, there are other reasons to separate different 'faces' of identity politics. When social movements mobilize against inequality and exclusion, they will be supported by disproportionate numbers of indigenous people and Afro-descendants, but that should not be taken as a reason for their demands to be met by policies directed at racially deprived groups alone, or predominantly by programmes in the field of culture. Inequality has to be treated in a universalistic way in the first instance, even if additional measures should be attached to deal with patterns of specifically racial and ethnic disadvantage. State-supported cultural programmes, such as bilingual and intercultural education and legal enactment of *usos y costumbres*, are eminently justifiable and desirable but no substitute for concerted policies to combat inequality.

The same applies to the disadvantages suffered by women – despite Kimberle Crenshaw's critique of the race-blindness of anti-discrimination laws, which arises in the unique context of the United States and its tortured history (Crenshaw 1989). Gender equality and the defence of women against violence in Latin America call for universal measures that would enable all women to exercise their rights as citizens, irrespective of their race, ethnicity, religion or social class.

Race and gender are powerful drivers of social movements which have brought to the fore the need for rights and protections that safeguard all genders and all races by laying the basis for citizens to be treated equally, irrespective of these attributes. An example is affirmative action to increase the number of black students in Brazil's public universities, which after much negotiation became affirmative action for students from low-income families and *among those* for blacks. In Mexico, 'intercultural' universities have been created to empower indigenous populations and meet their social and educational needs. Since it is neither possible nor legal to make entitlement to the label 'indigenous' a condition of admission, their purpose is achieved by locating them in predominantly indigenous areas with very poor populations. They are therefore open to any qualified student, thus revealing universalist practice operating under a 'cover' of particularist policies of recognition.

These are Latin American ambiguities that the cut-and-dried intuitive logic of Anglo-Saxon concepts of race has difficulty in grasping, as Peter Fry has repeatedly argued (Fry 2000, 2009).

Said as liberal

As used today, the term 'colonial' has become shorthand for structures of power implanted by the colonial system and perpetuated to this day, buttressed by racial classification, as in a standard formulation by Aníbal Quijano (Quijano 1992, 2007).[1] Later, the parallel term 'postcolonial' extended its connotations beyond racial classification, defining a 'postcolonial hierarchy' as a multiplicity of '[H]ierarchies of difference arising in the aftermath of colonialism when dominant understandings of race, masculinities and femininities, and imaginative geographies of rural and urban areas, were established under power relations that favoured the whiter, the urban, the masculine, and the wealthier over others' (Radcliffe 2015: 4).

This usage, with its overwhelming emphasis less on social class than on identity – first race and later race and gender – reflects a Latin American bend in a stream which has to be traced back to Edward Said's classic *Orientalism* (1978), an erudite book that crystallized sentiments in circulation for some time about the stereotypes underlying western fixations about other, especially Asian and Middle Eastern, cultures. One of the book's many agendas is to describe 'the metamorphosis of a relatively innocuous philological subspecialty into a capacity for managing political movements, administering colonies, making nearly apocalyptic statements concerning the White Man's difficult civilising mission, and to show how that imperial venture reveals a core weakness in 'a purportedly liberal culture, one fully committed to its vaunted norms of catholicity, plurality and open-mindedness' (Said 1978: 254).

His book foreshadowed some of the agonizing which threads its way through contemporary anthropology and decolonial efforts generally. I refer here to anxiety about 'the other' among people who painfully recognize the abyss which separates them as products of the West from that other – even if (like Said himself) they themselves were born as that other but educated and later employed in elite western institutions. The metamorphosis in the passage quoted above gets under way during and after the Great War as the European powers were portioning out the disintegrating Ottoman Empire, an enterprise which even involved relocating entire populations,[2] and a time when this field of scholarship and travel writing shifted from an emphasis on particularity, specialization and detailed knowledge to an approach which fitted the Orient into a grand imperial schema – as passive recipient of the attentions of the Orientalist. The texts quoted by Said have something in common with the development industry of the period after the Second World War, and they also foreshadow today's multiculturalism. The Orientalists may have been naive, but they were by no means mindless philistines – on the contrary they were scholars and travellers deeply concerned with understanding cultural difference, who were used by imperialist politics and military conquest. Like the most charismatic of them all, T. E. Lawrence (cf. *Lawrence of Arabia*), they somehow thought their activities would enable, for example, Arabs to better 'be themselves' – Said's phrase 'intimate estrangement' captures the relationship very well: 'All Orientals must be accommodated to a vision of an oriental type as constructed by the western scholar, as well as to a specific encounter with the Orient in which the Westerner regrasps the Orient's essence as a consequence of his intimate estrangement from it' (Said 1978: 248).

Contemporary interventions in support of indigenous causes may not be serving dreams of imperial domination, but in order to achieve their aims its practitioners do have to project some sort of essence of the cultural groups they are intended to support. Intimate estrangement, with its calculated contradiction, could well describe some of today's programmes aimed at the defence or recovery of indigenous cultures and languages, of which the Latin American version of multiculturalism, *interculturalidad*, is a leading example. *Interculturalidad* can be described ideally as covering a range of state policies to enable the bearers of marginalized cultures to function with ease throughout society and also to persuade the bearers of the hegemonic culture to recognize other national cultures, especially of course indigenous cultures, as equal in status within a national framework (García 2003, 2005). Inevitably, the implementation of intercultural policies struggles to combine bureaucracy and rationality with an anxiety to 'get inside the mind of their other' – an 'other' who, in pursuit of recognition or liberation, is nevertheless presumed subconsciously to occupy a position of dependence on the gatekeepers of identity politics. Illustrative examples include the establishment of government according to *usos y costumbres* in Mexico, programmes to teach indigenous people their own language (Lehmann 2013) and the imposition of an imagined pre-existing collective system of land tenure on black Brazilian beneficiaries of land redistribution (*quilombolas*) (Boyer 2014, 2106).

But the literature on these subjects, especially that written in English, too often overlooks the subtleties, the allusive usages and the ambiguities that are central to Latin American race relations, even in the most socially polarized situations. Edward Said himself later regretted the incorporation of his ideas into dualistic or binary *tercermundista* (third-worldist) polarization, which in some ways replicates the Orientalist mindset he was trying to undo. In the Preface to *Culture and Imperialism* (Said 1994), he praises anthropologists Janet Abu-Lughod and Leila Ahmed for doing away with the 'binary oppositions dear to the nationalist and imperialist enterprise', and he certainly does not offer the slightest hint of the denigration of western culture and its heritage in which some followers of a decolonial approach offhandedly indulge. His attack takes aim at the colonial freighting of Orientalist scholarship rather than of that scholarship itself. His description of the university as a 'utopian space' is out of tune with pejorative references to 'monocratic' western educational and cultural traditions found in the decolonial literature. In words which have added force 25 years after they were published, and which foreshadow the ideas of Silvia Rivera Cusicanqui, he goes on as follows:

> all cultures are involved in one another; none is single and pure, all are hybrid, heterogeneous, extraordinarily differentiated, and unmonolithic. This, I believe, is as true of the contemporary United States as it is of the modern Arab world, where in each instance respectively, so much has been made of the dangers of 'un-Americanism' and the threats to 'Arabism'. Defensive, reactive, and even paranoid nationalism is, alas, frequently woven into the very fabric of education, where children as well as older students are taught to venerate and celebrate the uniqueness of their tradition (usually and invidiously at the expense of others). (Said 1994: xxv)

He reiterates his aversion to the search for authenticity in many different contexts. One striking instance is the treatment in the late twentieth century of Protestant churches founded by European or American missionaries during the Ottoman Empire. It seems that 110 years after founding those churches by missionaries in the Middle East, their 'mother churches', beset by colonial guilt, decided they should return to the Eastern Christianity from which they had come – even threatening to cut off their financial support (Said 1994: 40). Somehow, the late twentieth-century European and North American church leaders had decided that the proselytism of their predecessors had been a violation of the cultural integrity of the converts and that it was time to force them out and cut them off. Said commented ironically, 'The missionary authorities had made a mistake one hundred years ago in severing Eastern Christians from the main church. Now they should go back' (ibid.: 40). It seems that eventually the 'mother churches' pulled back from their decision.

Said also attacks the scholarly defence of nationalist causes for what one might call the 'know-all essentialism' of those who assume 'that the African or Iranian or Chinese or Jewish or German experience is fundamentally integral, coherent, separate, and therefore comprehensible only to Africans, Iranians, Chinese, Jews, or Germans'. They 'posit as essential something which . . . is both historically created and the result of interpretation'. For Said, scholarship which aims to defend 'the essence or experience itself rather than promote full knowledge of it and its entanglements and dependencies on other knowledges' belittles the different experience of others (ibid.: 31–2).

Said's quarrel is not, however, with multiculturalism, or at least not with the everyday multiculturalism that weaves its way unreflectively through the social fabric. Rather, it is with attempts by agents of power to engineer ethnic relations. He does not think that actually existing everyday multiculturalism would – as feared by some of its enemies, who may also be disguising their hostility to racial equality – bring about a fragmentation of society. On the contrary, he claims, evidently with the United States in mind, that 'emancipation and enlightenment in their strongest form were also narratives of integration not separation, the stories of people who had been excluded from the main group but who were now fighting for a place in it' (ibid.: xxvi). The date of this Preface to his book, 1992, shows how times have changed.

There are two other dividing lines to be drawn between Said and the decolonials. One concerns different attitudes to politicization in the classroom and in scholarship, for although he was known worldwide for promoting and even defining the Palestinian cause, he was opposed to 'politicizing the classroom', and never gave a course on the Middle East (Brennan 2021: 222). His published work included numerous writings on authors such as Conrad or Kipling whose opinions he did not share, but whose works he could write about in a mode other than that of denunciation. Obviously, he wrote extensively and intensively on political subjects, but still he continued to publish interpretations of the classics, while also promoting the publication of contemporary Arab literature.

The other dividing line is marked by his growing affinity from the 1980s with Marxist and Marxist-influenced thinkers like Lukács and Gramsci and the Frankfurt School, and his parallel fierce attacks on postmodernism, deconstruction and the cult of theory in the study of literature (ibid.: 228–36), characteristic of the progenitors of the decolonial, especially Walter Mignolo.

Decolonials rarely quote Said, but I have found it necessary to mention these features of his vast and extraordinarily varied work because of his status as a foundational figure of the culture of the postcolonial and to show how the contemporary decolonial has carved out only a niche in that culture.

In his Preface to the Twenty-Fifth Anniversary edition of *Orientalism* (Said, 2003) he wrote that in writing the book he had intended to 'use humanistic critique' and 'to replace the short bursts of polemical, thought-stopping fury that so imprison us in labels and antagonistic debate whose goal is a belligerent collective identity rather than understanding and intellectual exchange'. He insisted on calling this 'humanism' despite the 'scornful dismissal'of the word by those he sarcastically called 'sophisticated postmodern critics' (Said, 2003: xv).

Fanon as psychiatrist

Frantz Fanon was a man of unbounded curiosity driven, in his tragically short life, to seek out an exceptionally wide range of experiences. When the island of Martinique, where he was born, was under the control of the *pétainiste* (pro-Nazi) Admiral Robert, Fanon, aged 17, escaped to Dominica (a British colony), returning shortly afterwards when the *pétainiste* was forced out with help from the United States, and then sailing to Europe to volunteer with the Free French Forces. Wounded and hospitalized, he nonetheless returned to the front and was decorated with the Croix de Guerre. After a disappointing return to Martinique, he went back to France to study medicine in Lyons, specializing in psychiatry. While studying, he read voraciously and by the time he qualified as a doctor he had already, aged 26, published the first of his two most famous works – *Peau Noire, Masques Blancs (Black Skin, White Masks)*.

Fanon's experience in the French army during the Second World War, his psychiatric training and his work as a doctor during the Algerian War contributed to his understanding of race and of violence. Fanon was not a 'team-player'; he was not usually interested in making others feel comfortable, and the story of his involvement with the Algerian revolution shows he cleaved very closely to his principles. His non-Algerian, non-Arab and non-Muslim background limited the extent of his inclusion in the Algerian Liberation Army or in the FLN (the National Liberation Front).

Fanon's denunciation and unmasking of French racism can be thought of as an emotionally driven counterpart to Said.[3] Said's writing, for all the force of his tracing of the underlying dehumanizing stereotypes that drove Europe's dealings with the Middle East and Asia, is erudite and humanistic, infused by Europe's very own grand traditions. Fanon's writing, now gathered together in two volumes from La Découverte (Fanon 2011, 2014), is expressed in vivid, sometimes even lurid, language. His words are often rough-edged but never demagogic and bear no trace of the grievance-laden prose of the minstrels of the decolonial. In Fanon, the fury is that of a man flayed alive – a phrase (*écorché vif*) used of Fanon by the Martinican poet and historian Edouard Glissant and by his first publisher at Editions du Seuil, the anti-colonial campaigner and writer Francis Jeanson, later appearing no less than six times in Macey's biography. As a psychiatrist, however, he enjoyed the confidence and commitment of his associates, encouraged fraternization among patients and was not afraid to express medical disagreements with his superiors.

Fanon did not use a typewriter: he dictated his works, mostly to Marie-Jeanne Manuellan and to his wife Josie, and they do convey an almost physical outpouring of anger, as well as occasional metaphorical excess. For example, in *The Wretched of the Earth*, he describes the building of a nation as 'facilitée par l'existence de ce mortier travaillé dans le sang et la colère' (in *De la violence*: 'moulded in a mortar with blood and anger') (Fanon 2014: 495). At one point, as if correcting his own empathy for indigenous beliefs and cures, he describes the future of the colonized, referencing the torture techniques used by the French army: 'up against the wall, with a knife to their throats or, to be precise, electrodes on their genitals, they will find themselves forced to *stop fooling themselves*' (ibid.: 468; emphasis in the original).[4] 'During the struggle for liberation, there is a singular loss of interest in these rituals ... The people will abandon the possession rituals, the dances and trances, the seances of possession and dispossession ... [which play] a key regulating role in ensuring the stability of the colonized world'. Instead, he prophesies that they will give birth in blood and tears to the liberation struggle (Philcox translation: Fanon 2004: 20). Despite his sensitivity to the supernatural lives of other peoples, and to the possibility that their rituals may represent imagined liberation, Fanon looks forward to the awakening from those trances and dreams – one might even say their exorcism – that comes with the struggle for liberation.[5]

Fanon's work, inspired by his psychiatrist mentor François Tosquelles at the Saint-Alban hospital and later by a fierce reaction against the ethos of French psychiatry as practised in Algeria before and during the revolutionary war, could be seen as a precursor to what later would be called psychiatry in the community (Aimé 2006). Both David Macey (Macey 2000: 148–9) and Jean Khalfa (Khalfa 2011) have described his work as 'social therapy' ('socialthérapie'). Observing the dissolution and fragmentation of the body and self in hospital, he hopes that occasional day-release would enable patients to hold their personality together against the debilitating effects of colonial integration.

In his work, Fanon tried to replace assumptions drawn from everyday life in France with everyday Algerian life, and to relax the tight controls dictated by established psychiatric practice.[6] His work was informed by an alertness to local cultures which, although seemingly common sense to our twenty-first-century outlook, did depart from the context-insensitive approach of psychiatry at the time. He introduced storytellers (who frightened European authorities because of their supposed role as messengers for the liberation forces), films, basket weaving for the women and farm work for the men. When asking patients to comment on a drawing of a cemetery, he realized that the crosses would not denote a cemetery to Muslims. In Tunisia, after leaving Algeria and resigning his position in 1958, he continued to work along these lines and continued to meet resistance from senior doctors.

Fanon's sensitivity to context can be described as 'everyday sociology' but also as psychiatric anthropology. For example, he realized the necessity that motivated a family who pleaded to have a relative discharged from hospital: as a saint (*marabout*), the offerings he received from his pious visitors provided income for his family. In a famous passage in the chapter 'On Violence', he describes a possession dance in language so vivid that he himself seems caught up in the trance: the spine bends forwards, then the body is thrown backwards, the entire group is caught up in a grandiose push to exorcise and liberate itself: 'Everything is permitted, for in fact the sole purpose of the gathering is to let the supercharged libido and the stifled aggressiveness spew out volcanically. Symbolic killings, figurative cavalcades, and imagined multiple murders, everything has to come out. The ill humours seep out, tumultuous as lava flows' (Fanon 2004: 20).[7]

Fanon as universalist

Although Fanon's experience of racial prejudice shaped his outlook on the deployment of colonial power, concepts of racial or ethnic identity did not dominate his understanding of where national independence should lead. This is how Said himself interprets Fanon: 'merely to replace white officers and bureaucrats with colored equivalents . . . is no guarantee that the nationalist functionaries will not replicate the old dispensation. The dangers of chauvinism and xenophobia ("Africa for the Africans") are very real' (Said 1994: 214). Said is saying that a nationalist programme based on racial identity is likely to lead to a repeat of the colonial order, advocating instead a national programme against all forms of subjugation.

For Fanon also, the idea of an 'African culture' was nonsense. In the chapter of *The Wretched of the Earth* entitled 'National Culture', he writes: 'There can be no such thing as rigorously identical cultures. To believe one can create a black culture is to forget oddly enough that "Negroes" are in the process of disappearing, since those who created them are witnessing the demise of their economic and cultural supremacy' (Fanon 2004: 169). He frequently expresses hostility against those who emphasize racial ties as a basis for political solidarity, as in *négritude*.[8] The implication of his writings was, in today's parlance, the hope that anti-colonial campaigns and struggles would build nations of citizens. But he did not spell that out: citizenship did not have today's resonance at that time.

And an almost shocking passage, again in *Peau noire*, spells out the underlying thought that the anguish of race hierarchies can be overcome only by an abolition of race categories:

> The black man wants to be White. . . .
> . . .
> The white man is sealed in his whiteness.
> The black man in his blackness . . .[9]

Fanon says his work is focused on putting an end to a vicious circle:

> It is a fact: white men consider themselves superior to black men.
> And there is another fact: black men want to prove to white men, at all costs, the richness of their thought, the equal value of their intellect.
> How to escape this vicious circle?[10]

And then a page later:

> Painful as it may be, we are forced to accept this conclusion
> For the black man there is only one destiny. And it is white.[11]

Fanon and Sartre: blacks and Jews

The influence of Sartre's *Reflexions sur la Question Juive* (1946),[12] which, Fanon wrote, contained some of the most beautiful pages he had ever read, is in full view: Sartre writes of 'le Juif ' and 'l'antisémite' like Fanon writes of 'le Noir' or 'le Nègre' and 'le Blanc'. Neither have any qualms about essentializing or stereotyping. Both ponder the impossibility experienced by Jews and blacks of extracting themselves from the condition which is imposed upon them. The tragic irony in Fanon's phrase is palpable. Sartre's Jew is also caught in an impossible trap: he (Sartre uses the masculine throughout) can be 'authentic', to use Sartre's word (which has caused a lot of unnecessary trouble since), or he can seek to join society, adhering to universal values in the hope of gaining the recognition he deserves, but it never 'works':

> His utilitarian psychology leads him to look for self-interest, calculation, and the pretence of tolerance behind the manifestations of sympathy that some people lavish on him. And he is rarely mistaken. Yet he seeks eagerly for these very manifestations; he loves the honors that he mistrusts; he wants to be on the other side of the social barrier – with the others, among the others, he caresses the impossible dream of being suddenly rescued from universal suspicion by real affection, evident proofs of good will. (Sartre 1948b: 94)

Authenticity in a Jew is the commitment to live his Jewish condition to its limit ('jusqu'au bout'), inauthenticity is to deny that condition. Yet, despite his stern statement of principle, Sartre does not see how Jews can extricate themselves from their dilemma.

> it is we who force him into the dilemma of Jewish authenticity or inauthenticity. . . . In this situation there is not one of us who is not totally guilty and even criminal; the Jewish blood that the Nazis shed falls on all our heads.

And he continues, alluding surely to the wartime German occupation:

> The liberal, when he met a Jew, was free, completely free to shake his hand or spit in his face; he could decide in accordance with his morality, with the way he had chosen to be; but the Jew was not free to be a Jew. (Sartre 1948b: 55)

Sartre does not align himself with liberals, nor does he think they can 'do something' about it:

> The fact remains, you may answer, that the Jew is free: he can choose to be authentic. That is true, but we must understand first of all that *that*

does not concern us. The prisoner is always free to try to run away, if it is clearly understood that he risks death in crawling under the barbed wire. Is his jailer any less guilty on that account? (Sartre 1948b: 121)

Sartre does not call upon Jews to give up on trying to be accepted and return to an authentic Jewish life. Indeed, it may be wrong to interpret his use of the word 'authentic', which is strewn throughout, as a positively or negatively charged value, let alone an injunction. Sartre is merely describing the facts – the facts in France, during the Second World War and its aftermath, a country from which more than 70,000 Jews were deported and 2,000 returned, as he says, to barely a celebration of their homecoming. (He omits what is well known, namely, that very many Jews and Jewish children were hidden and protected by their fellow countrymen.) In any case, his tract is not a description of all French people; it is a description of the anti-Semitic mindset and the choices its dominance poses to Jews.

So, in his chapter on the psychoanalytic (Adlerian) account of racism, Fanon quotes Sartre: 'Let us have the courage to say it outright: *it is the racist who creates his inferior*. This conclusion brings us back to Sartre: . . . It is the anti-Semite who makes the Jew' (Fanon 1986: 93; emphasis in the original). And, with extraordinary courage as a 26-year old new author, he writes: 'Shame and self-contempt. Nausea. When people like me, they tell me it is in spite of my color. When they dislike me, they point out that it is not because of my color. Either way, I am locked into the infernal circle' (ibid.: 116).

David Macey describes the *Reflexions* as 'not one of Sartre's more subtle texts' but to me its merit is precisely its rawness: 150 pages of barely controlled anger. His stereotypes would provoke surprise and even annoyance in today's readers, but the sympathy and empathy expressed is so strong that it feels almost as if Sartre, not yet the celebrity he later became, is projecting his own ambivalence as an intellectual and outsider. Maybe Fanon drew encouragement from that posture to write in the way he did – as a man 'flayed alive'.

Fanon and Sartre share a broad framework, especially in their understanding of the hold of anti-Semitic and racist stereotypes over the targets of their prejudice. They also both explore the pathologies engendered by identification with the oppressor. The black and the Jew struggle with what we might call their 'true nature' – except that whereas Sartre's Jew does have a 'true nature' of his own, Fanon believes that the tortured (and torturing) relationship with the White Man has expropriated his own and the Black Man's inner self – and he expresses this feeling by constant denunciations of authors, black and white, racist and anti-racist, who seek out something like the Black Man's interior being. (I use 'Black Man' because that was the usage of the time.)

Fanon's interpretation of the condition of blackness is bleaker. Sartre's Jew is able to 'fall back on' his authenticity, whereas Fanon sees none of that in himself or in the archetype he builds of the condition of blackness. Indeed the word 'authenticity' is notably absent from *Peau Noire*.

Jean Khalfa (Khalfa 2006) quotes Fanon, in a famous searing passage from *Black Skin, White Masks*, where he describes an experience so common for black people at that time, namely being pointed out, in this case by a small child in the street, as 'un nègre':

> On that day, completely dislocated, unable to be in the open with the other, the white man, who mercilessly imprisoned me, I took myself far off from my own presence, far indeed, and made an object of myself. What else could it be for me but an amputation, an excision, a haemorrhage that spattered my whole body with black blood? But I did not want this revision, this thematization. All I wanted was to be a man among other men. I wanted to come lithe and young into a world that was ours and to help to build it together. (Fanon 1986: 112–13)

The body which constitutes our exteriority, which situates us in the world, is reduced to nothing but a black skin (Khalfa 2006: 39).

The book concludes with an outburst – six pages of highly charged aphorisms, all in the first person, which reads like a prose poem. Fanon cries out to be freed of his colour, and for all people to be freed of their colour too: 'As a man of colour, I do not have the right to fix permanently on the White man the blame for the past of my race' (Fanon 1952: 205).[13] Or again, towards the end: 'The black man does not exist. Any more than the white man exists. Both must put aside inhuman voices that belonged to their forebears, in order to give birth to authentic communication' (ibid.: 207).[14] One can see here a distaste for a politics driven by hate of 'le Blanc'. Later, he would express a preference for the raw insurrectionary spirit of the 'peasant masses', directed against injustice and not labelled in racial or national terms. At this time, he was writing in France in response to the racism he saw around him and with the memory of his experience in the French army when he observed the racialized military hierarchy, placing Arab soldiers on the lowest rung.

Again and again, Fanon expresses a view that the colonizer and the colonized are both prisoners of their situation, and that by liberation is meant the liberation of blacks from the colonizer's conception of them. Later in life, in *The Wretched of the Earth*, we find the same thought: 'What we are striving for is to liberate the black man from the arsenal of complexes that germinated in a colonial situation' (Fanon 2004: 44), on a path towards what a recent commentator has called 'a genuine intersubjective empathy between colonised and coloniser based on a new humanism of equality' (Vieira 2019: 158).

In 2020, a volume of essays published in Mexico has taken up these themes in more polemical vein, bitterly criticizing the adoption or co-optation of Fanon by prominent decolonial figures, notably Ramón Grosfoguel, Maldonado-Torres and Walter Mignolo (Santos is spared). In their introductory essay, entitled 'Autopsia de una impostura intelectual', the editors, Gaya Makaran and Pierre Gaussens contrast the decolonial prioritization of culture and race, and their denunciation of Marxism, with Fanon's emphatically stated view, against the culturalists of his day, that in his own eyes and in those of the workers he knew in France it was through an end to the capitalist system under which they laboured that their condition of poverty could be overcome, not in the recovery of an ancient cultural ancestry or, quoting *Peau Noire*, 'a correspondence between a black philosopher and Plato', which would do nothing for the eight-year-old children working in Martinique's cane fields. When Fanon denounces the idea that specific values might be imprinted on his black skin, they say, he is refusing to subordinate himself to an abstract collective, be it 'black people', 'the black people' or 'black culture' (Makaran and Gaussens 2020: 12–13):

Fanon's ideas would not have been what they were without the breadth of his experience and competence: who else, at the age of 24, could convincingly adduce arguments and examples from psychology, psychiatry, phenomenology and existentialist philosophy and literature, and geographically from France, the Caribbean, and both North and sub-Saharan Africa? And who else at age 30 could call on lived experience in Martinique, as a soldier in the Second World War, in France itself, mixing in student and intellectual circles, in Algeria, in the midst of a war, and then as a participant in the international anti-colonial movement? All this before the age of 36.

Fanon as sociologist

Fanon's description of the Algerian family in *L'An V de la révolution algérienne* (also published in 1968 as *Sociologie d'une Révolution*), proved controversial among commentators (Hudis 2015: 101; Macey 2000: 397–407), but its importance for our present purposes is that it shows him as a revolutionary enthusiast engaging honestly, if also a little naively, with the society to which he had committed himself. He describes the respect women have to show to their fathers and brothers, the strict dress codes and the rules governing contact between girls and boys, and marriage. But he also envisions the liberating effects that begin when women are called on to hide bombs, messages or medicines in their clothing and continue when they leave to join the armed struggle. In a slightly romanticizing vein, their fathers are described as accepting these deviations from the norm.

On the other side of the violent divide stand the forces of colonial war, gripped by a French-Orientalist colonial obsession with the real woman behind the veil and the fantasy of freeing her from the backward customs of her society, now turned into a nightmare by fear of the bombs or weapons she may be concealing among her robes.

These observations tell us that Fanon was an unusually avid observer and tended to trust his instincts. Those instincts were shaped by an intellectually open disposition which led him to read avidly and widely with little respect for the dogmatisms that divided the French intelligentsia of his day. But it is hard to deny a certain romanticization of violence from the imagery of *Peau Noire* to this sociology of the Algerian family. He may not have advocated the political use of violence, but neither did he often openly disapprove of it when it served causes dear to him. As so often occurs when someone becomes the object of a cult, particular aspects of his writing and his action have been singled out in the name of particular causes: in the late 1960s, Stokely Carmichael and other Black Power spokespeople promoted Fanon's inclination to praise violence, especially the violence of the peasant masses already mentioned, which may have arisen from the despair of a man who witnessed at close quarters the Algerian War in which 400,000 Algerians and 35,000 French people died, and then became deeply disappointed in the postcolonial leaders. Similarly, the decolonial school has overemphasized his writing about racial exclusion and the violence of racism. David Macey, in his opening chapter 'Forgetting Fanon, Remembering Fanon', deplores numerous poor translations and misappropriations of Fanon's writings notably in the cause of racially or ethnically defined movements and cleavages and as part of a postcolonial canon. The last thing Fanon should be is a guru or cult-like figure because his life had so many facets, especially given its shortness, and his writing had the honesty of one who suffers and bears witness to the suffering of others.

Latin American and Latin Americanist postcolonial theories

The inclusion of Said and Fanon as background to the Latin American decolonial was designed to place the decolonial contestation of western and European liberalism in its genealogical context by focusing on particular texts rather than parading headline ideas or big names. The Latin American variant stands apart because of the place occupied by indigenous peoples and Afro-descendants in the region's culture, originating in the system of domination established under colonialism, and it is reflected in the fact that almost the only states to have adhered to the ILO's Indigenous and Tribal Peoples Convention 169 (1989) are from Latin America. The result in decolonial theory has been a version in which the politics of recognition has gone far beyond, for example, the advocacy of tolerance and multiculturalism in response to immigration in Europe, by instating indigenous cultures as the most authentically Latin American and by displacing the culture of white elites, denounced as the beneficiaries of the annihilation (or 'epistemicide') perpetrated during the colonial period. In this perspective, *mestizaje*, or race mixture, is but another face of the colonial domination that pervades entire societies, rendering illegitimate their political structures, their juridical institutions and also their knowledge systems.

Quijano, Mignolo, Santos

Latin American decolonial theory can be said to gain an audience with the 'conversion' of Aníbal Quijano (Quijano 1992).[15] Quijano had been known in Peru since the 1960s as a critic of the novelist and anthropologist José María Arguedas, a leading figure among the country's indigenists (Rochabrun 2011), but after a career as a prominent marxisant structuralist writing about rural trade unions in Peru and then, from a *dependentista* viewpoint, about urbanization and marginality in the UN Economic Commission for Latin America, he returned, writing tracts about imperialism and capitalism.[16] In the 1980s, he was born again as an advocate of the indigenous cause who saw race at the root of almost everything in society, in combination with the 'coloniality of power'. Coloniality imposed in the sixteenth century had left Latin America under the dominance of a European rationality attached to a single European concept of modernity and a dismissive European construction of indigenous knowledge. European science did harm to indigenous knowledge by separating science from ideology and subject from object, and Latin America's problems were due to the imposition of a European concept of modernity that suffocated indigenous knowledge systems.

Walter Mignolo, who came to the decolonial from Argentine semiotics via Paris in the late sixties and early seventies, deploys similar arguments, though his language is drawn more from the lexicon of cultural studies than from social science. He too is concerned above all to dismantle

European modernity, its myths and the colonial apparatus put in place to impose its rationality on the rest of the world. His repeated stock idea is that 'there is no modernity without coloniality, that coloniality is constitutive of modernity' (Mignolo 2007). Since the Renaissance, modernity has been driven by a sense of world mission and has been an all-powerful machine of political, economic and legal power. These ideas were first developed 50 years ago by the grandfathers of *dependencia* and radical development studies, for example André Gunder Frank and Immanuel Wallerstein, but the dimension now added, and which most troubles Mignolo, is the 'disqualification[s] over the centuries of non-European knowledge and non-European aesthetic standards, from the Renaissance to the Enlightenment and from the Enlightenment to neo-liberal globalization' (ibid.: 49).

The third leading figure is the Portuguese Boaventura de Souza Santos, who came to prominence as a sociologist of judicial systems and a critic of conventional concepts of the law (de Sousa Santos 1987). His much admired study of a land invasion in Recife combined structural background with a granular account of the interactions between land tenure, popular organization and micro-political management (de Sousa Santos 1983). Later, he evolved into a leading exponent, like Mignolo, of the idea that modernity has done nothing but harm to most of the populations of the world (though China is never mentioned). His main idea is the 'abyss' (*línea abismal*): it starts with colonial power imposing authority on colonies and decreeing that a 'state of nature' prevailed in a world of incomprehensible practices and knowledge, beyond *the line*, where the rule of law does not apply, where people possess neither rights nor even legal existence (de Sousa Santos 2010: 34). The 'abyss' is extended forward in time to divisions in the modern world between those who fall within the purview of the law and those without – the informal sector which now spreads across the globe within and between metropolis and periphery, between the world where the law rules and the world where traffickers and their allies in politics and security forces impose their own laws. The abyss sets aside people classified as terrorists, refugees and indigenous, and areas classified as ghettoes. From a proclamation of this overriding dualism, Santos moves on to laudatory remarks about the recent Latin American governments of Lula, Chavez, Mujica and former Bishop Lugo (Paraguay) and movements like the Brazilian MST (Landless Workers' Movement), as emancipatory ventures unforeseen by left-wing theories (de Sousa Santos 2010: 17).[17] Where once he would undertake detailed analysis of the local political economy of Recife's urban underbelly, Santos now bundles together governments and movements which have very different characteristics under a single heading of challengers to a global system of oppression. For example, Lula and Mujica both stayed within the institutional order under which they were elected, whereas Chavez destroyed it. Chavez's personality cult and centralization of all decision making also mark him out from the others.

Like Mignolo, Santos extends the deep global and national abyss to the sphere of knowledge, which they regard as just as much a field of exclusion as economics or politics. This they call epistemicide – an epistemological divide under which official science claims a monopoly at the expense of indigenous knowledge and the native wisdom of peasants, migrants and other excluded populations. At the end of a chapter on *ecología de saberes* ('ecology of knowledge') in *Descolonizar el Saber* ('Decolonizing knowledge') (de Sousa Santos 2010), he sets out to refound the philosophy of science starting from the polarization of abysmal and post-abysmal knowledge. How can we identify the point of view of the oppressed? How can we distinguish scientific from non-scientific knowledge? How can we distinguish solutions within and outside capitalism? He contests the claim of western science to a monopoly on setting standards of knowledge production and artistic creation (ibid.: 22), and calls for 'destabilizing individuals' to emerge from the excluded world of non-western knowledge, opposing conformity with their ability to 'swerve'.

Santos's belief that Latin American social movements ground their struggles in 'ancestral, popular and spiritual knowledge' which is foreign to 'Eurocentric critical theory' (de Sousa Santos 2010) confuses the symbolic role of inherited traditions and belief systems in mobilizing popular support with their application to political and practical challenges such as agricultural technology, social welfare or constitution making.[18] We shall see that the purpose of intercultural and bilingual education among indigenous populations is to counteract discrimination, to restore a sense of confidence among people whose cultures and language have been excluded and despised and to improve the competence of young people in dealing with both their inherited cultures and the dominant cultures, but that is not the same as applying non-western systems of knowledge. Likewise, the recognition of indigenous systems of justice, as a form of cultural regeneration as well as a way of 'making justice more just', is perfectly understandable in terms of modern 'European' concepts of justice. The extension of undoubted cultural and linguistic differences into the domain of epistemology, implying that cultural differences bring different ways of assessing evidence or reasoning, is unwarranted.

Mignolo, too, emphasizes colonialism's disqualification and suppression of indigenous systems of knowledge. In his *Desobediencia Epistémica* (Mignolo 2010), he extends this suppression through the

Enlightenment to the twentieth century, mentioning a list of prominent figures, including Ghandi, José Carlos Mariátegui, Amilcar Cabral, Aimé Césaire, Frantz Fanon, Rigoberta Menchú, the anthropologist Gloria Anzaldúa (ibid.: 15) and even Sayyid Qutb – the progenitor of political Islam whose interminable and chaotic torrent of hate and prejudice, *Milestones*, has served as al-Qaeda's doctrinal inspiration (ibid.: 24).[19]

The historical shortcuts that punctuate this sequence are exemplified by the insertion of the Andean colonial chronicler Guaman Poma de Ayala as the earliest figure in this genealogy of the 'delinking' (*desprendimiento*), advocated by Quijano and taken up by Santos and Mignolo, in flagrant contradiction of the work of ethno-historians. According to Frank Salomon (Salomon 1999: 45–8), although Poma criticizes the Spanish colonial authorities bitterly, he also inserts the indigenous world into the colonial scheme by incorporating Inca dynasties into a Judeo-Christian history going back to Adam and Eve, while Rolena Adorno, recognized as the leading authority on Poma, goes out of her way to stress his advocacy of 'evangelización rigurosa y completa' and of the suppression of indigenous practices throughout his *Nueva corónica y buen gobierno* (Adorno 2001).

A recent critique from within the postcolonial framework attributes to Mignolo, diplomatically, apropos of his notion of border thinking, a quasi-racial notion of intellectual or interpretative legitimacy: 'He analytically favours ethnically demarcated populations, such as African diasporas in the Caribbean and Amerindian communities in the Andes, as appropriate examples in critical border thinking and exteriority . . .' (Vieira 2019: 8).[20]

In a chapter on delinking, independent thought and decolonial freedom, Mignolo raises the delicate question of the reliability of local versus foreign experts and social scientists, creating a tension between ethnicity or nationality and scientific credibility. In the discussion, he comes close to conditioning the acceptability of an anthropological analysis on the nationality of the anthropologist. Eventually, he agrees that this only applies if they espouse colonial attitudes: thus 'US experts' who 'express . . . the belief that they can really decide what is good and what is bad for "developing countries"' are to be rejected. Although he is 'not saying that a Maori anthropologist has epistemic privileges over a New Zealand anthropologist of Anglo descent (or a British or US anthropologist)', he still claims that 'Maoris would know better what is good or bad for themselves than would an expert from Harvard or a white anthropologist from New Zealand' (Mignolo 2011: 137–8).

These three postcolonial authors share two interconnected ideas – that Europe is responsible for imposing on Latin America and other parts of the world not only a colonial system of government but a way of thinking, and that this way of thinking has suppressed equally valuable precolonial ways of thinking which survive precariously among indigenous peoples. Those ways of thinking embody a distinct type of knowledge, or way of knowing ('epistemology'). All three writers follow a radical relativism which contests the universal claims of what they call western science.

And yet, when it comes to specifics, to translating their ideas into even very abstract proposals for enactment in this world, the claim that western and other traditions embody radically incompatible modes of thought is moderated. Thus Santos, in his outline of a regime of transcultural human rights, adopts a cautiously eclectic approach (de Sousa Santos 2010: 72–96). Beginning by quoting Said, he reminds the reader that all 'subordinated cultures', like western civilization, are built on violent origins, and that cultures are always intercultural, even though the cultural mixture is unequal. None is monolithic and all are 'incomplete'. Cultures are divided by total incomprehension that leads him to propose a formulation of human rights as a *hermeneútica diatópica*, which means taking into account different points of view. Nevertheless, not all are acceptable: for example, he rejects Hindu and Islamic versions of rights because they subordinate injustice, freedom and autonomy to the collectivity or to a religious authority, and they neglect the individual dimension of suffering, and so he advocates a 'multicultural counter-hegemonic conception' (ibid.: 81). He also has no patience with the illiberal 'Asian concept of human rights' advocated by some political leaders. His main concern is to extend human rights to provide for solidarity and collective ties, which he says are hampered by western (i.e. current international) concepts of human rights. But he does not by any means reject the western corpus, connecting his ideas with those of Rousseau, as distinct from the Lockean tradition of 'possessive individualism'. He also seems to recognize that a western outlook is necessary in intercultural dialogue because only a powerful culture such as the West can recognize its own incompleteness without risking its own dissolution: the other cultures enjoy no such 'privilege'. He thus accepts the criticism that radical relativist points of view cannot logically denounce the western tradition from which they claim to depart since that tradition is itself the source of their inspiration.

Santos then enumerates his main requirements for an intercultural human rights order, which he describes as *ur*-rights (*urderechos*) – rights which pre-exist any institutional order and so have a similar status to human rights as they currently exist in international law. These are: the right to knowledge which leads to solidarity; the right to put capitalism on trial worldwide and to implement the verdict; a sphere of property rights which is private but not profit-oriented; the rights of nature; and democratic self-determination of all peoples, including those contained presently within states.

These alternative human rights, although contestable, are not all incompatible with the broad mainstream European and North American political thought. The concept of 'solidary property' is presented as a restoration of pre-colonial arrangements, but it is quite common in modern economies as well to find various forms of common ownership in which shares are not monetized, like cooperatives. If the proposal means to abolish property for profit, then it would be incompatible, but if the proposal is intended only to leave a space for solidary property, then that space already exists.

If we put aside his utopian proposal for an intercultural human rights order, Santos's positions are little different from mainstream contemporary western conceptions of human rights. He seems to have retreated from assertions about other epistemologies or about the harm done by western science. There is a shift in emphasis: although careful to criticize regimes which trample on individual rights, his emphasis is clearly on collective rights. His reluctance to recognize states as representatives of their entire populations, including different peoples, nations and cultures, and his emphasis on the rights of different peoples to self-determination within states is incompatible with modern state systems and even with ILO Convention 169 on the rights of indigenous peoples. None of the Latin American regimes who merit his praise (Lula, Chavez, Correa, Ortega) would admit such collective rights to territorial secession.

So what point is there in questioning human rights when the suffering caused here and now by massive violations across the globe would be recognized by any reasonable regime, western or transcultural, liberal or solidary? Santos sketches an outline of a new global economic and political order, but his divergences from the existing human rights regime are small. He is a ventriloqual universalist.

When one compares these writers with Fanon, the first contrast has to be between the utterly different worlds which they inhabit – the practising psychiatrist translating his raw fury into a prose of controlled emotion sometimes veering into prose-poems, but addressing a general public, in contrast to academics writing for academic readers. The difference in style, content and context is not a mere formality: it is a mistake to subject both types of writing to the same criteria when comparing the ways they illuminate the world. The sharp edge of urgency and anger in Fanon's writing coexists with an equally sharp perception of real ambiguities, stresses and tensions in the position of politicians, intellectuals and revolutionaries and in the situation of the 'people on the ground' (like the Algerian family). Fanon can hardly have thought of himself as a writer of theories, yet he pays more attention to the content of the authorities who have influenced his thinking than do decolonial gurus. They do nevertheless both come under the influence of phenomenology – Fanon via Sartre and the decolonials via Heidegger and Levinas, as we shall see – and that emerges in a very broad sense through the themes of essences and authenticity which figures in both. But the difference in their publics and in the subcultures they inhabit, between a world of action and the academy, remains extremely significant.

Said stands in between: he became a public figure and for a time was a member of the Palestinian National Council. He was vilified by *Commentary* magazine, who called him the Professor of Terror because of his support for Palestine.[21] In 1991, he resigned from the Palestine National Council in protest against the Oslo agreements: his disagreement was not just with the accords themselves, which in his view gave too much away to Israel, but also with the undemocratic character of the Palestinian leadership and its institutions. Said was a nationalist, but far from a nationalist in the mould of Arafat or Nasser. Rather, he believed in western-style democratic values – values which 'the West' or those who act in its name have all too often betrayed.

This decolonial literature is written by denizens of a global academic system and is pervaded by a jargon that can scarcely be comprehended by those unfamiliar with the decolonial subculture. This is not a criticism in itself, but it does serve as a reminder of the self-sufficiency of the academic public, with its thousands of professors and hundreds of thousands of students stretched across the world, and of how it can breed a self-referential discourse. It is reminiscent of Bourdieu's *Homo Academicus* (Bourdieu 1984), which describes the self-reproducing and watertight French academic field as it existed until 1968. Today, the field is infinitely larger and global, yet still it engenders its small enclosed tribes and specializations with their own jargon and systems of esteem (Walsh and Lehmann 2021).

Does it matter that a school of thought that inveighs against colonialism and claims to be the voice of the excluded of Latin America owes so much to US- and European-based scholars and institutions and to international funding? This is a sensitive terrain which few would dare to tread, but one of the foremost critics of colonialism, Sylvia Rivera Cusicanqui, has written forcefully out of her Bolivian base, denouncing the co-optation of subaltern studies by 'Mignolo and company' from the palatial surroundings of their US universities. In this distortion, they are joined by the Bolivian or Latin American intelligentsia with their 'postmodern or postcolonial poses', dazzled by the symbolic capital and clientelist networks managed from the North, to which indigenous and Afro-descendant intellectuals are also beholden (Rivera Cusicanqui 2010a: 57–8). If this were mere polemics, it might not matter much, but Rivera possesses a depth of scholarship to which the three gurus of the decolonial (Quijano, Mignolo and dos Santos) cannot pretend. We shall return to her conception of the colonial and of ethnicity later in this chapter.

The grounded decolonial

Sarah Radcliffe, who underpins her arguments with detailed long-term ethnography, begins her book *Dilemmas of Difference*, based on research in Ecuador, by defining colonial exclusion as a system of classification of social differences which, by reifying social categories in a static, essentializing racial-ethnic classification system, fixes them and inscribes their meanings on 'diverse bodies' (Radcliffe 2015: 15). She regards such essentializing as a defining feature of a system of cultural and socio-economic exclusion, thus placing clear distance between her approach and that of Mignolo. Coloniality, in her understanding, consists of a set of racial categories that perpetuate individuals' and communities' marginality. For 'racial' here means not just skin colour, but a host of other markers which act as exclusionary social devices: accent, dialect, language, dress, external signs of poverty, dwelling place ... the list is very long. Radcliffe's contribution from critical development geography, and from a postcolonial feminism which is quite different from the autonomous feminism discussed below, shows what the decolonial might be if it were rooted in the experience of those on whose behalf it claims to speak. Her engagement over many years with indigenous women in some of Ecuador's poorest rural areas has led her to declare her despair that postcolonial recipes, or recipes of any kind, can improve their lot: 'the postcolonial difference offers no secure or stable platform on which to construct a "solution" to development's lacunae, no rallying articulation of identity and culture through which to overturn the status quo in a neat political reversal' (Radcliffe 2015: 27).

Radcliffe is the only one of the Latin American or Latin Americanist postcolonial writers mentioned here who takes seriously a core implication of her ideas, namely the need to listen to the voices of the people and the collectivities who appear as one-dimensional victims in the decolonial narrative, and also to engage with the ambiguities and conflicting pressures which that listening imposes both on the observer/commentator and on the people being watched and listened to.

Listening in this context of extreme inequality brings doubt and self-questioning, and it was Gayatri Spivak in 1988 who predicted that the unspoken and unenunciated assumptions of these grand theories could end up reinforcing the subject positions of the theorists themselves (Spivak 1988: 273–4). Like Said and Fanon, Spivak is very often quoted in support of views about which an inspection of her writings would show her to be quite sceptical, and this is particularly striking with reference to her persistent attacks on the stereotyping and misleading homogenization which permeate discourses of victimization. Spivak is saying that the theorists, especially Foucault, are so dazzled by apparatuses of power that they think that the oppressed barely have voices at all or, if they do, they emit an undifferentiated or incoherent mass outburst. She quotes Edward Said's criticism that Foucault's use of power allows him 'to obliterate the role of classes, the role of economics, the role of insurgency and rebellion' (Said 1983: 243). Invoking Gramsci, she deploys a classic Marxist-structuralist approach: the subaltern has to be studied with the tools of political economy and an analysis of ideology, which are missing in the Foucault–Deleuze conversation.

Likewise, Radcliffe is pitiless in her dissection of some discourses of indigeneity which she finds to be largely exercises in propaganda and co-optation, with little real effect on the plight of advertised beneficiaries. Of the *buen vivir* slogan adopted by Ecuador's former President Correa (now in exile fleeing a prison sentence for corruption) to demarcate himself from neo-liberalism and project an environmentally friendly image in tune with the culture of the country's large indigenous population, she makes a point similar to Kimberle Crenshaw's remark that 'the primary beneficiaries of policies supported by feminists and others concerned about rape tend to be white women' (Crenshaw 1991: 1269). For Radcliffe, 'an implicitly racially unmarked female subject risks becoming the social referent for such policy formulations, whereas for racialized women working in agriculture or washing clothes, this policy paradigm creates as many obstacles as it removes' (Radcliffe 2015: 264). In other words, the development programmes that use an exclusively income-based criterion sidestep the effects of racial exclusion or do not seek to confront them. Yet as she picks her way through conflicting discourses, arguments and slogans, quoting extensive interviews from activist women, indigenous representatives and development planners, a web of intersectionality emerges in which the 'abyss' of the colonial does not insulate indigenous worlds from the influence of all sorts of ideas drawn from national and international spheres. One example is women's rights and environmental protection, which have filtered down from the international development policy community to the grass-roots organizations in some of the poorest areas of the Andes and Amazonia. Similarly, even though she writes of the 'Orientalist origins' of ideas of citizenship and development, Radcliffe does not dismiss them, describing rather how they become intertwined with indigenous ideas: 'This reconfigured political sphere is one where *indígenas* are knowledgeable interlocutors, able to consider well-being in relation to the Pachamama' (Radcliffe 2015: 278).

Radcliffe, like Spivak, avoids describing indigenous women in terms of their victimhood, preferring to emphasize their agency. She grasps the multiple strands which run across cultural boundaries and also the porousness of those boundaries, linking supernatural beliefs, communal arrangements, gender relationships, political organization, the many locations of indigenous representation in Ecuadorian society, environmental concerns and more. She is also a particularly fierce critic of the *mis*recognition of indigenous people: in her perspective they are 'racialized' by the others who come bearing the gifts of citizenship and development, yet who do not recognize the 'diversity within diversity' (Radcliffe 2015: 286). In the end, this has little in common with the oracular pronouncements of the men most prominently identified with the Latin American decolonial strand, save in the sense that, in Radcliffe's similarly over-determined perspective, the bearers of projects and programmes, however well meaning and however committed to participation, ethnic awareness and gender awareness, can never 'get it right'.

Philosophical lineage

Latin American movements for fundamental, structural change such as those which decolonials seem to envisage were heavily influenced in the period 1960–1990 by Marxism and its *tercermundista* offshoot, dependency theory, and later by liberation theology. This is borne out by the history and ideologies of the Cuban revolution, of Chile's short-lived Popular Unity government (1970–3), and of the disastrous revolutionary experiences of Central America in the late 1970s. The post-2000 leaders who have attracted the sympathies of Santos and Mignolo, sometimes known as the 'pink tide', have little interest in the language of theory or in any particular theoretical tradition, except for Evo Morales's intellectual Vice-President García Linera, who established a Vice-Ministry for Decolonization.

In the decolonial worldview, the ideal of freedom is not explicitly rejected but receives little consideration, perhaps on account of its connection to liberalism, whose association with individual freedoms and the free market, and with neo-liberalism, provokes widespread distrust. Nationalism and class struggle are also discarded in favour of the causes of indigenous peoples and Afro-descendant populations as historic and contemporary victims of colonialism. Environmental degradation gets hardly any mention, though it is implicit in the invocation of indigenous knowledges which can be assumed to stand for resistance against the ravages of mining and intensive and monocrop agriculture. The cause of women's equality is left, as we shall see, to feminists.

Decolonial theory can be seen in the context of tectonic changes which have drastically reduced the numbers and power of Latin America's working classes. If 'Eurocentric' baggage, including Marxism, are rejected, it is because the social base of classic European and Latin American movements of contention is no longer available: the protagonists of the decolonials' preferred social movements are not the party, the union and social classes but indigenous and *campesinos* of the highland Andes or the remote Amazonian forest or the *favelados* who live in peripheral neighbourhoods of big cities. Their demands are couched not in the language of socialism, democracy, development, or human rights but rather in terms of dignity, respect, cultural recognition, territorial self-government, *el buen vivir* and *Madre Tierra*. Patterns of organization have also changed: with the exception of Argentina, large-scale trade union mobilization is unusual, overtaken by contingents of students and women, while leadership tends often to be locally based. And that is without counting the millions of evangelicals who share those social conditions but are unlikely to take part in those movements.

For Santos, such movements are inspired not by (European) social theories but rather by cosmology and a distinctive episteme:

> They build up their struggles on the basis of ancestral, popular and spiritual knowledge which has always been foreign to the scientism of Eurocentric critical theory ... their ontological conceptions of being and life are quite different from Western shortsightedness and individualism. For them, beings are communities of beings rather than individuals, and their ancestors are present and alive in their communities like animals and Mother Earth. We are in the presence of non-Western cosmovisions which demand an effort of intercultural translation if they are to be understood and valued. (de Sousa Santos 2010: 17–18)[22]

The evidence for these claims is thin, as attested by the literature on the Brazilian MST and on the coca growers' union (*cocaleros*) which formed Evo Morales's power base: these are movements demanding land and associated requirements of a dignified life in the case of the

MST, and freedom to grow and sell their product in the case of the *cocaleros* – demands attuned to the left-wing European traditions which de Sousa Santos criticizes for being 'short-sighted and individualist'. They mobilize symbolic representations but in support of material and environmental concerns (Grisaffi 2019; Wolford 2016a, 2016b); for example, the MST campaigns against genetically modified seeds. Even a sympathetic observer like Sarah Radcliffe has, as we saw, expressed her scepticism about *buen vivir*, and Morales's co-optation of Aymara rituals to bolster his personality cult has been heavily criticized by Silvia Rivera and others.

Santos sometimes would like to see intellectual work more decentralized and grounded, like the movements he praises, as when he criticizes theory (in general) for merely confirming the successes and failures of the past, and calls for a new version of bricolage – more 'artesanal' than 'architectural' and more the work of a committed observer (*testigo implicado*) than a theoretical visionary, more rearguard than vanguard theorizing (de Sousa Santos 2010: 18–19).

Decolonial grand theory finds its expression in its philosophers, Enrique Dussel and Manuel Maldonado-Torres. For Maldonado-Torres, Husserl, the founder of phenomenology, and his successor Heidegger, and Heidegger's follower and critic Emmanuel Levinas, provide the underpinnings of the radical otherness of the victims of coloniality (Maldonado-Torres 2007).

The invocation of Heidegger is not entirely surprising. The decolonial theorists share with him what one interpreter describes as a search for a 'rootedness and for a "folkish" science [*völkische Wissenschaft*]'. It seems that Heidegger associated this folkishness with a 'thickness of Being' that contrasted with the 'flattening' represented by (modern) science. However, in his declaration of loyalty to the Nazi regime, Heidegger referred 'not to a science that with its rootedness in a people has grown certain of its stability, but rather to a science that has become all the more vulnerable . . . the rootedness of a "folkish" science is the originarity that is conferred upon it in its questioning concerning the originarity understood throughout his writings as Being' (Phillips 2005: 4). The passage is difficult, and is quoted here only to signpost the affinity between these important Heideggerian concepts and the decolonial yearning for indigenous science.

Levinas and the decolonials

It was Enrique Dussel who, having first studied theology, introduced the language and critique of phenomenology into the world of Latin

American left-wing, or critical, thought. Dussel starts his book *Filosofía de la Liberación*, first published in 1976 and written as a student text rather than as a formal philosophical treatise, by 'trashing' much of the history of philosophy, especially ontology: 'Ontology, the thinking that expresses Being, the Being of the reigning and central system, is the ideology of ideologies, the foundation of the ideologies of the empires, of the center. Classic philosophy of all ages is the theoretical consummation of the practical oppression of peripheries' (Dussel 1985: 5). He continues in this vein for one chapter before changing into a philosophical key, though often with a twist connecting the very specialized vocabulary with his everyday political concerns and those of his Latin American readers.

Dussel stands in the lineage of phenomenology, but phenomenology as redirected by the French philosopher Emmanuel Levinas who, despite the extreme difficulty of his writing, became one of the world's most admired thinkers in the late twentieth century. The decolonials were drawn to his development of a concept of responsibility, which would fit in with their hostility to western institutions like bureaucracy – a hostility to the opacity and exclusion that divides generous ideas of social justice or care for another from their implementation.

As a core principle, Levinas affirms that responsibility is responsibility for another, whatever that other does and whoever they are. It is not a choice but rather is constitutive of being human. It is prior to ethical reflection or moral debate, and he quotes Dostoyevsky from the *Brothers Karamazov*: '"my responsibility" is total, covering all the others and their responsibility – ego ("le moi") always incurs a responsibility beyond that of all the others' (Levinas 1982: 95).[23] Our responsibility is far more than a moral injunction to love one's neighbour.

The Other ('autrui' as distinct from 'l'autre') in these discussions possesses an absolute uniqueness which is revealed in the face and in the vulnerability of the face. That vulnerability enables me to treat them violently but also prevents me from doing so: I am bound to the other by this interhumanity. The interhuman relationship (he does not say 'relationship between people') is grounded not in any particular deed or feeling for that individual. Rather, it derives from the individuality of the Other, as expressed in their face, which stands 'more or less' for the body – an individuality which calls upon me and demands of me that I place myself at their service.[24]

But the Other is abstract in the extreme and cannot be concretized. In the words of one commentator:

> Insisting that the Other cannot be categorized, Levinas has abstracted the Other to the point that any specific Other would signify no

differently than an infinite number of Others. 'The other must be received independent of his qualities, if he is to be received as other.' Indeed, Levinas must hold that even the SS guard who has a face calls for an infinite ethical response. (Simmons 2011: 102–3)

Dussel, Maldonado-Torres and other decolonial philosophers, or philosophers of liberation, have found in these very abstract texts a legitimation for their much more imperative discourse, infused with partisan and politicized language. They have transposed Levinas's interhuman concept of the Other and the responsibility which binds the Same to the Other – who is also a Same – onto a platform of collective action and political alignment.

The decolonial reading of the history of Western European philosophy begins with a response to Descartes, besides whose 'cogito', following Dussel, Maldonado-Torres posits a 'conquiro'. Writing from exile in Holland a hundred years after the start of the colonization of the Americas, Descartes, we are told, facilitated subsequent race-based interpretations of American indigenous societies by establishing mind–body dualism: 'I think', they say, is a way of creating a category of those who do not think, and 'I am' creates those who have no being (who are 'desprovistos de ser') and are deemed disposable. (Maldonado-Torres 2007: 144). Furthermore, Descartes' dualism is then located at the origins of a system which has put science at the service of an apparatus of 'knowledge and control'. Maldonado-Torres attributes to Descartes and his successors responsibility for what he calls a 'misanthropic scepticism' and for raising common-sense racism to the status of a foundational philosophy at the very basis of knowledge (ibid.: 145).[25] He also criticizes Heidegger for developing his concept of *Dasein* at the expense of forgetting the 'coloniality of being'. In response to Heidegger's dictum that the absence of *Sein* is the great fault in European philosophy, Torres points to the absence of coloniality and the naturalization of war (Maldonado-Torres 2007: 146).

Phenomenologists do not write about structures or institutions: their attention is on consciousness and Being. Their concept of freedom as an attribute of consciousness has little in common with the French Revolution, with any other revolution, or with liberalism. This may account to some extent for their appeal to Latin American radical thinkers: they tend to see the rhetoric of freedom as a shield for the liberal rhetoric and free-market doctrines which have operated as a cover for very illiberal oligarchic rule and lopsided unfree markets, not to speak of slavery, ever since independence in the early nineteenth century.[26]

Torres draws on Levinas for a critique of freedom, seeing in his work instead a high value placed on sociality. The result is that 'ideals of freedom and equality make headway at the cost of the omnipresent death of fraternity or, rather, of altericity', i.e. responsibility towards one's fellow human beings (Maldonado-Torres 2007).[27] With his concept of trans-ontology, Torres is trying to recruit Levinas to a vision of a society grounded in the same–other relationship as a fraternal solidarity, but Levinas does not share such a vision. He places the law and justice above all else; the responsibility to the other is not a matter of feeling or solidarity, not least because it is prior to the very existence of the Other.

Dussel places Levinas's Other at the service of his own Manichean worldview. His foundational distortion is to take the Other to be either a person or a personification of a collectivity, and also to locate that Other exclusively among the globally dispossessed: '"Being is" summarizes all ontology. In the presence of Being, there is nothing to do but contemplate it, speculate on it, go into ecstasy over it, affirm it, and remain tragically in the passive authenticity [*Eigentlichkeit*] favorable for the dominator but fatal for the dominated. Gnosis is the perfect act of the ontological, aristocratic oppressor' (Dussel 1985: 49–50).[28]

Domination seems not to figure at all in the Same–Other relation as explored by Levinas. We have already seen the ethereal, even mystical, element in the Same–Other pairing, and we notice it also in his introduction of 'height' into it: the gaze of the other is the gaze of entitlement to everything, it is 'the epiphany of the face as face' and in looking upon an other one recognizes a hunger. 'To recognize the Other is to give, but giving to, and this recognition consists of approaches towards giving – giving to a master, a lord whom one looks up to on approaching' (Levinas 1961: 73).[29] The mystical abstract dimension begins to appear. The encounter may be one of openness, of placing oneself at the service of the Other, but that is not a response to the domination which decolonials would overthrow. In Levinas even the dominator is the Same.

The decolonial commentaries look to a concretization which in turn facilitates the development of political or ideological points. Dussel reduces *Sein* to a characteristic of either the dominator or the dominated and describes authenticity as a consequence of structure, and he pursues this schema in writing of the Other:

> In times of danger the other is transformed, thanks to ideologies, into 'the enemy.' In peacetime . . . the face of the other is exchanged for an ugly mask, weatherbeaten and rustic. The mask is not a face; it does not make appeals; it is one more piece of furniture in the environment. One passes near the other and says simply: 'A worker!' or 'A native!' or 'A black!' or 'An undernourished Pakistani!' (Dussel 1985: 54)[30]

Here the Other is personified as victim – of stereotyping, or of colonial violence – and the face, a concept woven in so many ways by Levinas, is reduced to a manipulated mask. For Davis, the face is 'perhaps the best known and the most mysterious' of all Levinas's terms (Davis 1996: 46): the face is not *simply* seen: to see the face would be to make of it an intentional object of the perceiving consciousness, whereas it is not the object of 'experience in the sensible sense of the term, relative and egoist' (Davis 1996: 46). The Other is 'not *with* me or *against* me'; it is simply there, 'present to me in an originary and irreducible relation' (Davis 1996: 45–6).

In a separate passage which tries to trace responsibility back to the other to an anteriority prior to anteriority, Dussel channels Levinas's concept into his own entelechy: 'To be responsible for the other in and with regard to the system is anteriority prior to all other anteriority . . . It is the metaphysical anteriority of the new or future order. . . . The mother is responsible for the defenceless child just as the teachers are responsible for their pupils and leaders for their people' (Dussel 1985: 60).[31]

One difference between Levinas and Dussel is that Levinas does not seek to allocate blame. When he uses the language of moral obligation, it is an aspect of the folding of the Same into the Other and the pre-conscious, pre-judgmental assumption of responsibility for the Other, which is not much of a guide to daily life, let alone to politics. To be near to an Other (*proximité*) has nothing to do with intentionality or with knowledge even of a human object or even with whether the Other is known to me (Levinas 1982: 93).[32] Nonetheless, he admits that this is an 'extreme formulation' and specifies that 'all sorts of laws intervene before justice can be put into practice, but justice only makes sense if it preserves the spirit of disinterestedness which drives the idea of responsibility for another man' (Levinas 1982: 96).[33] So even Levinas comes down to earth in incorporating the idea of impersonal justice – an ideal expressed in his exaltation of the Torah as the foundation and perennial expression of Justice as an institution.

So when he fastens on the face, the Other's face, this is a 'refutation of any totalitarian or absolutist form of the economy' (Levinas 1996: xi). The face is highlighted because it distinguishes our individuality, encompassing therefore 'any other typically human aspect that reveals the other' – voice, gait and other ways in which a person is recognized.

Phenomenology's apparent aversion to, or distance from, the notion of a system or a model, as in Marxism or liberalism, fits in with the decolonial rejection of the universalist and all-encompassing theoretical apparatuses which have dominated Latin American ideologies.

In the interview-dialogues published as *Ethique et Infini*, Levinas described his notion of the asymmetrical relation binding me to the Other (*autrui*): in the company of an other, whatever image I may possess of that person, their face, their expressiveness *instructs* or *orders* me to place myself at their service. He recalls that a basic theme of *Totality and Infinity* is the asymmetrical character of any interpersonal relationship ('la relation intersubjective est une relation non symmétrique' – Levinas 1982: 94). He then quotes Dostoyevsky from the *Brothers Karamazov*:[34] my responsibility is total, covering all the others and their responsibility – ego (*le moi*) always incurs a responsibility beyond that of all the others (1982: 95).

The interpretation of Levinas offered by Maldonado-Torres and Dussel is a distortion of his thought. The distortion is politicization, that is, an attempt to turn his expositions of the Same and the Other into a recipe for political action, and reinterpretation of the Other as shorthand for all the excluded of the world, a disembodied boundless collectivity in the place of the actually existing face.

There remains still the question of how it is that radical Latin American intellectuals can be so fascinated by a thinker whose political positions are so different from theirs. The practitioners of the philosophy of liberation and of decolonialism are nationalists, which Levinas is not; they place significant emphasis on the economic causes of injustice, which holds little interest for him; they support the claims of first settlers (i.e. the indigenous peoples) which he associates with European irredentist nationalism and therefore opposes; they take hostility to the western tradition of thought as their default position, whereas Levinas cleaves to it above almost anything else and sees his Judaism as entwined with it; and Levinas regards the Talmud as an embodiment of the universal values of that very same western civilization which they blame for the ills of the world on account of the colonialism which carried it across the globe.[35]

The next move undertaken by Maldonado-Torres and Dussel is their surprising approximation of Levinas and Fanon. The move is surprising, not least from the stylistic point of view: Fanon writes in a direct way which gives eloquent expression to his anger, though his works were far from exclusively an expression of that anger, while Levinas, as we have seen, makes a virtue of opacity and complex undercurrents. The confluence is facilitated by Dussel's term 'trans-ontology' (Irvine 2011), in response to which Maldonado-Torres coins 'sub-ontology' to denote the life of the colonized as 'a permanent struggle against an ever-present death' – a phrase taken from Alice Cherki's Preface to *The Wretched of the Earth*.[36] There is also a common ascendance in that Fanon too professes to have been strongly influenced not only by Sartre but also by Merleau-Ponty, both themselves, like Levinas, heirs to the phenomenological tradition of Husserl and Heidegger. Fanon, Sartre and Levinas all search for what might be called an inwardness (Sartre calls it authenticity) and the choices it imposes on us whether we like it or not; Fanon digs pitilessly into the condition of the Black man and, distressingly, finds a White man; and Levinas, closing in ever more tightly on the face, finds a 'same who is also me' and a responsibility which pre-exists our moral awareness. Perhaps then the decolonials have sensed a shared heritage through Levinas and Fanon (they do not mention Sartre), but they themselves are not imbued with this phenomenological inwardness. They are too interested in politics and in allocating responsibility in the form of blame.

The lesson I draw from Levinas is the centrality of the universal unrelenting archaeology of the concepts and terms he uses: he never lets them alone, but keeps explaining, fending off mistaken interpretations, carving out a conceptual and often etymological space for each concept. He rarely touches on politics or on social questions. Dussel, in contrast, goes on a rampage among received concepts, tears them down, mostly on the basis of a moralistic and geographical critique against the 'centre'. I sympathize with his anger, even if I do not sympathize with the way he chooses its targets (all outside his own region). Fanon, for his part, writes, as Francis Jeanson said, as if 'flayed alive', in such a way as to convey the experiences in which his pain has been forged, but he is immune to the decolonials' finger-pointing style of writing. He does not claim to be a philosopher, but some powerful and painful teachings find their way through his untamed writings.

The true taboo-breakers:
autonomous feminism takes on the world

It will not have passed unnoticed that the leading figures of decolonial grand theory are all men, that gender issues largely pass them by and that for the most part they are established in university positions. Many autonomous feminists, who have come also to call themselves decolonial feminists, live a different life, outside or on the fringes of academia, addressing sensitive issues like the funding of Latin American feminist organizations and sexuality. At times, they seem to engage in 'performance-theorizing', echoing performance artists.

Global feminism under fire

By 2019, a new wave of autonomous decolonial feminism had gained an audience, extending the scope of feminist intervention across the entire range of injustices, including climate and environmental injustice, and addressing an ever wider public.

Autonomous feminism dates back to a 1993 meeting in El Salvador which itself was the VI Latin American and Caribbean Feminist Meeting (VI Encuentro Feminista Latinoamericano y Caribeño), followed by the VII Encuentro in Cartagena, Chile, in 1996 and an XI Encuentro in Mexico City in 2019. The autonomous feminists were dissidents at these events and published separate declarations and books, starting with the idealistically entitled 1997 volume *Permanencia voluntaria en la Utopia* ('Voluntary Residence in Utopia') (Bedregal 1997). Their dissidence was, it seems, carefully planned, so for example in advance of the meeting in Cartagena, 150 Chilean feminists agreed to convene a preparatory committee (Comisión Organizadora) on an open basis. When it met, the *autónomas* found they were thirteen out of the twenty present and so, with this *número cabalístico* of thirteen,[37] they took control of planning the Cartagena meeting (VII Encuentro), while the *feministas de las instituciones*, the establishment feminists installed in their NGOs (*oenegés* as the text sarcastically transcribes them; cf. ONGs, the English equivalent would be NGO – 'njeeo'), were preparing for the UN Women's Conference.

The Cartagena meeting attracted an impressive 800 people, and a book published soon after in Mexico conveys the prevailing mood in combative and eloquent language, shot through with poisonous polemics. There had been a dispute with a Dutch NGO (ICCO) about the funding of the conference which complicated matters, and the Bolivian anarchist-feminist María Galindo, based at that time in Mexico, spoke contemptuously of this dependence as the 'feminine correlate of patriarchy' ('correlato femenino del patriarcado') (Artigas 1997: 15). Feminist organizations, she said, should be accountable to their rank and file and not to international bodies.

This version of the autonomous feminist ideology lays stress on pluralist feminism as a search (*una búsqueda* in the words of the Introduction), a force in constant movement rather than a defined campaign for specific rights (Artigas 1997: 7). Its spokespeople, like Ximena Bedregal, a Chilean-Bolivian living at the time in Mexico, portrayed their feminism as a project to transform the world. Energized by a struggle for public recognition of lesbianism, they were also driven by despair at the commodification of women as 'booty' in the wars over ethnicity, religion and drugs waged under the indifferent eyes of the world (Bedregal 1997).[38]

For them, women were not only bearers of rights but also bearers of ideas and beliefs which can change the world.

In March 2009, at the XI Encuentro in Mexico City, a further dissenting declaration was published, listing the names of various groups which preceded this one, such as the Chilean Las Cómplices and the Bolivian Mujeres Creando, culminating in the 'Permanencia Voluntaria en la Utopía' declaration of 1997 which they considered the founding statement of autonomous feminism.[39] It again denounced the control exercised by transnational organizations, and the lack of access for black, indigenous and other outcast groups. The declaration expressed a feeling that their presence was too complicit with prevailing bourgeois and patriarchal practices: for example, voting by show of hands in open session repeated the fallacy of bourgeois democracies, concealing *lógicas patriarcales* and silencing different (i.e. minority) ideas.[40] The declaration also drew attention to 'the innumerable connected forms of subordination and colonization of [women's] bodies and their subjectivities'.[41] Since the 1990s, autonomous voices had expressed a consistent set of themes articulated by people who, perhaps not by accident, seem to lead a peripatetic life as Latin American public intellectuals, born in one country, exiled to another, living in a third and returning once the latest repressive regime has departed.

This is a feminism without frontiers, heir to the struggles of *indios* and black women, latinas, chicanas and feminist lesbians. It opposes 'compulsory heterosexuality', as well as the treatment of women as a natural rather than a political category.[42] The condition of women is intertwined with a constellation of disasters afflicting vulva, rebelliousness, movement, the world economy, humanity and the planet, but also a confrontation with conventional morality, including conventional feminist morality. In 2009, their seven main themes included some which in 2021 might meet disapproval, 'orgasm, resistance, madness, sex toys, casual sex, solidarity, complicity', and their message of self-sufficiency was bolstered by videos of themselves armed with mops and posters, cleaning up a venue in preparation for their breakaway meeting.[43]

> Our feminist autonomy is a stand we take in the face of the world rather than a coordinated list of prescriptions. Autonomy does not draw on dogmas or mandates because it is free of regulation and of any attempt to separate us from our uniqueness and our responsibility as historical subjects committed to other ways of going about our lives and inhabiting the intimate, private and public spheres . . .[44]

The authors of these documents are not *habituées* of the academic circuit or of any policy forum. Their activism is elsewhere or on the edges of those circuits. Like the transgressive performance poetry of Diamela Eltit in Chile (Polgovsky Ezcurra 2019: 45–57), they exhibit a way of making their 'point' and their 'case' in other spheres, and so the language is less stilted and the forums more open – less 'elitist', in the words of some. It is not surprising that María Galindo (a leading light in Mujeres Creando) describes herself as an anarchist. Years later, she wrote of *despatriarcalización*: to ask for recognition from the state would be to allow the neo-liberal state to slot them into a uniform box. This slicing and dicing of a 'rights agenda' undermines a person's 'transformative potential and subversive force' (Galindo 2020).[45]

At a later stage, when the word 'decolonial' became common currency and a mutual approximation was under way with the academic world, the interventions of autonomous feminists began to fit into a tighter ideological or theoretical framework, distancing them from the unrestrained, but universalist, discourse we see in these declarations. New names appear, such as Ochy Curiel, who was to become a prominent exponent of decolonial feminism. Writing already on the eve of the 2009 XI Encuentro, her bibliography contained works exclusively by non-Latin American writers (except for her colleague Yuderkys Espinosa) and expressed a yearning for a synthesis of theory and practice and for a greater independence of Latin American feminist writing. The visible academic 'turn' away from the provocative tone of the previous autonomist meetings, especially from the 'performance' which overtook the 2009 meeting, is here illustrated precisely by extended discussion of the relationship between theory and practice (Curiel Pichardo 2014).

This newer decolonial generation appears in 'Tejiendo de *otro modo*' ('Knitting *otherwise*', or 'differently') (Espinosa Miñoso, Gómez Correal and Ochoa Muñoz 2014b: 25), easily available on the internet. The earlier declarations of 'feminismo autónomo' are mentioned but not reproduced, and many themes remain, such as a 'counter-hegemonic' posture in opposition to the institutional feminists. The emphasis now shifts to the decolonial, to an ideological confrontation with the white bourgeois feminism emanating from the 'North' or from Europe, and to an attack on the ideal of a feminist woman produced by western civilization – the myth of the 'universal woman'.

These themes come together in the late María Lugones, who had been writing about race, sexuality and love since the 1980s. Lugones aligns herself with decolonial feminism and draws heavily on Anibal Quijano, while criticizing his treatment of sex as a biological category (Lugones 2014: 62).[46] Not insignificantly, in tune with the enthusiasm for decolonial theory, Lugones's other references in the article reproduced in 'Tejiendo de *otro modo*' are, again, all in English.

THE LATIN AMERICAN DECOLONIAL

What if the Conquest had not happened?

Among explorations of the treatment of women in pre-colonial societies, Lugones picks up stories about Yoruba society which, according to some scholars, did not have a binary gender system until the imposition of colonial rule and with it a binary male-dominated system that was welcomed by Yoruba men. She also quotes the claim that North American Indians accepted homosexuality and intersexual individuals, until colonialism imposed a binary classification. This schematic narrative forms the background to a portrait of global Eurocentric capitalism in which colonized women are subjected to a heterosexual regime but without the privileges enjoyed by white women: whereas the latter are identified with 'nature, with children and with domestic animals', colonized women are reduced to the condition of animals in the 'deep sense of beings without gender' (Lugones 2014: 69).

Rita Segato, formerly professor of anthropology at the University of Brasilia, disagrees with Lugones's views about the 'pre-intrusion world' (*el mundo pre-intrusión*). In her portrayal of pre-Columbian societies, men had to pay a *tributo femenino* (in the form of obligations owed to women) and politics was conducted within the domestic sphere – later came the colonial destruction of masculinity, drawing politics into the public sphere under the command of white males, and leading to a regime of 'low-intensity patriarchy' (*patriarcado de baja intensidad*). She argues that in the course of colonial conquest the egalitarian discourse of modernity rearranged relationships within communities (*la aldea*) and accentuated pre-existing hierarchies, producing an inflated male role on the inside, and an emasculated one on the outside, as a result of the universalization of the public sphere and the polarization of the public and the private.[47] Women for their part were wrenched away from their own mutual solidarity expressed in ritual, in production and reproduction, and confined within the domestic sphere (Segato 2014: 81–5): an imaginary synthesis in which the idealization of untouched pre-colonial society merges with the critique of patriarchal colonialism and capitalism.

The decolonial drive behind these conceptualizations of women's condition is expressed in angry denunciations of those who speak of western civilization as if it were the only possible model, shrinking the world's womanhood into a uniform notion of a 'universal woman' created by the machinery of colonialism and capitalism. In a similar vein to Saba Mahmood and Judith Butler in their critique of liberal feminism (Mahmood 2005, 2006), they dissent from this homogenizing model propagated by white bourgeois feminism – mostly European but also Latin American – and denounce its hegemonic projects and the class and

THE LATIN AMERICAN DECOLONIAL

racial interests of its proponents (Espinosa Miñoso, Gómez Correal and Ochoa Muñoz 2014a: 28). White Eurocentric feminism is dismissed as an attempt to transmit the benefits of rights conferred by modernity to 'non-white, indigenous and black women' on the basis that patriarchy and gender domination are everywhere the same, thus ignoring the radical difference brought about by the irruption of colonialism and modernity in the non-European world. This underlies the hostility to international NGOs and their carefully crafted, gender-aware programmes. In their universalist conception, Segato sees the seeds of their failure: neverthe-less, she allows that if they were to promote equality among both men and women, they might facilitate the emergence of women leaders who stay in their communities and do not migrate (Segato 2014: 76–8). (Segato overlooks the innumerable women leaders who, instead of migrating in search of opportunities elsewhere, have become leading defenders of indigenous organizations and the environment, sometimes at the expense of their own lives, as we see with fearful frequency in the Amazon region and in Central America.)[48]

This colonial framework is taken up in more strident language by the organizers of 'Tejiendo de *otro modo*'. Even Gayatri Spivak is derided because she colonizes the experience of the subalterns themselves by speaking on their behalf (Espinosa Miñoso 2014: 320) – a tendentious reading of her classic essay 'Can the Subaltern Speak?' (Spivak 1988).

In an allusion to escaped slaves, Ochy Curiel speaks of a *cimarronaje intelectual*, referring to the search for a thought of their/our own (*pen-samiento propio*) which on the basis of concrete experiences begins to open a breach in the regime of *saber-poder* ('power/knowledge', as in Foucault). But then she raises doubts about those who profit from this decolonizing venture to gain credit by weaving theories about 'otherness' (Curiel Pichardo 2014: 328). This perpetrator-alertness also appears in the chapter by Yuderkis Espinosa who uses the pejorative *oenegisación* ('engeeoization') to refer again to feminist organizations funded by inter-national NGOs – even the word 'rights' is denigrated since those rights are consubstantial with modernity and the evils it has inflicted on the extra-European world. They emphasize the Eurocentric character of the feminism they oppose, arguing for a distinctively Latin American femi-nism, and noting that even prominent Latin American feminist thinkers tend to work in the United States or Europe, or write as if they do.

Curiel and Espinosa have adopted the decolonial 'guru' style. Compare their wide-ranging contributions, incorporating moral verdicts on entire periods of history, and their blanket contempt for entire groups of activ-ists and feminist aid managers, whose main sin is the colour of their skin or the country of their residence, with the more grounded contribution

57

of Aida Hernandez Castillo to the *Tejiendo de otro modo* volume (Hernández Castillo 2014). Though perfectly aware of the ravages wrought by global capitalism, Hernández turns the spotlight on the oppression indigenous women have to live with inside the household and the community, in addition to the discriminations and exclusions they face beyond their communities in the wider society.

As the two publics – the autonomist and the decolonial – began to overlap, they were tracked by Anders Burman in Bolivia through activist circles and government bureaucracies, including the Depatriarchalization Unit of Bolivia's Vice Ministry of Decolonization. Starting with an illuminating description of debates among anthropologists about the 'distinct Andean notion of gender', both complementary and conflictive, but different from western patriarchy (originally proposed by Olivia Harris in 1980), he follows them through the world of ethnic and gender activism – where *feminista* is sometimes used 'as an insult' by association with European feminism. There is then a discussion of the word *chachawarmi* – an Aymara word translated as 'man-woman' and often used to illustrate the distinctiveness of Andean kinship and gender. The result is a convoluted debate about whether that term denotes a truly complementary or perhaps egalitarian relationship or whether it 'conceals gendered asymmetric relations of power'. In one view, *chachawarmi* has been captured by 'male indigenous activists' who have positioned it as a 'hegemonic or unquestionable absolute of indigenous culture', while others consider that it opens up possibilities for 'indigenous women (negated, subordinated, rejected as political subjects, as citizens and, fundamentally, as producers of knowledge and enunciators of subversive horizons of socio-political change) to recreate and emancipate themselves as indigenous women in a colonial world, but in a way that differs from the modern liberal project of female emancipation in the North' (Burman 2011: 75–7).

The response of one of Burman's interlocutors – a 'male Indianista' – throws the question back in a way which makes discussion very difficult:

> As one male Indianista activist put it: In the Bible you can see that a prophet could have a thousand, two thousand, perhaps three thousand women, right? And then in the history here, they say that the Inca as well had his virgins. That is completely false, because then there would be no chachawarmi, right? History lies, because it wasn't created by us, yet. (Burman 2011: 83)

Burman concludes (ibid.: 90) by saying that the meanings of both *chachawarmi* and decolonization are context dependent and disputed. But his conclusion may also be a veiled way of saying that the discussion of origins is a way of avoiding or relativizing the discussion of structural inequalities.

Silvia Rivera Cusicanqui: gender, race and class

To unravel the loaded discourse around *chachawarmi*, we can consult Silvia Rivera Cusicanqui, an anthropologist and public intellectual who bridges the 'street' and the elite intellectual world.

After completing her university degree, Rivera went to work as a schoolteacher in a village 15 days' journey from the capital and observed at close quarters the humiliations inflicted on indigenous people. Subsequently, she studied anthropology in Lima and participated in the flowering of Andean anthropology and ethno-history inspired by John Murra and Xavier Albó, carried forward by a uniquely creative generation including Nathan Wachtel, Antoinette Fioravanti, Tristan Platt, Olivia Harris, Enrique Tandeter and many more (Lehmann 1982; Murra 1975, 1980; Murra, Wachtel and Revel 1986; Wachtel 1971, 2014). In the 1980s, she wrote the influential history of Bolivian *campesino* movements, *Oprimidos pero no Vencidos*, which combined class analysis with a recognition of the oppression of the indigenous population 'as society and as culture', while refusing to classify them in a single ethnic category (Rivera Cusicanqui 1986).[49]

Rivera seems to get far more 'views' on YouTube than Ochy Curiel or Yuderkys Espinosa or Aida Hernandez, though such numbers are no doubt open to various interpretations. In one of these appearances, recorded in Oaxaca, Mexico, in 2015, she takes a somewhat ambivalent position: '*mestizos* are even more colonized than the *indios* because they are neither *indio* nor white and they feel ashamed and sometimes even disbelieve their own words . . . and so they latch on to other people's theories . . . the *mestizo* has bought into the European ethos . . .' But she holds fast to a principle of openness to all cultures, and goes on to say that the leading epistemes have completely different features and a dialogue between them is necessary.[50]

There are echoes here of the decolonial concepts of different epistemologies, but she seems to avoid the idea of epistemicide, and has not developed those ideas in published work. She is averse to the word 'identity', and describes herself as a mixture of Indian, white and Jewish. Also, having mocked *mestizos* in her spoken words, elsewhere, in writing, she emphasizes the positive value of mixture. At that same Oaxaca event, she spoke of the everyday reconstitution of life in all its fluidity and messiness.[51] As if echoing Fanon, and rejecting the assignment of labels to each and every ethnic or linguistic group, she envisaged the prospect that 'once we are decolonized we will be *persons* (not indios, aymara, purhepecha or whatever)' ['ya que somos colonizados nosotros cuando seamos descolonizados, vamos a ser *gente*'], and she repeats the word *gente* in different indigenous languages. 'La carga pesada de los sellos se va a acabar . . .' [the heavy burden of labels will come to an end . . .]. Many phrases in her published work spell out a concept of decolonization which is trans-ethnic, or ethnically neutral, but also utopian, as in the following:

> My intention is to assemble teachings and utopias from the struggles of indigenous people in order to design a broader, shared utopia in which we women of this continent, in all our cultural diversity, can find inner mirrors in which we can see ourselves reflected in our many dimensions and thus build a base in which we can all, men and women, *indios* and subaltern classes, finally stop being strangers in our own land. (Rivera Cusicanqui 2010b: 180, 2010 [1997])[52]

The coincidence of that last phrase with the title of Arlie Hochschild's sociological bestseller (Hochschild 2016) merits reflection.

Rivera is sharply critical of interpretations of the history of colonialism such as Segato's, regarding them as merely the obverse of the 'manichean western' division of the world into North/South, civilized/ savage, Christian/heretic, white/black and so on (Rivera Cusicanqui 2010 [1997]: 189). Grounded in her own fieldwork and the landmark ethno-historical works of others, she presents much more carefully the intricacies of the pre-Columbian Andean kinship system.

In that system, women's and men's lineages each had their respective religious obligations: while the women operated in horizontal networks of affinal relationships (joining mothers and their son's spouses) and sisterly (sororal) relationships, the men were classified in male lineages. In these parallel descent systems, women were subordinated to their spouses' mothers in the *panaka* (kinship network) and sons to their fathers in the *ayllu* (territorial unit). Ethnic groups were often distributed over separated spaces because of the vertical ecology of the Andes, classically described by John Murra (Murra 1972; see also Lehmann 1982), and its implications for food production and subsistence, and this meant that there was much interchange between them, including of marriage partners. In this context, women had a central role in the horizontal texture of pre-Columbian inter-ethnic relations (Rivera Cusicanqui 2010 [1997]: 187). Despite superficial resemblances, the difference between Segato's and Rivera's accounts is that Rivera does not superimpose modern conceptions of power and gender onto the kinship and political arrangements of pre-Columbian society, and her schema sets aside the

THE LATIN AMERICAN DECOLONIAL

notion of a village (*aldea*) used by Segato, which is unsuited to the vertical economy of ecological niches (*pisos ecológicos*).

The violent irruption of large contingents of unmarried male invaders into this world was bound to disrupt the system, and Rivera traces the changes in women's roles wrought by colonization, appropriation of land and the demographic collapse of the sixteenth century, all of which laid the basis for the emergence of the *cholo* and *mestizo* strata of colonial and modern Andean society.

Ruthlessly summarizing several centuries of history, Rivera models the colonization of gender and culture: women undertake hypergamic liaisons and marriages to white(r) men and have to make their way on their own. This forced self-reliance laid the way for the predominance of women in markets all over the Andes and also for the seventeenth- and eighteenth-century adoption of Spanish dress (most visibly the multi-layered skirts) in the hope of 'passing' and avoiding taxes imposed on *indios*. By the nineteenth century, though, that dress code was relinquished by women of a higher stratum and remained, ironically, as a marker of *indio* identity – a subject to which we shall return later in a discussion of the Oruro carnival (Rivera Cusicanqui 2010 [1997]: 194).

Rivera is held in high regard by the autonomists: she is a fighter, an independent spirit and a captivating speaker and writer. Her performances and her writings sparkle with a rich vocabulary and constantly challenge other feminists and other decolonials. Like many of them, she operates independently of the structures of academia, having retired from the Universidad Mayor de San Andrés in La Paz. Like Gayatri Spivak and the subalterns, she thrives on being at once a consecrated figure of the movement and a critic of much of what is said in its name. But having achieved celebrity status, she pays the price: people quote her without reading her and the complex message suffers from oversimplification. Rita Segato, for her part, has achieved continental celebrity as the author of the words adapted by the Chilean collective Las Tesis for the song/dance 'El Violador Eres Tú', which went viral across the world in late 2019 and early 2020.[53]

In more recent work, written when she was fully engaged in – or in a sense against – the politics of culture and ethnicity, Rivera uses the Aymara word *ch'ixi* to describe the country's interwoven ethnicities. She also says she herself is *ch'ixi*, the word which most appropriately translates as the mottled mix represented by *mestizas* and *mestizos*. This is explained as follows:

> the word *ch'ixi* has many connotations: it is a colour that is the product of juxtaposition, in small points or spots, of opposed or contrasting

61

colours: black and white, red and green, and so on. It is this heather grey that comes from the imperceptible mixing of black and white which are confused by perception, without ever being completely mixed ... The notion of *ch'ixi*, like many others ... reflects the Aymara idea of something that is and is not at the same time ... (Rivera Cusicanqui 2020: 65)

The paragraph flows into musings around fused opposites which do not quite fuse, or the 'potential of undifferentiation' that joins opposites, eventually landing on the word *abigarrado*, coined by the revered intellectual René Zavaleta, rendered by the translators as 'motley' but which I would rather translate as 'mottled'.[54]

Whereas mixture in the region usually evokes mixture across hierarchical lines of race, she uses *ch'ixi* to denote mixtures across all kinds of linguistic, ethnic and racial boundaries, some more hierarchical than others. Therein, she concludes, lies the Bolivian population's modernity – in implied contrast with the modernity of capitalism, bureaucracy and standardized rationality. Paradoxically, her nemesis Evo Morales has found his way to a similar sort of conclusion by a different route, as we shall see.

Having supported Morales's electoral campaign, Rivera became disappointed by his development model. She confesses that she fell victim to a pretence by the 'educated *mestizo* elites' who joined the process and wrapped up in complicated jargon what turned out to be an updated edition of the country's 1952 national-popular revolution and its idealized (some would say deceptive) concept of a unified Bolivian nation (Rivera Cusicanqui 2015: 24).[55] Whereas the 1952 version proclaimed a national popular unity overlaying a racially divided society, the Morales version proclaimed an indigenous nation overlaying the class divisions produced by 'neo-developmentalism', driven by the exploitation of natural resources.

Rivera has also attacked Morales and his vice-president, García Liñera, for gathering the entire indigenous population of the country under a generic indigenous umbrella, leaving the Aymara, the Quechwa, the Guarani of the lowlands, the Laymi of Northern Potosí and others as nameless, or sometimes 'plain' Bolivian. In addition she opposes the usage *originario* and defends the modernity of the country's Indian culture and Indian population: for her *originario* evokes a 'static, archaic' past, and she is dismissive of their decolonization drive (Rivera Cusicanqui 2010a: 59). Her vision of a multicultural and decolonized country distances itself from standard decolonial formulae by affirming its bilingual, mottled and *chi'xi* vocation in a host of fields, but she also adopts some of those selfsame formulae by advocating South–South ties to neighbouring countries as well as Africa and Asia, so that, strengthened by 'our ancestral convictions', they can register the autonomy of their science from the 'academia of the North' and its hegemonic project (Rivera Cusicanqui 2010a: 73).

Rivera's outsider status is expressed in her preference for small publishers with original names and creative designers like La Mirada Salvaje and Piedra Rota. She fires in many directions, taking aim at both the Morales government and the bad faith that underlay its claim to represent the indigenous in the eyes of the postmodern or decolonial milieux in the United States, as well as of the international development community. But, like the autonomists, she does not tell us how her imagined social order could be translated into institutional reality or how the inclusive regime of recognition which she sketches could be also a regime protecting freedom and human rights. Her public adoption of an anarchist, or 'anarcho-feminist-indianist', political position is not an answer to those questions.[56]

Intersectionality

Since the 1992 anniversary, there has been a visible shift in social science writing about Latin America in both Spanish and English (less in Portuguese and, perhaps above all, in English) from 'class' to 'race', and a parallel shift from a marxisant climate of opinion to one influenced by Cultural Studies and its discursive accompaniments, culminating, for now, in a climate of opinion and scholarship heavily influenced by postcolonial ideas.

Neither Said nor Fanon offer support for these decolonial ideas, nor for the cultural politics of identity which marks the intellectual and academic superstructure of much Latin American indigenous and Afro-American mobilization. Their concern is with documenting and overcoming colonial systems of oppression and building nations to overcome them, and for them a nation, to be a nation, has to be democratic and respect a universalist regime of human rights. Although Silvia Rivera's emphasis on culture as a source of social division, and her use of the distinctive Latin American tradition of Marxism and class analysis, sets her apart from them, all three have in common a reluctance, and even a refusal, to see in the demarcation and thickening of cultural frontiers a basis for a just society.

Class and cultural difference and the racial cleavages that accompany or often underpin them cannot be separated from the inequalities of gender, and the word 'intersectionality' is frequently invoked to argue that class, race and gender march in step to drive social inequality ever deeper. But if we return to Kimberle Crenshaw, the law professor who coined the term, we see that the analysis in her 1991 paper, revolving principally around race and gender in rape cases, rests on intersection and not on correlation. Far from saying that race and gender dimensions of injustice (which include violence, institutional discrimination and socio-economic exclusion) always reinforce one another, she explains that sometimes they do and sometimes they do not: but they always *intersect*. As Lennon and Alsop explain:

> what the use of the term 'Intersectionality' tries to avoid is attending to these differences as simply additive. It is not that there is a pattern of discrimination that results from being gendered, and we simply add onto it a pattern that derives from being raced or assigned to categories of sexuality, ethnicity, class, or able-bodiedness ... It is rather that we cannot articulate the consequences of any of these positionalities without taking the others into account. (Lennon and Alsop 2020: 131)

Crenshaw's central message is well expressed in her explanation of the reluctance of the Los Angeles Police Department to release statistics 'reflecting the rate of domestic violence interventions'. The Department feared, she writes, 'that statistics reflecting the extent of domestic violence in minority communities might be selectively interpreted and publicized so as to undermine long-term efforts ... to address domestic violence as a serious problem'. That is, domestic violence might then be 'dismissed' as a minority problem. She was told that representatives of minority communities 'were concerned that the data would unfairly represent Black and Brown communities as unusually violent, potentially reinforcing stereotypes ...' And then she reaches her punchline: 'This account sharply illustrates how women of color can be erased by the strategic silences of antiracism and feminism' (Crenshaw 1991: 1253).

Using a series of clinical legal arguments, in a very different style from that of social science, she argues that:

> [A]lthough the rhetoric of both agendas formally includes Black women, racism is generally not problematized in feminism, and sexism not problematized in antiracist discourses. . . . The primary beneficiaries of policies supported by feminists and others concerned about rape tend to be white women; the primary beneficiaries of the Black community's concerns over racism and rape, Black men. (Crenshaw 1989: 1269)

Perhaps things have changed in the almost thirty years since the article was published, but my concern here is with the structure of the argu-

THE LATIN AMERICAN DECOLONIAL

ment. The dynamics of power within the black population on one hand and between women of different colour on the other, in a context of socio-economic inequality, undermine the notion that sexism and racism reinforce one another: rather, it is black women whose maltreatment they jointly reinforce while black men are, to some extent at least, spared. Furthermore, in quite strong language, she writes: '[T]okenistic, objectifying, voyeuristic inclusion is at least as disempowering as complete exclusion' (Crenshaw 1991: 1261).

If we return to the causes of indigenous exclusion, we may readily allow that they are intersectional, but that should not be taken to mean that they are compressed into a homogenized effect, or that the lives of indigenous people, their relationship with the supernatural, their systems of government, their legal systems, the languages they speak, their music, their dress codes, their socio-economic status, their occupations, should be interpreted only through the lens of race or ethnicity. Crenshaw's subject matter was made up of law cases which in principle make for a clear-cut database, although she included much broader sociological and ethnographic evidence, and she limited the main variables to sexism and racism. But we know from research in other fields how these interactions shift from one field to another, and how they interact with others. In education, we know gender effects interact with race among black populations so as to, very often and in many countries, enable girls to move ahead of boys, at least until they get to the labour market.

Intersectionality is an invitation to study interactions between race and many other variables rather than to focus on race or ethnicity as the leading correlative of all other factors. We can see how this can produce misleading results when we look at race mixture across generations. For example, in a 2009 paper, Luisa Schwartzman indicated that mobility can be underestimated and the perpetuation of black poverty overestimated if one forgets that as people acquire more education they tend to marry or have children with people of a similar educational level to their own. For upwardly mobile blacks, and in the light of evidence that black women in Brazil do better in education than black men (Braga and da Silveira 2007; Lopes and Braga 2007; Rosemberg and Madsen 2011), this means they are relatively more likely to have children with partners of a lighter skin colour. The resulting statistical pattern will *appear* to show that blacks are always and for ever pinned at the bottom of the distribution because it will omit those who have followed that path, which some would call whitening and others upward mobility (Schwartzman 2009). The intersection in this model shows social class operating against the grain of the racial hierarchy.

The tight focus on ethnicity and race diverts attention from the achievements of indigenous and black women as spokespeople, activists and intellectual leaders in grass roots movements and civil society organizations ranging beyond specifically women's causes and specifically indigenous causes. They cut across boundaries that separate the indigenous from 'the rest'.

Indigenous women in the rural environments where their cultures have developed over centuries have engaged in advocacy and confrontation in defence of their persons against violence and of their participation in the institutional life of their communities. This has occasionally been resisted from within, but the research in the volume edited by Rachel Sieder shows that the assumption that the idea of women's rights has no connection to indigenous cultures is misguided (Sieder 2017). Cultural inheritance has now, in some places, *intersected* with the boundaries separating indigenous groups from others and with the conflicts over land, education and distributive justice that attach themselves to those boundaries as indigenous women fight for their rights as women, not 'just' as indigenous women. The Ecuadorian indigenous women from the highlands who went to defend their rights at the Constitutional Assembly in 2007 did so as indigenous women, but the rights they went to defend were enshrined in international law (Lavinas Picq 2016). Their presentation of themselves as indigenous intersected with their demands as equal citizens.

'Whitening' is a Brazilian term used pejoratively as if to describe some sort of betrayal by Afro-descendant people of their heritage or even their race, but it is also used to describe a supposed project of white elites to diminish black populations by miscegenation. The upward mobility seems to consist mostly of women who move up the class hierarchy, possibly beginning to mix in lighter-skinned circles, yet are still vulnerable to discrimination as women. The intersection comes when their situation is compared to that of lighter-skinned women of the same socio-economic status. Yet people who mix freely with others of varying skin colour and social class can also claim to be counted as black or indigenous, and sometimes their rediscovery or reclamation of their origins contributes to movements in support of indigenous or black rights and full citizenship. A rare detailed illustration is provided by Sigrid Huenchuñir, a Chilean psychologist who, having been brought up by an indigenous father who had changed his name, reunited herself with her origins later in life. Her autobiographical essay tells how she experienced socioeconomic mobility, gaining an education far beyond that of her parents, and then in the process of recognition received an advantage from her reclaimed Mapuche status (in the form of an affirmative action Ford Foundation scholarship to study at the University of Texas). Thus she began to draw close to other Mapuche (Huenchuñir 2015). Many others who do not undertake this journey of rediscovery might nonetheless be claimed as Mapuche by activists. In Brazil, persistent pressure for people with brown or light-brown skin to recognize themselves and be officially recognized as black has met with success: the official categories of *preto* (black) and *pardo* (brown) are now in effect a single category for policy purposes (i.e. affirmative action), and the statement that half the Brazilian population are *negros* has come to be taken for granted in journalistic output (Lehmann 2018). (*Preto* and *pardo* are somewhat anachronistic words that remain in use in official documents and the Census; *negro* and *moreno* are the standard everyday equivalents.) In all such variations, we see intersectionality, and the intersections can cut across and against each other.

I can illustrate this by recalling the October 2018 FLICA literary festival (Festival Literario Internacional de Cachoeira) that took over the Bahian town of Cachoeira, a small estuary port two hours' drive from the capital Salvador, whose dilapidated but still imposing riverside grand hotel had once welcomed landowning dynasties arriving by boat for their holidays. The festival generated a hubbub of readings, panels, lectures, performances and above all enthusiastic chatter of an overwhelmingly youthful student public. The only white (and older) faces to be seen were a handful of authors and critics from São Paulo who conferred their celebrity on the event and were visibly disconnected from the hubbub, despite their official status as honoured guests. The guest of honour, though, was the black writer Conceição Evaristo, chronicler of black women's and children's suffering,[57] whose failure to be elected to the Brazilian Academy of Letters that year had caused much revulsion among black feminists. There were performances ranging from the recitation of the misery of *favela* life to angry hip-hop indictment of white elites (i.e. me, as the only white male present) by a group called Coletivo da Quebrada. The atmosphere in the street was of *estética negra*, or more precisely *estética femenina negra*; lesbian couples were transforming the event into a celebration of their established acceptability and the installation of their pride, their style and their fashions in Salvador's public spaces; militancy intersected with poetry recitals and learned panel discussions, and with a friendly disposition towards the politics of the moment (the sponsorship of the municipal and state authorities) and towards business (further sponsorship). Blackness embraced dissidence and respectability and all shades in between.

The festival was a space for intersectionality 'from below' in movements of resistance rather than mechanisms of exclusion. It gave expression to intersectionality in resistance and reflected a new stage in the development of Brazil's *movimento negro*. In the mid-1990s, the movement was principally a network of academics advocating for affirmative action in university admissions and had met with considerable success (Lehmann 2018). Then, from the mid-teens, black activism spread out to the world of culture, of fashion and of politics in the broader sense, and 'down' to the student population and also beyond the walls of the university into both official institutions and a proliferation of organizations dedicated to black people in different spheres of life. Its voice is heard in a widening range of instances – for example, advocating successfully for compulsory allocation of funds by political parties to black and female candidates in primary elections. In the year of COVID, much attention has been drawn to the disproportionate harm it does to the black-skinned and low-income population, along with the open hostility of the Bolsonaro government to everything the *movimento negro* stands for.

Intersectionality is also reproduced ideologically. Autonomous feminists may rail against the globalizing and modernizing feminists of Europe and the NGOs, but their advocacy of autonomy and of rights and recognition for lesbians and for women of colour, criticizing European models of feminism, has much in common with European and North American feminism. To some, this may seem contradictory since it seems to align them with the neo-liberal feminism they deride. However, in exchange, so to speak, they should recognize that their Latin American identity (which they collectively emphasize together with their colour and their diverse sexuality) does not comprehensively or exclusively define their intellectual or ideological affiliations. These are all intersections.

Intersectionality leads to a universalist conception of justice because it allows for multiple sources of injustice and thus is an obstacle to an insistence that oppression comes from a single source of a person's identity. Thus Fanon's diagnosis of the malaise of intellectuals in the period of decolonization: his bitterness against the colonial system, which in his view co-opted those who fought against it, twisted some of them into quasi-collaborators or turned them into postcolonial dictators, is inspired by the same values and instincts as those which led him to denounce the vicious internecine battles of the Algerian political and military forces themselves and the deeply rooted prejudices that ran through French society and were by no means limited to the political right.

Cultural and ethnic difference also intersect

The leading figures of Latin American decolonialism have ploughed a different furrow with their attacks on western modernity and on the

THE LATIN AMERICAN DECOLONIAL

natural and social science which have grown out of it. They do not claim expertise as natural scientists and they do not undertake evaluation either of the science which they denigrate or of the indigenous scientific knowledge which has indeed been marginalized and ignored by academic and political institutions. The position loses consistency when confronted with a few stylized facts. On the one hand, colonial indigenous science is not alone in its marginalization: European and North American popular science or folk biology are similarly marginalized. But on the other hand European health authorities are quite relaxed about homeopathy and exotic non-medical treatments derived from eastern religions. Those eastern or New Age streams bring us full circle back to the *machis* who receive patients in their hospital consulting rooms in Chile, drawn not by an ancestral faith in Mapuche rituals, but as aficionados of New Age or homeopathic treatments. Those other knowledges, then, are not to be found exclusively in indigenous communities. For decolonials, however, it seems that the reliability, trustworthiness and integrity of scientific claims reside in the identity of those who make them – as exemplified in Mignolo's discussion, which might be titled 'Who will speak for the Maori?'[58]

The claim that trust or mistrust in modern science is conditioned by differences of culture is misplaced – if, that is, we can agree on what constitutes a 'difference of culture'. Religiously derived beliefs about the creation of the world, or panics around vaccination (seemingly more prevalent in Europe and the United States than in poorer countries[59]), or the worldwide receptivity to conspiracy theories exist within the same cultural sphere as trust in modern science. Recent political and epidemiological developments in the United States and in Europe have spawned a widely shared folk-anthropology reflecting deep disagreements between swathes of their populations about values and scientific expertise – differences marked apparently by education and geography more even than social class. Thus an analysis of the United Kingdom's 2016 Brexit referendum, which was preceded by a campaign infused with conspiracy theories and folk-anthropology, found that 'voting Leave is associated with older age, white ethnicity, low educational attainment, infrequent use of smartphones and the internet, receiving benefits, adverse health and low life satisfaction' (Alabrese et al. 2019).[60] The 2016 referendum is widely considered to have revealed deep rifts in British society between segments of the population who inhabit 'different universes', have different notions for example of what counts as evidence and radically different levels of trust in expertise, yet those differences are not superimposed on ethnic or quasi-racial lines as implied by those assumed to divide indigenous from non-indigenous populations in Latin

America. In the United States, Pew exit polls reveal an astonishing polarization among 'white-born again/evangelical Christians' (so excluding black evangelicals) of whom more than 75 per cent have voted for the Republican candidate in all elections since 2004, reaching 81 per cent in 2016, reflecting even more radical differences in worldview than those revealed by the UK referendum.[61]

Since 2010, opinion polls asking about the priority accorded to environmental issues found not only that political alignment was related to a lower level of 'belief and urgency' on climate change, but also that 'education, self-rated knowledge, and science comprehension are positively related to belief among Democrats and liberals, whereas the relationship for Republicans and conservatives is weak or even negative'. The conclusion was that 'providing more information to climate sceptics will do little to lead them to belief, and it may even backfire' (Egan and Mullin 2017: 216–17). In other words, belief or disbelief in scientific information is more than a question of ignorance or knowledge and has the characteristics of deep social divisions, especially when linked to party loyalty and religion.

Disagreements between supporters of Republican and Democrat parties seem to go beyond 'normal politics', especially when touching on the wedge issues of abortion, gun control and religious freedom. Although biblical sources or religious doctrine are invoked in such discussions, the disagreements do not originate in Bible study: Bible study serves to supply a text in support of any position. This is a world in which, according to Hochschild, 'a survey' in 2010, had found that 33 per cent of Democrats and 40 per cent of Republicans would be 'disturbed' if their child married someone from the other party (Hochschild 2016: 6). Despite claims about not just cultural but epistemological differences between them, I doubt whether such profound differences about science or even such resistance to intermarriage would be found in Latin America between indigenous and non-indigenous people. Indigenous leaders are in the forefront of mobilization on climate change. In Latin America, conceptions of the supernatural, kinship codes, beliefs about science, personal morality, skin colour, language or dialect, degrees of community inwardness, and so on should not be assumed to be superimposed and highly correlated.

The same point can be made, in a contrasting movement, with reference to indigenous movements and their leaders, who claim support for their cultural heritage while also promoting climate science and mobilizing to stop practices which cause environmental destruction and global warming, not to speak of damage to their lives and their habitats. The politics of recognition do not oblige us to say that they are somehow departing from their own heritage and culture when they embrace the findings of modern science.

It is a mistake to think of the recognition of indigenous rituals and medicine in terms of knowledge, or 'knowledges'. Even if it does have therapeutic qualities, this claim to recognition is couched in terms of cultural authenticity, not of efficacy.[62] Spiritual invocation and ritual performances are not to be taken as a sign of 'another knowledge': they are ritual performances to display shared identity and heritage, to show deference towards a tradition, to mark moments of a chronological cycle (weekly, monthly, annual) or a life cycle (Bloch 2004, 2007), or simply to honour a prominent political figure – like Evo Morales in his heyday. Rituals performed to ward off an evil spirit or to summon spirits of good fortune are not undertaken on the basis of 'knowledge', that is, on the basis of claims about cause and effect, but rather to demonstrate loyalty to community and deference (again) and for the sake of preserving the social fabric. They also accompany herbal treatments administered by *machis* to their fellow Mapuche in Chile – and to others who do not claim any Mapuche ancestry at all.

This does not mean to say that those treatments have no scientific basis. 'Another knowledge' is knowledge which has been developed by procedures other than those of conventional science, probably by trial and error across many generations. It may well have desired effects and a certain validity, and there may be non-pharmacological placebo or psychological effects, but it is local knowledge, not generalizable or transferable beyond the immediate context. Not, so to speak, peer reviewed.

It is therefore not surprising that whereas in Mapuche rural communities in southern Chile curative procedures are accompanied by ritual, in the capital, Santiago, which is home to the largest number of people who recognize themselves as Mapuche, they are separated. In their projects of cultural renewal, Mapuche associations have set up locations for their ritual practices, which are separate from the curative activity undertaken by *machis* in their allocated space in hospitals (Brablec 2019). The ritual revival of heritage and the claim to recognition are detached from the question of Mapuche knowledge in the sense of the efficacy of their medicine.

I have used the concept of intersectionality to show how ethnic and cultural divisions do not necessarily always correlate with one another. In the following chapters, I will pursue these themes with respect to religion and to the politics of ethnicity, culminating in a section on evangelical religion which undermines so many of the assumptions of the decolonial.

2

Indigeneity, Gender and Law

In the 1960s, when Latin American Studies was born as a profession, hostility to imperialism and capitalism was a default position, drawing on feelings of national dignity and of solidarity with working classes and peasant populations. Those ideas spread their influence and even contributed to the birth of Cultural Studies as an outcrop which has come almost to overshadow the study of literature. Cultural Studies seems to have grown out of a search for analytical coherence, or theory, among students of literature, perhaps inspired originally by the now forgotten contribution of Warren and Wellek's *Theory of Literature* (Warren and Wellek 1949: 105) and eventually turbo-charged by the spirit of hostility to US power, then imperialism, then multinational corporations and eventually world capitalism and neo-liberalism, which overtook US humanities and social science in the wake of the civil rights movement, Vietnam and other wars. In general, Marxism in many guises provided the theoretical framework until displaced in its 'anti-system' role by postmodernism and the current decolonial turn.

The decolonial has many ramifications, placing race at the forefront of the interpretation of contemporary societies and emphasizing nontranslatability of cultures and the epistemological differences between them. In exploring these ideas, I begin by returning to the use of the word 'colonial' in Latin American, especially Mexican, social science. One of my purposes is to show that despite reiterated claims that they are contesting the dominance on the global periphery of western-oriented bias in science and in conceptions of the law, anthropology of indigenous society and advocates of *interculturalidad* largely share a universalist outlook under which the legitimacy of collective rights remains subordinate to universal human rights, equality and dignity in the face of the state.

The colonial in modern Mexican social science

In Latin America, the term 'colonial' was extended and to some extent redefined as 'internal colonialism' by Pablo González Casanova in his bestselling *La Democracia en México* (1965) – creating a revised concept of colonialism as the perpetuation of enclaves, normally of indigenous people and communities, condemned to dwell forever in a state of economic dependence. The community structures persisted in such a way as to fit the requirements of dependent capitalism. It was also a reformulation, in the language of structural Marxism, of the *regiones de refugio* coined by state anthropologist Gonzalo Aguirre Beltrán. The concept was simultaneously developed by the anthropologist and later indigenist campaigner Rodolfo Stavenhagen (Stavenhagen 1981 [1965]),[1] whose innovation was to combine the previously separate indigenous and peasant (*campesino*) questions in a single framework, thus creating a unified imaginary of domination.

The indigenous question was subsumed within Marxist approaches as they stood in the 1960s and 1970s, and it took decades for its cultural and linguistic dimensions to gain prominence. González Casanova estimated the number of *indígenas* in Mexico to be far greater than those enumerated by official statistics, extending the concept to include the entire 'marginal' population (González Casanova 1965: 107). Forty years later, taking up the anti-neo-liberal cause, he would go even further, including within the word's coverage nations, peoples and ethnicities gathered in the vanguard of a world-historical revolt against the 'end of the welfare state, socialist or populist', opposing all sorts of material, ideological and religious forces which block the way to 'universal values of democracy, justice and freedom' (1965: 429). Evidently, by then he had in mind Mexico's Zapatistas – the Zapatista National Liberation Army. But this vision of a worldwide upsurge of popular forces did not include any cause identified with what we would now call *interculturalidad* or multiculturalism – terms that do not mean precisely the same thing (Lehmann 2013, 2016a). Indeed, already in *La democracia en México*, González Casanova had expressed his indifference to the cultural dimensions of exclusion by dismissing the religious rituals practised in Indian communities as a tool of economic and political manipulation.[2]

Mexico's anthropological establishment (led by Manuel Gamio, Alfonso Caso and Gonzalo Aguirre Beltrán), like Gonzalez Casanova, spread across two or three post-revolutionary generations, regarded indigenous cultures as an obstacle to economic improvement and integration into national society. But that establishment came under attack in the late 1960s when many things began to change in Mexico. In 1968, student mobilization gathered strength, fuelled by violent police repression at the Politécnico in Mexico City. As the cycle of protest and repression intensified, and the government grew ever more anxious in view of the impending Olympic Games, it brought down a fearful wave of repression culminating in the massacre of Plaza Tlatelolco in October. To this day, there has not been an inquiry into those events and many people remain unaccounted for.

Amidst the turmoil, the National School of Anthropology and History (ENAH), an institution offering university-level qualifications but attached to the 'leviathan' of the INAH (Instituto Nacional de Antropología e Historia)[3] became the scene of a confrontation between contestatory Marxist or quasi-Marxist students and professors (among them Stavenhagen) and the bureaucracy of archaeologists and anthropologists, like Aguirre Beltrán and Alfonso Caso. For these, their profession was a branch of the state devoted to the excavation and preservation of archaeological sites as the emblematic symbols of Mexican nationhood and its indigenous origins, as well as to the integration of indigenous communities. The rebels' frustration was expressed in the sarcastic title of a book published in 1970: *De eso que llaman la antropología Mexicana* – translatable as 'Of Mexico's *so-called* anthropology' (Warman et al. 1970). Ever since the revolution, the ruling elite and the hegemonic PRI had found a niche for Marxist intellectuals, but now Marxism became the default framework for social sciences throughout universities in Latin America as a whole and became less indulgent towards the nationalist rhetoric of Mexico's political class. Eventually, anthropologists took another direction, distancing themselves from a state whose grandiose memorialization of pre-Columbian civilizations sat uneasily beside what many of them saw as a supposedly indigenist policy of integration that guided the country's Indians towards cultural oblivion and perpetual marginality.

Deep Mexico

The shift was marked by one emblematic anthropological text, Guillermo Bonfil Batalla's *México Profundo* (1987). This work may today appear dated, oversimplified and even 'essentialist', but, along with some others, it provided the impetus for a new direction in Mexican anthropology around the same time as the network of social research and graduate teaching centres, CIESAS,[4] came into being. Indeed, CIESAS was the successor to CIS-INAH (Centro de Investigaciones Superiores del INAH), which itself had been created in classic Mexican co-optative mode in 1973 by President Luis Echeverría, who as minister of the interior had been responsible for Tlatelolco, to accommodate the dissidents.[5]

Bonfil had been director of INAH between 1971 and 1975 and then of CIS-INAH between 1976 and 1980, and later occupied important posts in the state's cultural apparatus, including as founder of the Museo Nacional de Artes Populares, devoted to popular arts and crafts. Like Gonzalez Casanova and others, he embodied the figure of the loyal dissident, more an in-house prophet than a court jester, cultivated over decades by the PRI – the Revolutionary Institutional Party which acted as the support apparatus for 80 years of highly centralized presidentialism till the end of the twentieth century. While the dissident, even angry tone of *México Profundo* might lead one to think of it as the work of an opposition intellectual rather than a member of the cultural establishment, its content is perfectly compatible with the official indigenist rhetoric of the period, reserving harsh words rather for the overall development strategy in which that rhetoric had little say. Bonfil wrote passionately of the cosmovisions of indigenous peoples and the reserves of knowledge they had accumulated over centuries but deplored the enclaves to which colonial domination had confined them. His purpose was above all to reclaim the integrity and ubiquity of indigenous cultures in Mexico and to affirm their common origin in a single Meso-American civilization, despite the abundant evidence of their variety. He emphasized the durability of a cultural complex which 'confers transcendence and meaning' on men's actions, adapting the deep meanings of their civilization but also bringing them up to date with the modern world (Bonfil Batalla 1987: 28). The cosmovisions of deep Mexico contained all sorts of knowledge preserved in colonial *regiones de refugio* (Aguirre Beltrán's term) which under a different development pattern could be liberated for the benefit of the country as a whole. Bonfil deplored the prevailing state-led *desarrollista* or *dirigiste* pattern of development, inspired by what he called an unreal 'imaginary Mexico', derived from the technocrats' arrogant assumption that no other path is valid and treating human beings as mere inputs and outputs (Bonfil Batalla 1987: 202).

Bonfil's vision was not entirely of cultures as blocs fenced off by symbolic or physical frontiers, for he saw that Mexican society as a whole was pervaded by Indian influence and habits: even if Indian cultural life was disintegrating in the heartlands, it pervaded the peasant and *mestizo* cultures of villages and provincial towns. Like Gonzalez Casanova, he criticized official agencies (notably the Census) for using a narrow, language-based criterion which led them to underestimate the number of Indians in the country (Bonfil Batalla 1987: 45) – an approach which has only recently been replaced by self-assignment. This was not, by any means, an anti-western manifesto, for Bonfil took care to say that the West has produced much that is useful which other cultures can apply without undermining their character (ibid.: 204).

To anthropologists of later generations, this book should be deeply problematic: while recognizing cultural mixing, it leaves no space for concepts like frontiers or hybridity or the construction of identities; it offers a stereotypical version of Indian communities as places where wage labour is almost unknown and families live in harmony; it has little time for gender; and it has no reference to ethnography. At the same time, its freewheeling style, interspersing the rhetoric of indignation with occasional lyrical evocations of life in remote times and places, shaped the outlook of generations of students for whom it has been a basic text.

Bonfil tapped into a multi-generational unease among the Mexican intelligentsia. His message fitted in with the compliant dissidence that the state had nurtured for decades, yet with clear red lines – red lines that became rivers of blood after 1968 under Echeverría's presidency, during the country's guerrilla episode and the dirty war associated with Lucio Cabañas's Partido de los Pobres in the state of Guerrero. Later, the Zapatistas knew well how to respect those red lines by retreating to a few municipalities in Chiapas. That unease is engendered by the spectacle of gargantuan bureaucracies like the Instituto Nacional Indigenista (INI, charged with development projects in support of the indigenous population),[6] which have provided secure lifetime employment to some anthropology graduates but are also widely charged with cultural insensitivity for their policies of integration at the service of a doctrine of the *mestizo* nation.

The Zapatista uprising of 1994 in Southern Mexico

Indigenism in government and in scholarship

On 1 January 1994, while recovering from a currency crisis and celebrating the first day of NAFTA (renegotiated and renamed in 2018 as USCMA – the US–Canada–Mexico Agreement[7]), Mexico experienced a rude awakening. Awakening literally, for early that morning the unknown Zapatista National Liberation Army (EZLN) had seized ephemeral control of five highland towns in Chiapas state, bordering on Guatemala, including the colonial town of San Cristobal de las Casas (Tello Díaz 1995: 17). The EZLN, switching within a few months from a Marxist discourse to one more attuned to indigenist demands, and building on the 1992 Quincentenary, reignited the indigenous question and the poten-

76

tial that indigenous political mobilization might hold for the country's redemption. Academics in Mexico, the United States and Europe were also drawn to the Zapatistas, whose leaders invoked inspiration from the works of Marx and Mao that they had read as university students. The enthusiasm was contagious: Guillermo de la Peña, a distinguished anthropologist representing a less activist strand, announced a new phase of Mexican nationalism, grounded in a multicultural imaginary of the nation. That multiculturalism had already been foreshadowed in the constitutional reform of 1992 promoted by the same President Salinas who signed the NAFTA agreement, and it now found further expression in initiatives in intercultural education and the institutionalization of indigenous procedures in municipal elections and local justice (de la Peña 2005, 2006; Recondo 2007; Román Burgos 2019). This and similar initiatives elsewhere inspired the term 'neo-liberal multiculturalism'. Unlike previous versions, de la Peña explained, this was a nationalism driven by an inward-looking focus on the nation rather than on anxieties about its external vulnerability. The Chiapas-based anthropologist Xochitl Leyva, less wide-eyed and closer to the action, spoke of an 'excess of ideology' in much of the literature and an 'excessively "external" position' standing in the way of a comprehensive 'global' appreciation of the conflict (Leyva Solano and Ascensio Franco 1996: 109). The Zapatista leadership soon grasped the 'signs of the times': they deployed indigenist rhetoric in support of participatory democracy and gender equality, neither of which were rooted in the traditions of indigenous communal life, becoming a leading voice in worldwide anti-neo-liberalism as well as campaigning for environmental sustainability and peasant agriculture in the face of agribusiness and competition especially from US agro-industrial maize exports. And, as we shall see, those commitments went deeper than mere rhetoric: as far as we can tell, in the areas under their control, democracy and gender equality were taken very seriously.

The interpretation of what and who the Zapatistas stood for, and what their leaders were seeking, soon became tied up in ideological and political agendas. A strongly worded but well-documented 2004 article by the Spanish anthropologist Pedro Pitarch confirms their then leader Subcomandante Marcos's switch from a Marxist to an indigenist rhetoric soon after the uprising began, and mocks international observers, and anthropological and activist sympathizers, for their naivety: it seemed, he wrote, 'as if the whole country had lain down on the analyst's couch in the Lacandón jungle', referring to the colonization region of Chiapas where the Zapatistas had their social bases (Pitarch 2004: 300). Pitarch, who has done deep fieldwork in Chiapas (Pitarch 2010) and seems familiar with at least one of the indigenous languages spoken there, described

Marcos's appropriation of indigenous modes of speech as a 'pastiche' which 'could be heard amongst Mexican pro-Zapatistas, international visitors, journalists, and even began to spread amongst congressmen, senators and government workers' (ibid.: 298).[8] He also questioned the existence of a nationwide indigenous leadership in Mexico. His polemics, though, should not lead us to think that the Zapatista movement is a charade.

Polemics around the deployment of indigenist credentials by governments and the *engagé* intelligentsia have spread far beyond Mexico. Carmen Martinez Novo, in a similar vein to Pitarch, takes up the term 'ventriloquism', defined by Pitarch as 'the art of giving one's voice distinct intonations and altering it in such a way that it appears to emanate from a different source'. For Martinez, it refers to the use by Ecuadorian President Correa (2007–2017), variously described as 'populist' or 'left-wing', of a 'colonial and indigenist repertoire' to disguise his true attitude of contempt for indigenous voices (Martinez Novo 2018a, 2018b). As an example, she notes that his slogan 'Sumak Kawsay' (also 'el buen vivir') is a 'propaganda tool' fashioned by 'environmentalists, decolonial scholars, and other *indigenistas*', and, like Silvia Rivera, she bitterly attacks various prominent names in the Latin American decolonial firmament – Walsh and Escobar, for example (Mignolo and Escobar 2013; Walsh 2009, 2012) – for their complicity in lending a decolonial aura to Correa's anti-indigenous government.

Pitarch's and Martinez's strictures, with their allusions to 'international visitors' and 'decolonial scholars', reflect the transnationalizing of anthropology's activist engagement with indigenism, announced by US anthropologist Charles Hale in 2002 and then further promoted by his advocacy of 'activist anthropology' (Hale 2002, 2006). Hale too was unimpressed by contemporary indigenism, but his interpretation differed from Pitarch's. Hale attributed the disappointments of indigenist initiatives to neo-liberal co-optation of indigenous leaders, designed to avoid confronting the need for broad-based policies of social justice.

Maybe in some cases indigenist policies really are a cynical ploy by politicians who hand over the keys to minor institutions with few resources and limited powers to readily co-opted leaders – a description which fits Slavoj Žižek's 1997 parody of multiculturalism (Žižek 1997). But such criticism can go too far, as can the idealization it seeks to demystify. Hale himself did not regard these doubts as a reason for demobilizing indigenous movements – after all, if indigenist 'multicultural' demands are the best that the state might contemplate, why set them aside? – and the literature shows many examples of multicultural initiatives which seem to bring improvements in opportunities or treatment for at least some of those concerned. Their defect, in the eyes of someone seeking a policy of recognition, is that they bureaucratize genuine political engagement and drain it of emotional content.

We can see how this works in the Chilean government's micro-targeted development and agricultural credit programme 'Orígenes', designed to support Mapuche agricultural producers and artisans (de la Maza and Bolomey Córdova 2020; de la Maza, Bolomey and Ahues 2018). These programmes may be directed at indigenous beneficiaries (as defined by the country's singularly bureaucratic criteria[9]), but they contain no element of recognition of collective existence, neither are they designed to be of benefit to the indigenous population as a whole. The 1993 Chilean 'Ley Indígena' recognizes the country's 'pluri-ethnic' character but does not offer collective recognition to *pueblos indígenas* (indigenous peoples) or indigenous institutions (Boccara and Ayala 2011; Boccara and Seguel-Boccara 1999). It has to be added, however, that in the truly tragic case of the Mapuche Indians in the south of the country, their institutions of governance were comprehensively and violently destroyed in the nineteenth century and all that are left are their shamans (*machis*), who since 1990 have undergone a renaissance (Bello 2011; Bengoa 1985). The destruction was so comprehensive that there is little in Chile to compare with Andean and Meso-American confluence of indigenous and Catholic religiosity. Whereas in other countries indigenous movements strive to create or revive institutions of self-government, in southern Chile they rally round the *machis* as representatives of an aspiration to autonomy and resistance to rampant industrial forestry and dam projects. Too often there have been cases of violent repression, even deaths, of people shot by police in rural locations, and prolonged poorly justified imprisonment of *machis*,[10] who have become symbols of Mapuche resistance (Bengoa 2014; Pairícan Padilla 2014).

The Zapatista army as social movement

The 1994 revolt was the culmination of several decades of peasant expulsion, demographic explosion, migration and colonization, and land conflicts, with involvement by several different left-wing revolutionary groups and the diocese of San Cristobal. Chiapas is in a tropical region stretching from chilly highlands to humid lowland forests (the *selva*). The region has historically been associated with extreme poverty and concentration of landholding, and with a caste-like stratification system (similar to neighbouring Guatemala) which had barely been touched by the Revolution or by the agrarian reform that followed. On the contrary, the PRI had strengthened Chiapas's landed oligarchy. Still, in the late twentieth century, significant percentages of the population, especially the women, knew no Spanish.

The seeds of revolt were sown when, from the 1950s, estates in the highlands, the Altos de Chiapas, abandoned maize cultivation for cattle rearing and expelled large numbers of workers subjected to semi-servile conditions as *peones acasillados* (living and working for an estate and tied to it by debt bondage or serf-like labour obligations). This led to a mass migration to the unexploited forests of the Selva Lacandona, where people took de facto ownership of smallholdings which they cleared in the hope of eventually achieving legalization under the agrarian reform legislation. Population growth in the *selva* from 1950 was very high – rising from 62,000 to 290,000 between 1960 and 1990 (Leyva Solano and Ascensio Franco 1996: 49). Chiapas's poor connections with the rest of the country held back migration northwards. The *colonos*[11] were drawn from all the main Chiapas language groups (Chol, Tojolabal, Tzotzil, Tzeltal) and came to form what Leyva calls a 'diaspora of Indian peoples' or a 'new ethnicity' shaped by colonization and religious diversity – which must mean that they included a sizeable number of evangelical Protestants (ibid.: 104). Social conditions were atrocious: schools and health provision were almost non-existent, and people had to penetrate ever deeper into the forest to find a piece of land. Furthermore, the highland cattle ranchers were also extending into the jungle, having benefited from a skewed redistribution by the government in the early 1970s which conferred 600,000 hectares on only 66 families – a decision corrected in 1989 (ibid.: 112).

The *colonos* lived their condition of *indios* as racially discriminated and socially marginalized, but they did not live in indigenous *communities*: in the estates, they had been dependent on landowners, and now their condition was that of uprooted proletarians. In the colonized areas, they formed *ejidos* (communal land tenure associations, but not *ejidos* emerging from an official process under the Agrarian Reform) to jointly manage the land while working it on an individual family basis. Some descriptions have them struggling to produce maize on cleared forest land and using more than half of the production to feed pigs which they would fatten and sell in the hope of eventually buying some cattle – the store of their meagre capital. Here, as for example in Colombia (Molano 1992, 1994), this combination of an uprooted population, ill-defined land rights and desperate poverty provided fertile conditions for the preaching of revolution. At first, various groups of Maoist or Castrist persuasion came there from other regions, notably from among the student population of the industrial city of Monterrey. Simultaneously, the newly installed bishop of San Cristobal, Samuel Ruiz, began to apply the ideas of liberation theology and to develop a new relationship between priests and the religious and the laity. In this, he was following the teachings of the Second Vatican Council reinforced at the landmark 1968 meeting of all Latin American bishops (CELAM) in Medellín, Colombia (Lehmann 1990; Levine 1980). In 1974, with government support, the bishop, who was the leading figure in the Mexican church's engagement with indigenous populations, convened a Congreso Indígena de Chiapas. But the event slipped out of the government's control (Tello Díaz 1995: 67).[12] That moment marked the beginning of a long period of tacit and sometimes open collaboration between the Chiapas diocese and various revolutionary groups – groups which were recovering from severe losses incurred in armed confrontation with the security forces in Chiapas and also elsewhere in the country. The bishop brought people from the colonization areas to San Cristobal for training as catechists, which meant learning about liberation theology and also learning Spanish. He welcomed Dominican friars who came to live among the *colonos* and preached social transformation, occasionally hinting at the role of violence. The numbers were not negligible: summarizing Womack, Krauze writes of catechists numbering in their thousands (Krauze 1999; Womack 1999). Morales Bermudez's slightly hagiographic life of Ruiz tells how the catechists and priests encouraged colonizers in their study groups to use the story of the Exodus to describe their own epic journey, like the *Igreja Popular* (People's Church) in Brazil and the revolution-ary priests in Nicaragua during the same period (Lehmann 1990). They used the analogy, and perhaps more than just the analogy, of God's covenant with Abraham to underwrite their claim to the land: one of the new versions of the catechism devised for this reborn people spoke of their customs emerging 'from God's thought and the agreement of the entire community' (Morales Bermúdez 2005: 226). Morales Bermúdez recounts a classic conjunction of themes that pervaded the various movements inspired by liberation theology throughout the continent: the people seeing the very creation of the world as the creation of them-selves as a people, God conferring on them the wisdom and the right to take stewardship of the land, as in the biblical creation story;[13] their migration from the highlands to the jungle as a new Exodus; the divine origin of their customs, the *selva* as the Promised Land, and an almost mystical vision of indigenous rebirth, giving rise to a new society in the whole country inspired by the poorest and the most downtrodden. The poorest would also form the crucible of a renewed Christian community, guided as in Brazil by a People's Church – even though the phrase itself seems absent from the Mexican vocabulary of liberation. In the words of Samuel Ruiz, 'the resurrection not just of the indigenous, but of society as a whole, lies with the indigenous' (ibid.: 231).[14] Out of Chiapas would be born a new Christian civilization (*una nueva cristiandad*) in the image of the early Church – the Church that existed prior to its adoption by the Roman emperor in the fourth century.

All this may sound fanciful, but there was a parallel engagement with the everyday challenges of organization, production and politics, and on this terrain the diocese operated in a fluctuating alliance with the various revolutionary groups. The achievements in terms of organization were impressive, as the *colonos* (*indios campesinos* or *campesinos indígenas* in Leyva's usage) organized cooperatives in support of production and marketing of their produce side by side with a system of *autogestión* – self-government known as the *comon*, an indigenous version of the Spanish term *común*. Leyva reproduces an organigram comprising an assembly of all inhabitants as supreme authority and an intricate hierarchy of committees responsible for policing, for credit, for pasture management, for a hostel, for health and much besides. This apparatus, whose members numbered some 23,000, was responsible for and to the inhabitants of the Las Cañadas subregion of the Selva Lacandona with its population of several hundred thousand (Leyva Solano 2001: 31). Their social organization had little to do with either the corporate communities that were at the basis of colonial and post-Independence indigenous society, and of the internal colonialism entrenched after the Mexican Revolution, or with the revived *usos y costumbres* arrangements encouraged by contemporary multiculturalism. The population of Las Cañadas was mixed linguistically, by ethnicity and also by social class, recognized by themselves and others as Indian in a generic sense, occupying the lowest rungs of a profoundly racialized, caste-like society. Migration and colonization, however, provided no basis – in land tenure or in social networks – for the institutional reconstruction of corporate indigenous communities. Instead, with the help of the diocese and the revolutionary factions, they constructed the Unión de Uniones, as the *comon* was known, which shaped various ethnic and linguistic groupings, a congeries of revolutionary groups and an array of quite different class locations into 'a completely homogeneous sociopolitical landscape'. The Unión de Uniones was 'able to grow into a hegemonic institution because it connected and integrated four "paths": the Catholic faith, Castrist-Guevarist and Maoist socialist ideologies, and an ethnic consciousness opposed to the *caxlanes* or *ladinos*', who held them in humiliating subordination (ibid.: 21–2).

By the early 1990s, Monseñor Ruiz's positions were out of step with the views of his colleagues and especially those of Pope John Paul II, and the Nuncio in Mexico was rumoured to be plotting his removal. By 1994, the bishop and the insurgents began to diverge, particularly over the question of violence, which Ruiz had earlier tacitly tolerated, while the revolutionary leadership, especially Subcomandante Marcos, began to reveal their religious scepticism. After the uprising, the apparatus became subject to political divisions and different economic interests, as Leyva explains. Although repression by army units continued sporadically, including the murderous attack by unofficial paramilitaries at Acteal in 1997, after January 1994 the national government invested previously unheard of resources in roads, health services and schooling in Chiapas, including an intercultural university in pastiche colonial style in San Cristobal, which I visited in 2009.

So the Zapatistas were one branch of the broad-based movement of *indios*, but that movement was not primarily indigenist in the sense of seeking recognition of indigenous institutions, although mention was made of Indian culture and religion in the speeches and literature of the diocese. After the uprising, the Zapatistas 'rebranded' themselves as an indigenous movement, but even then they did not try to reorganize the communities they controlled along indigenous institutional lines. Rather, they developed concepts of local democracy and participatory government.

Seen from the vantage point of 2020, two themes are conspicuously absent from the literature in support of the cause of the *colono* Indians and *campesinos*. One is that of evangelical Protestantism, which had already grown very fast in Chiapas. According to the Census, it had risen from 5 per cent to 14 per cent of the state's population between 1970 and 1990, but in the Selva region it had reached 30 per cent in 2000 (Rivera Farfán et al. 2005). Censuses are not very reliable on evangelical head counts, but the scale of these changes leaves little doubt. The book by Farfán and colleagues indicates that Protestants tended to be out of sympathy with left-wing tendencies and more inclined towards the PRI while, according to Leyva, Protestants first withdrew from community institutions and even from the community areas after January 1994, but later often returned and took part in reconciliation among local groups and with the government (Leyva Solano 2001: 28). But I have not found detailed ethnography, and the tone of Farfán and his peers betrays a certain distrust of the diocese and its political engagement.

The other absent theme is gender. Although mention is made of women among the officers of the armed revolutionary organizations, and among the catechists, and although passing mentions allude to women in holy orders as very active participants in the diocese's campaign of consciousness raising and institution building, the position of women in the society of *colonos* receives scarcely any attention. This theme, as we shall see, was later taken up by anthropologists when the state of revolutionary mobilization no longer existed and the internal structures of indigenous life came under the spotlight.

One lesson from this account is that we must separate the observation of indigenous people's participation and protagonism in a social movement from assumptions about the purposes of the movement. It is possible that the imaginary projections of a movement may include the re-establishment, the recognition or the institutionalization of culturally distinctive practices (*usos y costumbres*) when there is such protagonism by people who speak indigenous languages or who recognize themselves as indigenous, but it is not inevitable. Their aspirations, which are most likely shaped by their leaders and their advisers (cf. Samuel Ruiz and the catechists or the various revolutionary groups), may well be those common to excluded and racially subordinated classes and peoples: a life of dignity in which human and civil rights are safe; and social justice in the form of equal opportunities, schools, health care and a decent income. Often the two distinct imaginaries will overlap or coexist in the same movement, and if their social base is indigenous, they would be called indigenous movements.

The Zapatista experiment in local democracy hardly seems to draw much in practice from traditional forms of indigenous representation or judicial authority, even if they use the *mandar obedeciendo* formula derived from Tojolabal practice: rather, according to research by respected but committed scholars, they are looking for a form of strictly egalitarian representation, with equal rights for men and women and constant accountability, and readily admit that more than 20 years on they are still experimenting (Harvey 2016).[15]

This interpretation of the Zapatistas is not intended to 'reveal' supposedly hidden purposes and agendas behind the indigenous rhetoric. Rather it shows that the leaders have sought both a remedy to historic injustices inflicted on indigenous people as indigenous and a form of participatory democracy which has little connection with indigenous systems of governance.

Interculturalidad: cultural difference in knowledge, education and law

In the wave of indigenist enthusiasm that followed the 1992 anniversary, a new word was born: *interculturalidad*. Its widespread acceptance in Spanish America owes much to the flexibility of meaning which has enabled it to be adopted by different interests and constituencies.[16] For politicians not preoccupied with analytic refinements, it opened the way to policies of recognition without encouraging sharp separations, while among anthropologists, as especially educators involved in bilingual and intercultural education and in teaching at intercultural universities, it has stimulated lively discussion about the meaning of cultural difference and the tensions between recognition and economic opportunity: a former minister of education in Peru once told me of a visit to a highland community where parents had told him that they saw no point in teaching Quechua in school. 'We can teach our children Quechua,' they said, to which he replied, 'So what do you want them to learn?' and they answered 'Inglés – para que nos vayamos' ['English, so we can get out of here'].

In the view of the experts, the promise of *interculturalidad* is parity of esteem among people identified with different cultures and the prospect of an ideal future in which individuals would be as competent socially and linguistically in one as another cultural frame (García 2005). That is the vision of Luis López, a leading figure in Latin American Intercultural and Bilingual Education (EIB, Educación Intercultural Bilingüe) (López 2005; López and Sichra 2004). But López also argues that EIB needs to go together with social structural changes. Similarly, the teachers at intercultural universities in Mexico whom I interviewed in 2006 and 2012 conceived their vocation jointly as cultural recovery and consciousness raising that would awaken students' awareness of the broader society and its injustices (Lehmann 2013, 2015). At the same time, I repeatedly heard that intercultural education was a drive to challenge the myth of a unified *mestizo* nation promoted by the state ever since the Revolution with the purpose of diluting indigenous identities. Theirs was a project of strengthening identities, of consciousness-raising and confidence boosting among students whose parents might have taught them to be somewhat ashamed of their indigenous language and origins. Ideally, recognition would bring change in both the hegemonic and the indigenous cultures. Questions of authenticity were less important than the empowerment and encouragement that an intercultural education could provide to the bearers of those cultures and languages: identity provides a sense of solidarity and a shared motivation to pursue social and racial justice, but the pursuit of justice need not be tied to a pursuit of authenticity.

Epistemology

It is sometimes argued that the recognition of other cultures implies the recognition that they have different epistemologies. Yet profound epistemological differences exist within what would normally be considered the boundaries of single cultures where people share religious beliefs and language as we saw in the discussion of trust in science in the previous chapter.

The idea that knowledge is culture bound has a distinguished genealogy (in Lévi-Strauss's *La Pensée Sauvage*, notably), but recently it has been extended far beyond what Lévi-Strauss might have imagined to cast doubt on whether criteria of truth and verifiability in science can ever be detached from the tradition in which they have been developed. To accept claims of this sort is to admit there will always be a basis for questioning scientific findings on the grounds that they are biased at their very root, to which it is added, explicitly or implicitly, that the bias is not accidental, not 'purely cultural', but manipulated, designed to favour certain interests – for example, of a colonialism which has never disappeared from the social fabric. A further claim would be that epistemologies differ between different cultural contexts and should be equally respected, as in the notion of 'other knowledges' (*otros saberes*). If this means that the differences are incommensurable, and if they are extended to hard sciences and to the realm of morality, then we step into deep waters.

Epistemology tries to answer the question 'On what grounds can you say that you know what you claim to know?' If someone says that they learned from their grandparents and that is sufficient justification, then it will be hard for them to persuade others who do not share their presuppositions, unless they can show that there is something about grandparenthood which endows them with special expertise. Although this may sometimes be convincing, since grandparents have experience which goes with their role, it is not their kinship status in itself which renders their opinions convincing but rather their experience. Extending the generalization to grandparents is just part of the everyday proclivity to stereotype and create ontologies – a proclivity without which it would be hard to communicate at all. Such generalization occurs in the case of both modern scientific findings and indigenous knowledge – for example, folk wisdom about Vitamin C and the common cold or about herbal remedies. We can also readily allow that practices honed over dozens of generations and enshrined in folk botany and biology are effective in, say, agriculture and in the medicinal use of plants. But there is still a world of difference between accepting opinions on the basis of the status of the speaker and accepting them because *in addition* they have been subjected to verification, especially verification set up to ensure the exclusion of personal tastes and prejudices.

Equally misleading is a conception of a world divided between societies and cultures in which scientific reasoning based on impersonal verification is universally accepted, and others where it is not. In an infinity of subjects – like child-rearing – impersonal verification and definitive answers are extremely difficult to obtain, especially if they concern not a general question and probabilistic results, but a particular case, like 'How can I handle my hyperactive child?' Such questions will probably not produce verifiable impersonal answers. But even the availability of scientific answers (in a conventional sense) does not ensure universal consensus: those scientific findings themselves can morph into folk wisdom which is similar in its logic and in its reliability to 'other knowledges' or 'indigenous knowledge'. Every day we hear beliefs about Vitamin C and cold prevention or cure and about the virtues of this or that diet, sometimes accompanied by references to 'findings' or 'evidence'. Even our trust in heavily regulated biomedicine has an element of irrationality – we do not usually know why the medications prescribed for us 'work'. And that is the point: it is precisely because most of us do not know how or why medicines work, or how or why buildings stand up, that we place our trust in doctors and architects – or in the Inca builders who were also experts in that field. It is when we come to discuss folkloric wisdom such as that mobilized in campaigns against vaccination, and the severe social fractures they expose, that we realize that there has to be a limit to relativism: modern societies and the professional ethos which governs many institutions, notably science and medicine, have produced a culture of trust in impersonal professionalism and therefore a basis on which knowledge can be verified in an impersonal way on the basis not of a person's name or status but on the basis of an institution. Although that impersonality has become dominant, many individuals and organizations do not trust impersonal institutions, and others seek to profit politically from popular paranoia invoking allegedly scientific findings, notably today in the case of climate change and the coronavirus. The consequences can be serious, as evidenced already before 2020 in the upsurge of measles in recent years in Europe and North America, where campaigns against vaccination have gained traction,[17] and what the campaigns show is that there is a difference between doubt and disagreement within the science profession, which has been known to commit catastrophic mistakes, and the phobias, hysteria and conspiracy theories encouraged by anti-science campaigns driven by an ideological agenda. 2020 has shed disastrous light on this.

So impersonal verification is only decisive in certain sorts of cases – for example, cases that can be studied using statistical sampling and double-blind testing and conducted under controlled conditions in a hospital or other circumstances where several individuals can agree on what they are seeing or hearing. There will still be instances where an individual's personal authority may be the best available basis for making a decision, as where team leaders must be deferred to in certain circumstances.

In social science, where personal judgment is pervasive, it happens all the time, and not without reason: if the opinion of women is regarded as indispensable, this is not just a matter of tokenism: lived experience counts in making professional judgements and statements, and by no means only on the subject of gender: the 'judgement calls' and interpretative frames which feed into the interpretation of data benefit from input by people of different backgrounds. The objection to the advocates of 'other' epistemologies, which for present purposes means indigenous epistemologies, is that they call for the recognition of scientific authority based on a person's status, for example, on indigenous belonging or the claim of indigenous background or identity.

A certain strand of thought claims that modern science and more broadly the modern mindset are prejudiced against 'knowledges', which use 'other epistemologies' that are no less valid than those of modern science, and these claims raise several questions. The first points to long-standing and deeply rooted prejudices whose effects are to humiliate practitioners of, for example, indigenous medicine. To humiliate people is wrong, but that does not oblige others to recognize the effectiveness of indigenous medicine simply on the grounds that it is indigenous. In the words of Charles Taylor in his classic essay 'The Politics of Recognition':

> half-baked neo-Nietzschean theories ... [d]eriving frequently from Foucault or Derrida ... claim that all judgments of worth are based on standards that are ultimately imposed by and further entrench structures of power ... A favorable judgment on demand is nonsense, unless some such theories are valid. Moreover, the giving of such a judgment on demand is an act of breathtaking condescension. No one can really mean it as a genuine act of respect. It is more in the nature of a pretend act of respect given on the insistence of its supposed beneficiary. Objectively, such an act involves contempt for the latter's intelligence. (Taylor 1992: 70–1)[18]

He goes on: a 'favourable judgment made prematurely would be not only condescending but ethnocentric'. In other words, one humiliation is replaced by another.

It must be true that the *theories* of knowledge underlying shamanic practices, for example, are different from those underlying modern science. The charismatic authority, ritual and tradition, comparable to those that operate as legitimators of a shamanic authority, may play a role in the life of science, but they are circumstantial, and if they are found to impinge on scientific findings, those findings are discredited. Conversely, there is no reason to believe that a shaman is unable to comprehend the claims of science.

Culture versus epistemology

Assumptions about internally homogeneous cultures coexisting in different life-worlds are contradicted by the mutual interaction and porous boundaries that mark contemporary life. More importantly, they confuse cultural differences with epistemological ones. Indeed, the renewed prominence and diffusion of conspiracy theories in high-income countries remind us that epistemological differences in interpretation of the material world are not cultural differences. The argument is illustrated by referring to conspiracy theories, that is, disagreements which are truly epistemological about facts and their explanation, about science, but also about shadowy, quasi-supernatural and often malevolent forces that gain control of a population – yet which have little to do with cultural differences. The difference separating them from other ways of interpreting the world could be compared to religious differences, and cognitive psychologists have made a direct comparison between conspiracy theories and religion (Franks, Bangerter and Bauer 2013). Drawing on Boyer, Sperber and Atran (Atran 2003; Boyer 2001; Sperber 1996), they note that, like religion, conspiracy theories are not totally absurd or unbelievable but rather, like religious beliefs, 'minimally counterintuitive', plausible in all ways except one. For example, the Zande people of Southern Sudan, studied by Evans-Pritchard in the 1930s, know that houses fall down because of termites, but they want to know 'Why now? Why me?' (Evans-Pritchard 1965 [1937]). Further features, according to Franks and colleagues, are that religious ideas refer to connections between phenomena which adherents cannot fully understand and so they defer to experts (priests, gurus, charismatic seers . . .) whose authority is bolstered by some sort of community (at one extreme a cult). Most important is the standard human inclination to interpret events via the activity of sentient agents, an evolved disposition to see agency where there is none ('hyperactive' agency detection). Should then the possession cults (also known as Afro-Brazilian) be taken to represent a different culture from Brazilian hegemonic culture? Not really. People who frequent their *terreiros* are drawn from many spheres of social life and many levels of the social and racial hierarchy – they may be scientists or lawyers or wage earners or domestic servants, and they may be from a Christian or Jewish or agnostic background – but they live in the same cultural complex as other Brazilians.

These are not the only epistemological differences within Brazilian culture: in the same towns and cities as the *terreiros*, Pentecostal preachers share a fear of these entities but anathametize the mediums (*maes* and *paes de santo*) who 'incorporate' them, accusing them of tying their clients to these evil forces. But the churches and their followers do not inhabit another culture.

Sometimes the invocation of a separate epistemology seems to derive from a political rationale, as evidenced in the use of the word 'epistemological' to refer not only to ideas about supernatural causation prevalent in possession cults, but also to conceptions of history and projects of identity formation among Brazil's black population. This appears in a study of a cultural centre and *terreiro* in Ribeirão Preto (São Paulo) which, combining the fixation on difference with the decolonial, speaks of 'creating possibilities to mobilize other epistemologies that counter coloniality's devalorization and delimitation of the meanings, uses, and significance of Candomblé' (da Costa 2014: 50). 'Epistemology' is not the appropriate word for difference in social science and historical methods. Different perspectives and different biases are not different epistemologies. This use of the words 'epistemology' and 'epistemic' portrays the minds of black or indigenous people as different from others merely on the basis of the colour of their skin, in particular when possession cults are invoked as prime bearers of their historical consciousness, as thinking about history and injustice in religious or supernatural ways. Candomblé originates in the cultural inheritance of the descendants of slaves brought from West Africa and Angola under indescribable conditions and treated with extreme cruelty in Brazil, but its followers and practitioners are racially diverse and its supernatural beliefs do not provide a way of thinking about history.

It is, however, not easy to define what is meant by a shared culture or for that matter by 'a culture'. To say, for example, that people who share a culture coexist in a world where they speak a common language, possess a common epistemology, share common ethnic identities and even skin colour, follow the same religious traditions and attend the same educational system may make intuitive sense, but it cannot be coherent because extra factors or variables can always be added, and, in any case, cultural variables do not move in 'sync'.

The consciousness-raising role of interculturalidad

In the course of my research on intercultural universities in Mexico between 2007 and 2012 (Lehmann 2013), many of the members of the teaching staff I spoke to saw established institutions and pedagogical practices as forces perpetuating the exclusion of indigenous people. For them, as enthusiasts for intercultural education, raising competence in indigenous languages and encouraging a re-encounter with indigenous heritage went together with a liberating project enabling people from an indigenous background to achieve full participation and respect. Intercultural programmes are usually sponsored and implemented by non-indigenous individuals and institutions who assemble cultural and linguistic packages for the benefit of people whose culture and language they do not share. Insiders appear to be less worried about authenticity than outsiders because they see such activities in the light of a claim for citizenship as much as of a project of language revival. Decolonial theorists look to interculturality as a way of recognizing radical differences as expressed in the idea of 'other knowledges', but Gunther Dietz and Laura Mateos, leading exponents and practitioners of intercultural higher education, write that instead of 'reifying knowledges', educators must draw on a wide range of 'discursive sources' (Dietz and Mateos Cortés 2011: 169).[19] Recognizing that they are working in societies divided along many fault lines, of which linguistic and cultural differences are only two (ibid.: 136ff.), they envisage a confluence of knowledges.

Drawing on experience in the state of Oaxaca (Gonzalez Apodaca 2009), they observe that recently educated generations took up an empowering discourse centred on indigenous ethnogenesis, while others, notably schoolteachers armed with skills and experience acquired in the wider political world, returned to take an activist role in indigenous organizations or local authorities. They speak of the revival of community institutions and of a new *disidencia indígena*, an increasingly diverse intelligentsia who, rather than seek a career in the state apparatus, are returning to community leadership (Dietz and Mateos Cortés 2011: 112–13). They also note that graduates and staff of the UVI (Veracruz Intercultural University), where they are leading figures, have found their way to elected office in local government. These observations, about the universalist vocation of intercultural education, echo Bret Gustafson's study of intercultural and bilingual education among the Guarani of lowland Bolivia, when he writes that they understood interculturalism as, in their words, 'seeking to walk and speak out loud among the *karai* [the whites]' (Gustafson 2009: 23).

Dietz says that for most *indios* belonging to a community is more important than belonging to an ethno-linguistic group. The thrust of the argument is local democratization, educational methods drawing on insights from local conditions, recognition that cultural variation exists both nationally and locally, rejection of fruitless binarisms between 'indigenism and normalism' or between 'ethnic particularism and universalist nationalism' and thus a rejection of any kind of cultural essentialism in unusually strong terms.[20] Intercultural educators also emphasize the style of teaching and learning, setting intercultural education against the notorious authoritarianism and rote-learning which characterizes

Mexican public schooling, and speak of providing an empowering education in the radical tradition of Paulo Freire, Vigotsky and others and the *educación liberadora* inspired by liberation theology. My research also found that the quality of teacher–student relations in the intercultural universities was quite different from those generally assumed to exist in Mexican schools and universities – class sizes were much smaller, the students older, and teacher–student relations informal and supportive. Interestingly, the ('pastiche colonial') Intercultural University of Chiapas, (UNICH), located exceptionally for an intercultural university in the large town of San Cristóbal, had a more urban student population, larger classes and a more conventional university atmosphere (Lehmann 2013).

The intercultural identity of these universities lies in their name, in their location and in a curriculum which includes, among many other things, indigenous language and culture. They are not required to restrict admission to indigenous students – a stipulation that is both practically impossible and in Mexico unconstitutional – but, by virtue of their name and of being located in or near areas of indigenous population, they ensure that a high proportion of their students will recognize themselves as such. The core programme in many of them in 2007–2012 was designed to equip indigenous people with skills suited to the prevalent model of national development: 'Tourism and Development', 'Regional Development', 'Environment and Development' and 'Indigenous Language and Culture', though it was not always easy to find teachers qualified to teach indigenous languages.

Similarly, when we look at the proposals from indigenous organizations which have their own educational programmes, we find the priority for them is a degree of political autonomy and recovery of land, with cultural regeneration coming in its wake. For example, the Zapatistas in their Chiapas redoubt, where they exercise de facto autonomy, design their own educational programmes and appoint their own schoolteachers. Their intercultural education grows out of a two-way interaction, rooted, but not exclusively, in the indigenous culture so as to achieve a 'critical and creative dialogue between traditions' (Baronnet 2015: 98).[21]

The Colombian Consejo Regional Indígena del Cauca (CRIC), which has operated since the 1970s, has produced a cadre of scholars, some counted as 'outsiders' and others, coming from an indigenous background, as insiders, devoted to sustaining the indigenous culture in pursuit of a relationship of equality of respect with the national culture and with the academic culture of anthropology, and benefiting from the guidance of the anthropologist Joanne Rappaport (Rappaport 2005, 2008). The struggle for autonomy by the Guambia and Nasa (formerly Páez) peoples goes back a very long way (Rappaport 1990) and has unfolded in costly struggles, often armed, to recover land lost at various periods – a struggle which has brought about a reaffirmation of cultural values and a regeneration of authority structures originally conferred upon them in the colonial period (Rappaport 2005). Their political autonomy – recognized by the Colombian constitution – and the recovery of their land take priority. In the wake of those conflicts, their culture was surely transformed by building the structures needed for an engagement with the modern state. When one considers the list of those who have threatened the Nasa – land grabbers, different indigenous groups, guerrillas, *paramilitares*, the state itself – legalization and institutional stability inside 'the system' must be a rational option even if so many threats remain and even though the state does not offer all the guarantees to which they are entitled.

The involvement of the state in combination with demands for authenticity can generate many complications, as we saw in the Chilean examples of land allocation and recognition of indigenous medicine. This 'patrimonialization' (Boccara and Ayala 2011) has been criticized as a form of forced political clientelism inspired by neo-liberal multiculturalism, to which I would add that the Chilean zeal to create a tight legal framework and respect for private property has made state indigenism into something of a simulacrum of indigeneity (Cuyul Soto 2013: 261–70).

These complications lead me to an approach to the intercultural which recognizes a multiplicity of *intersecting* dividing lines: cultural and linguistic, to be sure, but also political, territorial, and socio-economic. The *indigena–no indigena* polarization should give way to a recognition that these societies are at once infused with race mixture and with deep race-based inequalities, calling attention to everyday racial discrimination, which can be sanctioned in concrete ways, as well as support for cultural regeneration, which is invaluable but has a less immediate effect.

An egalitarian concept of citizenship would dictate that *interculturalidad* should have as its target the majority population living in the hegemonic culture, requiring for example that mainstream state education teach the history of a country in ways that recognize its diverse cultural heritage and the history of exclusion suffered by indigenous peoples and other minorities, notably Afro-descendant or black people. But in practice the programmes of *interculturalidad*, such as those already described by Dietz, by me and by many others (Aguado and Malik 2009; Baronnet 2011; Dietz 2009, 2012; Saldívar Moreno et al. 2004; Schmelkes 2009), which are mostly implemented in the education field, are designed to enable people from indigenous groups to study their *own* history and languages or to pursue standard curricula in a manner attuned to the cultures of indigenous people. Strictly speaking, then, the parity envisaged by ideal versions of the intercultural is not on the horizon, although the existing programmes are not promoting the sort of rupture, or de-linking, contemplated by the decolonials. Rather, they are trying to reconcile pride and knowledge of indigenous difference with an enhancement of citizenship in the national state. Ten years later, it is to be hoped that all this will not be buried by COVID and its sequels.

Anthropology, indigenism and gender

The critique of neo-liberal multiculturalism by anthropologists in Mexico came after President Salinas's imposition in 1992 of a 'pluricultural' amendment to the Mexican Constitution.[22] This change opened the way for the country's sub-national states to institute plural electoral and judicial regimes, recognizing indigenous procedures for selection of local authorities and settling disputes. But while educators and many politicians promoted indigenist programmes and laws, prominent anthropologists were sceptical, denouncing them as a device to offload government responsibilities onto local authorities and indigenous organizations in the name of decentralization and budget-cutting, while not ceding real power (Hernández Castillo, Paz and Sierra 2004). For them, the way to recognize the existence of indigenous peoples was by granting territorial autonomy, while the Zapatistas demanded a high degree of autonomy in which indigenous regions would be governed by indigenous peoples on their own under systems of their own devising with, for example, jurisdiction over the exploitation of mineral resources and land ownership.

To pacify the situation in Chiapas, Salinas's successor Zedillo established a public dialogue between his envoy and the Zapatista leadership, attracting a large number of Mexican and international left-wing dignitaries and onlookers. This took place over several months in the town of San Andrés Larraínzar and culminated in the 1996 San Andrés accords which included a generous formula whereby indigenous peoples would hold rights collectively and constitute entities in public law, able for example to draw and redraw municipal boundaries. It was not difficult to see that the process was a sham: the president had sent a political rival, Manuel Camacho, to lead the government delegation, the presence of celebrity left-wing intellectuals from Mexico and beyond drew international media attention, and the government-appointed Secretary of the Peace Commission which emerged was evidently instructed to do nothing.[23] The Accords themselves reproduced many Zapatista demands, including this version of autonomy, but the weakening of central power that they would have brought were inevitably unacceptable both to Salinas's successor, President Zedillo, and to the Congress.

Unsurprisingly, the Mexican anthropological profession has been supportive of indigenous movements, and sceptical of official *intercul-turalidad*. One reason is the above-mentioned distrust of the state and especially of the neo-liberal label affixed to all governments from Salinas to Peña Nieto (2013–2019), while another is the essentialism and official classification inherent in any government policy in this field. Also, the anthropologists had been replaced in the making of indigenist policy by educators who led the intercultural and bilingual education initiatives.

The anthropologists most prominently committed to the indigenous cause in Mexico are dismissive of official *interculturalidad* and adopt some positions consistent with universalist concepts of human rights and women's equality. They distance themselves from other agents, not least the state itself through its intercultural initiatives, for whom respecting indigenous society means casting a blind eye to its tensions and conflicts, especially those affecting women. This is the 'culturalist' bias of governments, in the words of activist indigenous women, that are unwilling to question discrimination within indigenous communities. Sometimes, for pragmatic reasons, indigenous leaders go along with the culturalist approach but seek to overcome its limitations by 'expand[ing] their definition of culture to include demands for rights to land and greater municipal autonomy' (Hernández Castillo 2003: 69). One group quoted in Hernandez' ethnography criticized the 'Indianist discourse' emanating from the state: according to them, indigenous law was 'essentially democratic and based on consensus', and they 'stressed the need to work on the construction of a democratic communitarian culture' (ibid.: 80). This laid the way for her activist commitment to indigenous women's rights and her alignment with decolonizing feminists, such as those quoted in the previous chapter, who had distanced themselves from the dominance of discourse analysis with its relativism and anti-essentialism and turned more to anti-capitalist advocacy (Hernández Castillo 2008a: 274). Opposing the idea that indigenous people are 'different, "pre-modern" or opposed to the values of progress', she came to the view that the defence of indigenous peoples and indigenous women also necessarily involved supporting their defence against the capitalism that undermined their society (ibid.: 264).

Hernandez and her colleagues chip away at culturalist assumptions, reminding us that indigenous society, like any other, is not frozen in time or space (Hernández Castillo 2016). She refers to changes in the behaviour of indigenous men and also, importantly, to the influence of external political forces, and not only those coming from government bureaucracies and programmes: her description of the mobilization of Nahuatl women in the state of Puebla in the early 2000s implies that their organization drew on their experience of left-wing organizations and even of Central American liberation struggles with which some of them had had direct contact (ibid.: 146).

This approach means taking it for granted that indigenous people are part of a national society, whatever their linguistic and other cultural differences, and being part of (integrated into) that society means being vulnerable, in accordance with the works of Gonzalez Casanova and Stavenhagen, to the dynamics of exclusion derived from Latin America's development models (both the *dirigiste desarrollismo* and neo-liberalism). In this view, the discriminations inflicted on indigenous populations are in addition to the exclusion suffered by low-income groups, especially women and the rural poor.

Likewise Teresa Sierra, a legal anthropologist and co-author of Aida Hernández, approaches the subject with circumspection. Avoiding the direct criticism of local juridical arrangements, such as dispute settlement and even penal punishment, often made by those who saw them as leaving individuals, especially women, unprotected in unregulated or uncodified proceedings, she also distances herself from those who would 'romanticize' them, analysing them in isolation, privileging age-old traditions and underemphasizing their articulation with the wider society (Sierra 2002: 248, 254). The argument continues to find a middle way, recognizing difference in legal and social norms between local and national legal systems and societies, but also recognizing the variation among innumerable local systems and the negotiation and power dynamics between and within, eroding the national–indigenous binary. We see something similar years later in her case study of indigenous justice in Guerrero, which would be better described as local popular (rather than indigenous) justice in content, save in the important sense that it was conducted by indigenous people (Lehmann 2016b; Sierra 2013: 39).

This feminist school of legal anthropology finds its culmination in the region-wide case studies edited by Rachel Sieder (Sieder 2017), which document in often painful detail the exclusions suffered by indigenous women. Centred on the anthropology of law and legal pluralism, the studies repeatedly refer to the need for a possibility of appeal from indigenous to national legal instances in cases of sexual violence – see for example the Ecuadorian case study (Cervone and Cucurí M. 2017: 151) – and highlight the dynamic role of women's mobilization in building a system of justice free of privilege and impunity. The Bolivian case study describes women getting organized in the context of a new system of territorial autonomy (Estatuto Autonómico) and through meetings and debates persuading their own authorities, which would also include women. Their activism leads to a reformulation of the time-honoured

Andean principle of complementarity in terms of *despatriarcalización* – which is described as the true decolonization (Arteaga Böhrt 2017). The author envisages kibbutz-style arrangements for child care (p. 177), quoting the late Sally Engle Merry's phrase 'remaking human rights in the vernacular' (Merry 2006). The concluding chapter raises the prospect of something like a decolonization of the relationship between their anthropologists and those they are studying: contrasting themselves with their own teachers in the 1970s, Hernandez and Terven describe how they have put aside their self-image as missionaries come to raise the consciousness of the women with whom they are working (Hernández Castillo and Terven 2017: 296). In addition to those assumptions about intellectual authority, they are distancing themselves from the hypostasized notions of indigenous culture implicit in some versions of *interculturalidad* and are prioritizing women's rights over indigenous self-government, autonomy or collective rights.

Further evidence that, when faced with a tension between respect for indigenous cultural practices and women's rights, Mexican anthropologists who study the subject tend to give precedence to women's rights is found in the collection of documents, testimony and ethnographic studies of the Zapatista movement assembled by Hernández with Lynn Stephen and Shannon Speed (Speed, Hernández Castillo and Stephen 2006). The book, published in 2006, draws on the mature experience of a movement which by then was more than 12 years old and had been administering several townships and their surrounding areas, as it continues to do today. The book opens with a Women's Revolutionary Law and a further document produced by women from several indigenous groups entitled 'Women's Rights in our Traditions and Customs' ('Los derechos de las mujeres en nuestras costumbres y tradiciones'). Both these documents focus almost exclusively on the sufferings of women in indigenous society: pressure to marry young and have many children, violence suffered at the hands of their men, exclusion from education, exclusion from community decision making, and more. They ask for teachers who speak their languages, but they also want their children to learn Spanish so they can go to university; they welcome official medicine so long as it respects their traditional medicine. The underlying theme is respect: respect from their menfolk, respect from the authorities, respect for them as persons and respect for their way of life.

In their introductory essay, the editors criticize 'the essentialist approaches by some sectors in the Indian movement that mythologize cultural traditions', and remind us that 'organized indigenous women have pointed to the way in which gender inequalities are equally apparent in national law and in what is referred to as indigenous law'. So careful are they to avoid essentializing and homogenizing that they write of 'what is referred to as indigenous law', lying that official discourse on the subject is a simplifying construction (Speed, Hernández Castillo and Stephen 2006: 44). In her essay, 'Between Feminist Ethnocentricity and Ethnic Essentialism . . .', Hernández challenges various assumptions underlying what might be called naive indigenism, reformulating gender as a 'multidimensional category' and recognizing the role of 'both ethnic and class issues in understanding identity processes'. Criticizing Maxine Molyneux and Alain Touraine somewhat unfairly for casting doubt on the strategic potential of Latin American social movements, she elevates indigenous women as 'constructors of their own history' (Herrnández Castillo 2006: 66, 72). In a later article, Neil Harvey also describes the pains taken by the Zapatistas to include women, as well as the cultural and practical obstacles they encounter (Harvey 2016). Harvey refers to educational documents for study in primary school produced by the Zapatistas in 2013 which provide extensive evidence of their attention to women's participation and to the details of administration in a range of areas, each with its own committee and extensive provisions for consultation and feedback. Obstacles to full female participation are enumerated and include discussions which freely admit to problem areas. Although these booklets are to some extent propaganda exercises, the detail and the inclusion of discussions of failings do carry conviction.[24]

Following Lynn Stephen in a separate chapter, it is necessary to separate the collective ethnic identity, which acts as a force for solidarity, from the content of demands and ideals embodied in a movement. The women whose mobilization and commitment is so enthusiastically described in the book edited by Speed and her colleagues, and who proudly proclaimed themselves Tzeltal, Tzotzil, Tojolabal and Mam, learned to organize and to speak in public in 'educational and inspirational meetings of Catholic and Protestant groups' (Stephen 2006: 164). This shows that the Zapatistas did not then confine their campaigns to demanding a space in which they could preserve a separate culture or practise a medicine based exclusively on medicinal herbs, and they certainly expressed no interest in reconstructing an authority system based on the rotation in office (*cargos*) of men alone.

Legal pluralism as ventriloqual universalism

Normative questions, with special reference to India

Legal pluralism, then, begins to appear not as a coexistence of different systems, with different concepts of proof, responsibility and impartiality, but rather as *métissage,* or mixture. We see this in Sally Engle Merry's plural conceptualization, which recognizes that ever since the spread of colonialism across the world, legal systems have been variously overlapping and superimposed, resulting in a 'layered legal pluralism' (Merry 2006: 68). Globalization has shaped legal cultures in the most varied of circumstances and, by implication, decoupling is not an 'option'. Legal culture therefore cannot be defined in terms of a set of principles or doctrine (like 'common law', or even 'Nuer law') but rather has to be couched in terms of the practice of a fairly well defined collectivity or set of institutions like 'Brazil' or 'England', shaped by the overlapping layers prevailing within them. In this conception, indigenous legal arrangements cannot stand on their own because there is no fixed original to which they should conform and also because they are shaped by national and occasionally international law. It is hard today to reproduce the optimism Merry expressed in 2012, when she foresaw the emergence of '[g]lobal legal regimes such as human rights, women's rights, and indigenous rights ... along with mechanisms to regulate the circulation of intellectual property, trafficked persons, and illegal migrants' and the redefinition of sovereignty (2012: 69), but the interweaving of ideas and traditions in codifications far removed in time and space from their multiple birthplaces is evidently an ancient and unending phenomenon, albeit accompanied by violence and coercion.

A few years earlier, using the notion of 'vernacularization', Merry, together with Peggy Levitt, wrote of how international institutions, and indeed the 'West' itself, brought 'magic and financial influence' and 'appeal, power and legitimacy' to the 'global women's rights package' just as 'ideas about democracy, the rule of law and good governance had become part of the development portfolio' (Levitt and Merry 2009: 447). The keynote of vernacularization is the incorporation of international human rights norms and perhaps culture into local legal practices across the world, in New York as much as in India and Peru. What might be called the senior status of international human rights is taken for granted – a position that cannot be reconciled with an assumption that indigenous legal cultures all have equal right to recognition. Nonetheless, Merry had already enumerated some of the tensions that arise 'when the sovereign commands different bodies of law for different groups of the population varying by ethnicity, religion, nationality or geography, and when the parallel legal regimes are all dependent on the state legal system' (Merry 1988: 871).

In her 2012 article, Merry describes a women's village council (*panchayat*) in the Indian state of Gujarat 'inspired by a women's development program funded by the Dutch government and administered by the Indian government's Department of Education' that led to the creation of 'women's courts to handle domestic violence, divorce, and other family conflicts' (Merry 2012: 74). She describes a tense hearing in which a husband, supported by his father, defended his maltreatment of his wife on the grounds that she 'deserved to be beaten because she was such a poor cook' (ibid.: 75). In the end, the husband was 'upbraided' and the article's verdict is that '[d]uring this public event, new standards were articulated for how husbands should treat their wives, performed in front of this mixed-gender audience.' We live in hope.

Merry and her co-author should not be afraid to admit that they do believe in universal values. Nonetheless, the claim, or aspiration, to universal relevance and applicability of ideas about rights raises serious questions, for even if we do accept the concept of a human being with rights and with the 'right to have rights', why should it be only the concept developed in European culture, especially when we know all too well how some forces claiming to be inspired by that same European cultural patrimony have contested and violated that concept in the most violent way imaginable both in Europe itself and across the world?

All these concepts are culture-bound and their conception and application are tainted with the consequent ready-made assumptions and vested interests. Notions of 'European' and 'western' are themselves idealizations in which purified versions of certain liberal philosophical strands are taken to represent the whole of 'the West' and 'Europe'. It is a matter of convention to question and even reject these assumptions and interests in the case of western hegemonic cultures (embodied in supranational institutions), but to retreat into a position where non-western cultures are exempt from the sins of empire and colonialism and mass murder is a dead end. There too we find cultural complexes with a history of war and conquest that explicitly reject human rights, yet at the same time we also find 'western' universals in eastern cultures – as Amartya Sen eloquently explains in *The Argumentative Indian* (Sen 2006) – just as we find very un-'western' values within Europe and the Americas.

One approach to the problem is that of Martha Nussbaum, whose interventions on human rights, inspired by her experience in India, provoked much controversy (Nussbaum 2000). In a chapter boldly entitled 'In Defence of Universal Values', she focuses above all on women living in extreme poverty and lacking the independent social or economic resources to protect themselves against exploitation. Whatever their rights in law, they cannot exercise them. Nussbaum's guiding principle is 'each person as an end'. She is sharply critical of those who attack her positions as out of tune with Indian traditions, like Veena Das whom she describes as believing that 'Indian women are simply unable to form the concept of their own personal well-being as distinct from the well-being of family members' (ibid.: 55). Cuttingly, she asks: 'Has Das, not at all from a peasant background, mistaken her own background for a special "Indian essence"?' (ibid.: 58). She dismantles other over-homogenized versions of Indian traditions and points out that western opinion tends to homogenize other cultures in ways westerners would never do in relation to their own. Her rejection of arguments of any kind from tradition even extends to those who would use tradition to defend women's rights, pointing out that those who would invoke the Mahabharata[25] for its defence of those rights should remember that it invokes the law and not the power of Krishna (ibid.: 44–7). Nussbaum's purpose is to dismantle cultural homogeneity and to show how change over time and influences across space make a nonsense of communitarian arguments. Amartya Sen makes similar points in his essay 'Indian Traditions and the Western Imagination', where he writes that '[T]he contemporary reinterpretations of India (including the specifically "Hindu" renditions) which emphasize Indian particularism join forces in this respect with the "external" imaging of India (in accentuating the distinctiveness of Indian culture)' (Sen 2006: 140). In the end, the implication of both Nussbaum and Sen is that relativism and essentialism overplay cultural differences, entailing the risk of sliding into intolerance and incompatibility. Edward Said would surely agree.

An alternative approach would be to state what might be the irreducible minimum guarantees for protection of human beings. In an essay on 'Justice, Gender, and International Boundaries', written several years before Nussbaum's book, another philosopher, Onora O'Neill, argues that relativist approaches are no more free of theory and ideology than are idealized discussions (O'Neill 1993: 316). Idealized concepts of justice for their part belong in an ideal world, which is not where we live. But whatever the concepts of justice at work, she says that if 'impoverished providers' (people, especially women, responsible for providing for others) are to be 'treated with justice, others who interact with them must not rely on these reduced capacities and opportunities to impose their will. Those who do so rely on unjust institutional structures that enable deceit, coercion, and forms of victimization' (ibid.: 321). Unlike Nussbaum, she keeps to one single element, namely the providers:

although she does not use quite these terms, she is looking to institutions to ensure that the weak are not placed at a disadvantage in their dealings in the market, in the family and with power.

This is where we can rejoin the discussions of legal pluralism, for in place of debating the substance of norms which are changeable and subject to debate, the focus now is more on procedure. Universalist rights in contentious areas may be forever contested, but it is hard to contest the claim that a person, however poor and however bereft of supporting networks, is entitled to equal treatment before authority. This is where western bias of some kind has to be introduced: if justice is conducted in very local contexts, the impartiality of the procedure is vulnerable to the pressures of friendship and kinship. The impersonality of judges and others involved is a minimum requirement for the prevention of deceit and coercion. This minimum rests on a concept of the citizen and of the impersonality of authority: a collectivity of people of equal rights irrespective of their personal characteristics. It would follow that the vernacularization advocated by Sally Merry and Peggy Levitt would be more durable if in addition to campaigns for women's empowerment like the one they describe, supported by the state and an international development agency, and many in Latin America described in the essays collected by Rachel Sieder and by Sarah Radcliffe and her colleagues (Andolina, Laurie and Radcliffe 2009), more emphasis was placed on the importance of impersonality, impartiality, bureaucracy and professionalism in the adjudication of rights, though not at the expense of the local.

Determined efforts to reconcile such differences under a single jurisprudential roof were made, also with discrete but significant input from the Constitution-Building Processes Programme of the Swedish intergovernmental organization International IDEA (Institute for Democracy and Electoral Assistance) in the 2008 Bolivian Constitution, which 'established the basis for a plurinational state with thirty-eight separate and distinct legal systems' (Goodale 2019: 70). Whereas Stavenhagen and Boaventura de Sousa Santos (de Sousa Santos 1995), as quoted by Goodale, describe legal pluralism as operating under the aegis of a national legal system which ensures the protection of basic human and civil rights, this plurinationalism 'anticipated hardened cultural and institutional boundaries that were meant to create both ideological and territorial spaces in which Bolivia's separate nations could preserve their distinct cosmovisions and develop their own autonomous forms of law and governance' (ibid.: 90). Quite apart from the risk of perceived inconsistencies and injustices in such an extreme version of legal pluralism, the indigenous systems would have to be moulded into positive law if they were to work as *systems*, yet that would undermine the philosophy of legal systems inspired from the grass roots and reflecting the many coexisting local arrangements, or 'cosmovisions'.

Goodale blames an unwillingness on the part of the lawyers and politicians working for the Morales government 'to take the vision of plurinationalism to its logical conclusions because of an enduring, if unacknowledged, commitment to a unitary conception of the state' (ibid.: 93), but apart from Morales's own well-known centralizing inclinations, the objective requirement of clarity and impersonality is circumvented in Goodale's account.

Mexico

Laws governing indigenous land tenure are not necessarily products of recent intercultural or multicultural initiatives. In Mexico and Colombia they go back to colonial times. Judicial decisions within that framework are subject to precisely the pressures which justify the establishment of indigenous justice under a regime of legal pluralism – as witness the endless chicanery and not infrequent organized violence surrounding indigenous land titles in the very dangerous Mexican state of Michoacán. Unfortunately, recognition of indigenous authorities does not necessarily put an end to violence, as observed in the case of Cherán in 2007–8 after the Supreme Court recognized it as an official 'indigenous municipality' entitled to make its own security arrangements. In an admittedly controversial interpretation, Denisse Román Burgos describes how a generation of intellectuals, more educated than their predecessors, successfully challenged the PRI-dominated order in the town and were themselves able to operate in their newly discovered guise of indigenous people. (Known locally as the 'generation of '88', Román Burgos recalls that when they were students in the 1975–1988 period, they would say they were studying to 'stop being Indians' [Román Burgos 2019: 266].) In the name of democracy and human rights, they ran a campaign against nefarious political practices, even gaining a meeting with President Calderón, extracting the municipal government from a competitive party system and entrenching themselves at its head. At the heart of their ascent to power in 2011 were bitter conflicts over control of communally owned timber forests which had been a source of wealth for various interests for a century, but at its culmination under the protection of *usos y costumbres* they were able to establish their own militia. For Román, the multicultural regime in this case has placed power and access to state resources in the hands of those who gain recognition as Indians and has excluded others who do not, irrespective of the socio-economic and

103

security problems affecting them (Gledhill 2012, 2015; Román Burgos 2019). (For a different view, see Aragón Andrade 2013.)

The experience of another Mexican state, Oaxaca, where a reforming PRI governor introduced a state-wide change overseen by the State Electoral Commission in the system covering 570 municipalities in 1995, is more nuanced. (Oaxaca is unusual in having this large number of municipalities.) The change was conducted after extensive consultation, and a vote in the municipalities to decide which ones wanted to choose councillors in accordance with their traditions, often involving open meetings and therefore not a secret ballot, and which ones chose the party system (Recondo 2007). This reform was a response to the uprising in the neighbouring state of Chiapas, motivated both by a desire to respond to indigenous pressures in Oaxaca and also to reduce the corruption and even violence of the state's municipal politics. Paradoxically, under the previous regime the secrecy of the ballot had been a cover for rigged elections, so that secrecy of the ballot may have been considered less trustworthy than open meetings. After eight decades of rule by the PRI through local notables, it could be claimed that the true indigenous system was, in Jan Rus's formula, the 'comunidad revolucionaria institucional' whereby the PRI negotiated privately with local notables and then an election was held to confirm the outcome (Rus 1995). The practice of open town meetings, known now as 'sistemas normativos internos', thus stood in contrast to 'tradition', especially with the revolutionary introduction of full rights for women.

Gender equality did not come easily. Despite the requirements of the law, women represented an infinitesimal proportion of elected councillors in Oaxaca until 2016 when they jumped from 3 per cent to 10 per cent – still a low number. To overcome open resistance to their election, they had to take their case all the way to the Federal Electoral Tribunal. That Tribunal, invoking both human rights and the 2014 Constitutional Reform, which had introduced complex measures to ensure gender parity in Mexican elections and elected bodies, imposed a system to ensure they would not be frozen out, scared away or frustrated by visible vetoes or invisible circumvention of procedure, and ordered a rerun of the local election in which the plaintiffs had been unfairly defeated (Fernández Tapia, Robles Torres, and Hernández Ríos 2018).

The case shows that indigenous government can benefit from the presence of a state regulator overseeing its laws and procedures, if the regulator is transparent.

Colombia

In Colombia, to a greater extent than in Mexico, the judicial system (unlike the security agencies) seems to enjoy a degree of trust among citizens of all classes, ethnicities and racial groups, and legal pluralism operates within parameters laid down by the national judicial system. It is therefore possible to combine a conventional concept of due process with continuing functioning of indigenous law, as described by Sandra Brunegger in her study of the institutionalization of indigenous law in Tolima, where we find judges in indigenous courts sending offenders to state jails and receiving training in judicial procedure from international aid agencies (Brunegger 2011).

Colombian recognition of indigenous territorial rights and of *usos y costumbres* in law owes much to the CRIC (Consejo Regional Indígena del Cauca), founded in 1971. It is the largest and most enduring of Latin American indigenous organizations. According to the 2018 Census, Colombia has a much smaller indigenous population than other Andean countries, numbering less than 5 per cent (1.9 million), based on self-assignment, as well as 115 *pueblos nativos*, although many must live in towns and cities and the overall figure seems to be an underestimate.[26] The Departamento del Cauca, home to the CRIC, accounts for about one-sixth of them and rises from the sea to the high Andes in the south of the country, bordering Ecuador. Like the Zapatistas, the CRIC has created a system of self-government benefiting from the rediscovery of Law 89 of 1890 under which the colonial institution of the *resguardo* was confirmed as the institutional form of indigenous ownership of land with their own councils – *cabildos*. This law rendered subsequent usurpation and encroachment invalid, enabling legal restitution (Gros 2010: 83). The movement for land recovery and institution building found further support in the country's very liberal and pro-indigenous 1991 Constitution.

CRIC is not an armed organization, although it emerged in parallel with the Quintin Lame armed land recovery movement and has had intermittent alliances with the M-19 guerrilla. When it set out on its campaign to recover land rightly belonging to the *resguardos*, CRIC and its leaders suffered attacks and murders from landed interests affected by its claims and by state repression (Jimeno and Klatt 2014: Introduction). Over the years since then, like the rest of the country, it has had to face up to the exactions of paramilitaries, traffickers and the FARC guerrillas. Quintin Lame laid down its arms to take part in the 1991 Constitutional process.

The hallmark of CRIC is institution building. It achieved success recovering *resguardo* territory and establishing elected *cabildos* to manage it.

Its semi-official history states that 'most of the land has been recovered' through claims based on *resguardo* title (Bolaños et al. 2012: 80). CRIC rebuilt *cabildos* where they had disappeared, removed them where they were under the control of non-indigenous or other adverse interests and redirected them to support CRIC and its struggle for land (Gros 1991).[27] Despite a sometimes hostile environment, it has enjoyed a favourable disposition from some state institutions or at least from officials in those institutions and in the judiciary. This relationship can be dated back to the country's brief 'left-liberal' opening in the early 1970s during the presidency of Carlos Lleras, when CRIC benefited from land redistribution by INCORA (the Instituto Colombiano de Reforma Agraria) and also from the migration of some INCORA officials who came to work with it. Later, with other indigenous movements, the CRIC gained representation in the Constitutional Assembly which created legislation recognizing indigenous legal systems in the 1991 Constitution. The two indigenous representatives in the Constitutional Assembly which drafted the Constitution achieved a public recognition far out of proportion with their number. It was not, however, out of proportion with the land area occupied by indigenous people, who are the majority population in the lowland Amazonian region that accounts for 40 per cent of Colombian territory.

The CRIC's institution building has far outpaced the Zapatistas or perhaps any indigenous movement in the region. It has established a Guardia Indígena for *resguardos* which is unremunerated, unarmed or only very lightly armed (the source does not specify) and is trained to provide security during meetings and demonstrations, and to give first aid treatment. It has also set up an intercultural university – the Universidad Autónoma Indígena e Intercultural (UAIIN) – which in the first decade of the century offered courses lasting from four to thirteen months, of which the largest, in Gestión Etnoeducativa (Educational Management for Minority Ethnic Groups), had 111 students from 43 different indigenous peoples (Bolaños, Tattay and Pancho 2009: 158), and hosts a Nasa-UNESCO *Cátedra* that awards a Masters in Traditional Wisdom (Maestría en Sabiduría) (Rappaport 2005: 120).

There have inevitably been tensions between the indigenous authority and the elected municipal authorities, but decentralization has also opened the way, both in the Andean highlands where CRIC operates and in the lowlands, for new generations of educated Indians who have their 'feet in both worlds' (Gros 2010: 97): they are leaders in their home base but are adept at operating in national or regional politics. Furthermore, unlike Mexico, the literature on Colombia does not mention patronage relations between indigenous leaders and the state.

Colombia also provides the famous case in which a Constitutional Court judge entered into an anthropological analysis of indigenous law. The case started in 1996 in the Cauca region where over several decades a variegated system of indigenous government and politics has developed, sometimes against and sometimes with the support of the state, impelled from below by the CRIC. In the town of Jambaló, a local leader was sentenced to be whipped for his remote role in the assassination of a rival. There was no question of his direct implication. Rather, the issue was whether he had contributed to creating the climate in which this murder could be committed – a crime known as *tardecer* in the local context. He was tried by a *cabildo* and sentenced by the recognized indigenous judicial instance to sixty lashes (*fuetazos*) plus exile and exclusion from political office. The state's own municipal penal court ruled that the process had been deficient and that whipping constituted torture, but appeals succeeded one another right up to the Constitutional Court, whose president ruled in 1997 that 'concepts such as human rights and torture could only be defined in culturally specific ways' (Rappaport 2005: 247–52; Van Cott 2000). The ruling was not couched in terms of a fossilized concept of tradition: he said that the case could only be resolved 'from an intercultural dialogue capable of establishing minimal standards of tolerance that encompass different value systems', and since *usos y costumbres* is 'a dynamic process', the issue was not one of demonstrating that 'the ancestors' proceeded one way or another. 'What is required is compliance with those actions that the accused can anticipate and that approach the traditional practices that assure social cohesion' (Rappaport 2005: 250).[28]

But if judges can use a concept of social cohesion – rather than a concept of identifiable individual or corporate responsibility – in their judgements, this introduces anthropological interpretation, with all its recognized relativism, uncertainties and margins of error, into a field where judicial rulings are expected to make matters as cut and dried as possible. The ruling created an uncertain situation by authorizing judges to decide what tradition prescribes. Rappaport, in a carefully balanced paragraph, observes that 'cosmological references are muted, almost absent, in the highly pragmatic utterances of Nasa politicians regarding this case' (ibid.: 251). In other words, while some highly prestigious external authorities incline towards emphasizing the 'otherness' of indigenous practices, the indigenous leaders themselves are more wary, even when the law might validate their traditional procedures.

Returning to the case itself: the initial execution of the sentence was forcibly interrupted after eight lashes by the daughter of the accused and a group of associates (ibid.: 248), though he did leave his community.

Ideally, the case shows that vernacularization can be an institution, more than a programme or a campaign, which not only respects indigenous laws and procedures but also grants them initiative and protagonism. It has the great merit of legitimacy and visibility in contrast with the physical and cultural remoteness of national judicial systems. The reasoning of the judge in the Colombian case is buried in the past and in any case unusual, so we need more cases of appeals to the higher national courts to discover a balance between vernacular justice and the national courts.

For Rappaport, the ideal remains in the world of the ideal: the rival claims of *usos y costumbres* and of human rights were being confronted in the shadow of paramilitaries and of the guerrillas who had been the authors of the assassination for which the convicted local leader – who had himself apparently had prior connections with a guerrilla force – had supposedly set the scene, and there was a need to 'induce . . . confession and halt a chain of events that might lead to violent retribution' (ibid.: 253) rather than pursue the court's verdict to its bitter end.

The other background element was a shift at the turn of the century in the guiding concepts among the indigenous intelligentsia. The CRIC was born in the early 1970s and for the subsequent two or three decades the indigenous struggle was, in the marxisant outlook of that time, seen as equivalent to the struggles of other oppressed classes. But then a rival conception emerged, in tandem with *interculturalidad*, framed by a 'discourse of peoplehood' and an emphasis on cultural difference (ibid.: 259). The tension between these was further sharpened, but their conceptual bases were also clouded, by the external sponsorship of the more cultural approach.

At times, the discourse verged on the oneiric, as when a group of *cabildos*, calling themselves the Indigenous Communities of the Ancestral Territory of the Nasa people of Caldono, 'affirmed and ratified the teachings of the elders about our laws of origin and the Greater Right[29] founded in and lived through cosmovision'. They asserted that the territory was at once cosmic and earthly and they couched their demand for political autonomy in the language of self-determination combined with that of the spirit world in guiding indigenous authorities (ibid.: 268). Yet when these deliberations gave way to a public meeting where the overriding cosmic institutional system was to be explained, it was external experts, including the surprised Joanne Rappaport herself, who were called upon. Her Epilogue, which retells these events looking back several years later, ends with a virtuoso exercise in diplomatic anthropology. Recognizing that local intellectuals have to operate in the heat of urgent and conflicting demands – in implicit contrast to the tranquillity of academe – she concludes that their ideas must be judged by their outcomes: looking to 'trace the ramifications of the constructs in a variety of settings and among a range of social actors', she measures their accomplishments 'by how effectively they engage communities to bring projects to fruition in the local sphere' (ibid.: 274). She is not invoking a yardstick of conformity to tradition.

Bolivia and 'prior consultation'

Another example of the *intersection* of collective indigenous recognition and rights with universal rights of citizenship is analysed in the case of the right to prior consultation of communities affected by state initiatives, such as infrastructural and mining projects, by Fontana and Grugel (Fontana and Grugel 2016). These rights derive from ILO Convention No. 169 (1989) and the UN 2007 Declaration on the Rights of Indigenous Peoples (UNDRIP). All Latin American states save Cuba have ratified Convention No. 169 and are therefore bound by law to 'consult the peoples concerned, through appropriate procedures and in particular through their representative institutions, whenever consideration is being given to legislative or administrative measures, which may affect them directly', while the UNDRIP speaks of consent, rather than just consultation. The formula has been incorporated into national legislation with varying degrees of strength or dilution, giving rise to the standardization of the concept of 'free, prior and informed consultation' (FRIC). Although in principle such consultation applies whatever the ethnicity of those affected, the platform provided by this provision is particularly effective for indigenous mobilization, to such an extent that anti-mining movements have become synonymous with indigenous movements (Rodríguez-Labajos and Özkaynak 2017).

Once again, the line between the rights due to indigenous people, deriving from their membership in a collectivity, and the rights due to them as citizens is hard to draw in law. How can different judicial arrangements and institutions be applied to groups who cannot be classified differently by a consensually agreed, or objective, criterion? In Bolivia, indigenous representatives (lowland *indígenas* and highland *originarios*) fought hard in the years following the approval of the 2009 Constitution to restrict the law regulating FRIC to themselves and to exclude *campesinos*, even though that would have been contrary to the Constitution. 'Indigenous leaders repeatedly appealed to international agreements on this matter, claiming that peasant organizations do not meet the criteria of authenticity, nativeness and a pre-colonial existence', claiming that Convention 169 'clearly says that indigenous native people must have historical continuity, and the peasants have no historical continuity' (Fontana and Grugel 2016: 264). These distinctions were in any case largely political, dividing MAS supporters from the others as Morales's conflicts with the indigenous of the lowlands grew in bitterness over the TIPNIS conflict, to which we shall return. In the end, the prior consent law was applied to them all – it had to be recognized that the material disruption brought about by a mine or a highway is not altered by the indigenous or peasant classification of the community affected. Either way, the TIPNIS highway was only temporarily suspended.

The difficulties involved in implementing consultation with legitimate representatives, as stipulated by international law, can be compounded if local institutions operate according to inherited uncodified procedures and where there are parallel representatives – in the Bolivian case 'traditional' authorities, unions and indigenous organizations. Although those bodies can cooperate, such diffuse representation can be exploited by governments and politicians for their own purposes. In any case, no Latin American state would concede to local communities of any kind a veto over mining projects which are central to their development model.

Whereas the literature contains accounts of the germination of conflicts, few ethnographies follow the story to its conclusion, and there is a danger that we become over-impressed by the dead ends and interminable conflicts to which the law can lead if it is too strictly interpreted. The judicial case from the Cauca Valley in Colombia did however show that there is room for negotiation and mediation. One reason for this may be that, unlike Bolivian movements, the CRIC has tended to keep its distance from national political rivalries.

State-sponsored indigenous classification

The discussion so far has focused on the conceptualization of cultural difference and questions of law. It has concluded that concern with difference operates in an implicitly universalist framework. However, the politics of recognition often involve allocation of resources in the gift of the state, notably land, and this creates problems of classification: when the definition of beneficiaries has an unavoidable subjective element, how is eligibility decided and how are the resources allocated?

In innumerable projects overseen by NGOs and by government agencies such as Secretariats of Indigenous Affairs, the state only rarely demands strict criteria for people to qualify as beneficiaries. We saw that there was never any question of Mexico's intercultural universities restricting entry to indigenous students. But we shall see that in Chile the state has devised a bureaucratic criterion for the conferral of *calidad indígena*. First, though, we go to Brazil where the state has found various creative ways around this question.

Brazil

The Brazilian state has created separate agencies to provide for different types of Amazonian population: Indians are the responsibility of FUNAI (Fundação Nacional do Indio); people claiming descent from escaped slave settlements, or *quilombos*,[30] apply to the federal government's Fundação Palmares and submit land claims to INCRA (Instituto Nacional de Colonização e Reforma Agraria); and the Instituto Chico Mendes de Conservação da Biodiversidade (ICMBio – Chico Mendes Biodiversity Conservation Institute) can set aside land for conservation purposes for usufruct by 'traditional populations' – rubber tappers and people who live along the river banks, principally through fishing, hunting and rubber tapping. Clearly, this last category is a 'residual' – those who do not fit the other two, frequently known as *caboclos*. The state can formalize categories, but it cannot impose identities on groups or individuals so as to fit them into one or other of these categories, so people are able to choose, and it can happen that groups which have long coexisted in neighbouring settlements or villages, and have even intermarried, decide to go in different directions, with different land tenure arrangements. In one well-documented case in the north-eastern state of Sergipe, people who lived from the land and had no history of indigenous lifestyles or names or religious rituals, engaged in a campaign, involving local politicians and a group of friars, to have themselves recognized as Indians (Boyer 2014, 2016; French 2009).[31]

In an as yet unpublished survey of a multifarious literature combined with her own accumulated ethnographic experience, Boyer describes (Boyer forthcoming) the evolution since the late colonial period of the Amazonian region's highly mobile population: in addition to de facto enslavement and transportation of, and sometimes by, the Indian population, she brings to light the fluidity of boundaries and transferability of customs. There were many polygamous alliances between Portuguese merchants and Indian families whom they joined as the equivalent of *cunhamenas* (a Tupi term best translated as 'compadres') (Harris 2013: 87; Sommer 2006). The trajectory of the Gamela Indians of Maranhão (as they were named by the Portuguese) is illustrative: they absorbed fugitive black slaves and joined *quilombo* settlements during the eighteenth and nineteenth centuries and divided into two groups, one of which was dispersed or decimated by military expeditions while the other received

111

from the authorities a grant of *sesmaria*, a land grant normally reserved for Portuguese colonists, and eventually came to be classified as *caboclos* (Varga 2019). Faced with this bewildering array of social 'types', Mark Harris asks:

> Who were these people? Indians with highly varied experiences of colonial life; Africans sent as slaves from various nations in southern and western Africa; colonists, mostly poor soldiers, artisans and peasants seeking fortunes, or criminals sent to Brazil as punishment [. . .] This mobility gave people the confidence to function in a range of contexts and to pursue their own interests rather than those expected of them.

And he concludes that 'there were no stable or fixed frontiers between the variously identified ethnic groups in colonial Amazonia' (Harris 2013: 88–9).

Boyer also quotes Barbara Sommer along similar lines: 'In contrast to the old tribal versus acculturated dichotomy, historians now interpret the adoption, exchange, layering, and convergence of native and western concepts and the creation of new meanings and identities in the colonial context as a selective innovative process without a predetermined outcome' (Sommer 2014: 110).

Fast forward two centuries and in contrast to the chromatically graded and hierarchical race relations regimes found in Spanish America or in urban Brazil, the Amazonian population has been divided in common parlance and official thinking into Indians and blacks, with a white urban elite in the background. There is no customary equivalent of the *cholos* of the Andes or the *morenos* of urban Brazil, or *criollos* of Mexico. Instead, there are the *caboclos*, who are the main concern of Boyer's text: they rarely use the word to describe themselves as a collectivity, and it is not used by others when addressing them because of its pejorative connotations: they are everybody's 'other'. Like a set of empty sets, they are not singled out by identifiers in terms of skin colour, language or religious practices. In contrast, for Deborah Lima (Lima 1999), *caboclos* are defined in contrast with other groups and therefore count as an 'intermediary category' in the system of social classification, and they have also been defined by their liminality, their location in several in-between spaces, in terms of where they live, what they subsist on and the rituals they practise (Valentin 2001).

The 1988 Constitution instituted indigenous territorial rights, but left *quilombola* rights for later decision, and after 2000 the *quilombolas* became an officially recognized category. The Indians and the *quilombolas* fitted into a narrative of social mobilization and claims to reparation for past sufferings through land restitution or redistribution. Since fugitive slave settlements (*quilombos*) were by definition unregistered, the concept was eventually broadened to permit applications without evidence of *quilombo* origin. This left the vast low and very low-income population of *caboclos*, comprising, among others, riverine populations, rubber-tappers and collectors of tree crops. It does not seem to matter that these socio-economic categories could also overlap with the ethnic categories of Indians or blacks. Considered to be deserving of land and resources, in 2007 the category of *populações tradicionais* ('traditional populations') was invented, whereby *caboclos* could gain access to land under a National Sustainable Development Policy for Traditional Peoples and Communities through the ICMBio Institute. The title they would receive is for usufruct only under the supervision of the environmental agency and, as ever, obtaining it involves laborious bureaucratic procedures. Some have criticized the label 'traditional' as condescending, labelling the people concerned as not modern, but it was probably chosen as a convenient neutral label for the 'set of empty sets'. At least from now on the *caboclos* have a name they can use without shame.

As a result, the Amazonian forests offer to specialists and bureaucrats in search of clear-cut differences a field for classification of the population by way of life, by religious practice and by ancestry, while the population choose among the alternatives on offer. The heavy bureaucratic machinery reflects a corporatist approach to redistribution, under which beneficiaries petition designated agencies to act as their sponsors, and also a consensus that existed until the election of Bolsonaro that social justice and reparation are best pursued on the basis of ethnic and racial claims rather than universalistic policies such as land reform, which ground to a halt after the election of Lula in 2002.

The involvement of the state in assigning people to racial categories has also appeared as an unintended (but for some not unexpected) consequence of affirmative action policies designed to increase the proportion of black students in universities, especially public universities. Affirmative action gradually built up momentum in the private sector of education (on behalf of the state) and was institutionalized by a law in 2012 which allocated 40 per cent of places in federal public universities to students from state schools (who are assumed to be from lower-income backgrounds), of which half are reserved for those who claim black or brown skin colour or indigenous identity (Lehmann 2018). The system is therefore designed to combine both socio-economic and racial criteria, but it is universally known as 'quotas for blacks'. The numbers are not insignificant: in 2018, for example, 90,000 places in federal and state universities were filled on the basis of affirmative action by students claiming black, brown or indigenous status (de Freitas et al. 2020: 16, 23).

At first, classification was left to self-assignment but eventually it became a matter of controversy. Brazil has seen a growing movement of black consciousness among young people, and black students, notably in Rio, São Paulo and Bahia, have begun to organize around topics such as biased curriculum content and the limited representation of blacks among their professors, but also around the question of whether, in order to qualify for the quotas, people were falsely describing themselves as black. Although the idea that skin colour can be 'falsely' or 'fraudulently' or 'correctly' described is surely offensive to many if not most people, the issue became a matter of heated debate and of administrative action. Furthermore, since in Brazil the majority of non-whites classify themselves as *'moreno'* (brown) and there is no binary division of skin colour as there is, according to conventional wisdom, in the United States, a degree of reasonable disagreement about a person's qualification for the black quota is inevitable and no easier for a judge or administrator to decide than for a lay citizen.

It might be thought that the idea that a judge or administrative instance would decide on fraudulent allegations of self-assignment is also offensive, but this is what has happened. Students who have had their applications rejected take them to court, and judges have little choice but to decide. Universities have also begun to recognize the possibility of *fraude*, distancing themselves from the flexibility inherent in the principle of self-assignment (Guimaräes, Rios and Sotero 2020). In 2021, the highly prestigious Federal University of Minas Gerais (UFMG) concluded a four-year long inquiry into allegations that, in 2017, 61 students had made 'irregular' use of the quota provisions – that is, they had falsely declared themselves to be black or brown. The inquiry allowed them all to be heard individually and to be 'amply' defended, and it must have involved about a hundred academics and administrators in various committees. After withdrawals and elimination of improper allegations, eventually the cases were reduced to 29, of whom the University Council expelled 22 while suspending the other seven for one semester. The reasons for the more lenient sanctions were interesting for the light they shed on the substance of such decisions: 'their self-declaration as black arose from relevant social references that reflected that they had acted in good faith.'[32] It would appear that the lengthy inquiry (during which presumably they continued with their studies) explored with the students the motivations for and context of their self-assignment.

Universities have introduced procedures that require students applying to enter via the race quota to write a statement explaining their self-assignment and to appear before a commission which will evaluate their claim in accordance with their phenotype and, according to the

Vice-Rector for Student Affairs at the UFMG, whether their claim to be classified black or brown is 'compatible with the way in which society perceives it'.[33] The rector of the UFMG put out a statement deploring denunciations that might lead to 'virtual lynching' on Twitter.

The federal civil service has also introduced a quota system for filling staff positions, and the relevant law contemplates sanctions in cases of *fraude*. Commissions to check on 'declarations of racial identity' were instituted and norms established for their functioning in 2016,[34] as has also been done in some municipal governments and universities.

Protests around racial quotas have followed contradictory reasoning: in some cases, they have objected to students being deprived of their black quota places as an example of violation of the principle of self-assignment or an attack on quotas generally, while in other cases there have been protests against students fraudulently passing themselves off as black. In late 2018, at a Research Day at the Federal University of Bahia, I listened to a presentation by a consultant to institutions in the formation of these commissions and she stated forcefully that 'white students' were dishonestly 'stealing' black students' quota places.

The opening up of these race-specific opportunities, accompanying changes in urban youth culture and the readiness in academia and the press to recognize and forefront the specifically racial character of inequality have resulted, as Antonio Sergio Guimarães has observed, in a shift away from a 'classificatory system of colour which secularly opposed racialization' to a 'tendency to reaffirm racial categorisation' encouraged by affirmative action policies. To account for this, he has drawn on a modified version of Omi and Winant's concept of racialization and racial formation in which 'a positive racial counter-identity emerges' involving 'the formation of racial collectives', eventually transforming 'stigmas into charisma' (Guimarães 2019: 83, 87; Omi and Winant 2015)).

Chile

Chile requires people claiming *calidad de indígena* (indigenous status) to register (Law 19,253 of 1993 and Decree 392 of 1993).[35] Thus if someone wants to apply for land distribution under the procedure for land restitution to Mapuche people in the south of the country, or for an indigenous scholarship to attend university, they must qualify under criteria established by the National Indigenous Development Corporation (CONADI) which include having a Mapuche surname, living in or being descended from parents or grandparents living in a Mapuche *comunidad*, or simply leading a Mapuche way of life. In the elections for the 2021

Constitutional Convention, the criteria are slightly broader in that a person has to register with the electoral regulator (SERVEL) and can be considered indigenous even if they have ancestors beyond the second generation and no longer have an indigenous surname. Chile is the only country to codify indigenous status other than by self-assignment.

The difference compared to other countries in the Andes and Meso-America is that in Chile the land to be awarded is not usually land with which a Mapuche community has a historic connection. It has to be purchased on a 'willing-seller-willing-buyer' basis, supported by a subsidy from CONADI. Purchasers must form a 'community' of ten people, but they need not necessarily share a common family or community background and in the vast majority of cases the land is bought in individual holdings, though it should not be assumed that those holdings can support a family without recourse to wage labour (Mallon 2005: 210).

In a formal sense, the Chilean response to the Mapuche renewal takes recognition seriously: it is a structured reparations programme acknowledging three attacks on their land and their institutions: in recent decades they suffered from the violent reversal of the Agrarian Reform of 1968–73 and then, in 1979, the military government proceeded to the dismantling through compulsory parcellization of the legally constituted indigenous communities established through land grants (*títulos de merced*). In addition, it recognizes the usurpation of that land under the *títulos de merced* during forced resettlement of their people in so-called *reducciones* in the late nineteenth and early twentieth century, to make way for European immigrant farmers brought to Chile with government support.

The reparation was not designed to restore Mapuche institutions, even if that were possible, which distinguishes it from the Mexican path of reclaiming land on the basis of colonial title and from the Bolivian *ayllus* whose spokespeople look to restoring or preserving community land tenure arrangements. It differs from the Brazilian *quilombola* approach because the Brazilian INCRA only grants land in the form of collective tenure even though the *quilombolas* have no experience of it. It differs from the Brazilian opening of opportunities to the 'traditional populations' because the latter have no shared ethnic identity. There is no talk of legal pluralism or of establishing local government on Mapuche principles (as we saw in Oaxaca and Colombia), so there follows no institutional restoration.

Yet the Mapuche case stands out because of the growing strength and militancy of Mapuche movements, even though they are not linked to the reconstruction of their institutions. In the sphere of culture, they press for the recognition of the Mapunzungun language in schools, and in the national sphere they speak of territorial autonomy – something unheard of until recently. But the most widely supported protests are those that target infrastructure projects like dams and the environmentally damaging forestry industry (Pairícan Padilla 2014). The forestry industry, which has benefited from very generous treatment from the state through governments of all stripes and has destroyed hundreds of thousands of hectares of primeval forest,[36] has also been the object of violent attacks.

We thus find that the land restitution programme, although born of and carried forward on a proclaimed debt to and solidarity with the indigenous population, resembles in many ways a conventional moderate land reform in which poverty is a criterion to becoming a beneficiary and the resulting holdings are held as private property with no restrictions. Although *calidad indígena* is required, the procedures are guided by impersonal socio-economic indicators and take little account of the indigenous background to the land claims. The Mapuche movement likewise is carried forward by strong, even fierce, ethnic sentiment, but the causes it espouses are causes of concern to society as a whole, and, in addition to a widespread sense of solidarity with the Mapuche and their tragic history, reparation of historic wrongs is the source of its legitimacy.

Repression has become an established feature of life in the Mapuche regions of the south and has invigorated protests in the name of human rights. The broadening of their demands has gone together with their increasingly urban character and the gradually improving (though still below average) level of education of the Mapuche themselves: more than 40 per cent of Mapuche live in urban areas, 35 per cent of them live in the metropolitan region of Santiago and 14 per cent have higher education (Cerda 2017). In addition, untold numbers of people who would count as indigenous under the definition of Law 19253, which established CONADI, do not admit to their indigenous status or maybe are not even aware of it. Beyond these parochial concerns, they have come to symbolize the struggle for deeper and fairer democracy than that allowed by the Constitution imposed by Pinochet on his departure. This was highlighted when the demonstrations in Santiago's Plaza Baquedano (renamed Plaza Dignidad by vox populi) in late 2019 featured no political party emblems or flags, but only the national flag of Chile and the Mapuche flag.

These features of the country's indigenist policies and of the Mapuche movement go together, and further exploration would show how they are also connected with what makes Chilean society different from other Latin American countries.

Conclusion

This discussion began with a brief history of the concept of internal colonialism in Mexican anthropology, showing how, despite drawing on stereotypes of the indigenous community, it shifted away from over-racialized versions of the indigenous by recognizing the economic drivers of indigenous exclusion and also the existence of a *mestizo* society especially in small towns. I then followed the generations of anthropologists, showing their estrangement from the state and their adoption of the viewpoint of the indigenous themselves and especially indigenous women. The subject of legal pluralism that arose from that literature seemed to me to show that recognition of indigenous law is best thought of as a recognition of popular justice – in a general sense that encompasses indigenous justice, not in the sense of summary justice. In a similar vein, insofar as the limited available evidence allows, we saw that the Zapatista movement, under 'cover' of its indigenist demands, has introduced participatory democracy and has opened positions of authority to women.

We can see now how *interculturalidad*, when translated into practical programmes in education, the law, health and politics, is a vehicle for making local institutions more responsive to the needs not only of indigenous people but also of low-income rural populations (education) and making them more transparent at the local level (the law). Intercultural universities also have had a role in the formation of an indigenous or more broadly local leadership at least in some cases. The revival or reinvention of indigenous institutions of self-government in Oaxaca and Michoacán had very different effects, and both brought about profound changes in local government, but to describe the resulting structures as 'more indigenous' than those which had gone before is to overlook their wider successes and failures: in Michoacán, they perpetuated bandit rule, and in Oaxaca they had the paradoxical effect of replacing a system of co-optation and patronage which had become 'tradition' over many generations with another which was regulated by state authorities but created more openness in the election of local leaders. Furthermore, the changes required the intervention first of state authorities, starting with the governor, and more recently of the federal authorities, at the behest of women candidates, to open up Oaxaca's municipalities to gender parity. The case of Chile's sponsorship of intercultural health is the only one which explicitly encourages untouched indigenous practices, but even then it does so on hospital premises and as a result has to conform to regulatory standards imposed by the state.

The chapter also criticized the notion that differences between indigenous and hegemonic cultures were so profound that they could be described as epistemological. I have argued that anthropologists committed to the indigenous cause nevertheless pulled back from pursuing this idea in practice because of its connotations of romanticization or folklorization, and also because they do not accept that indigenous communities exist outside modernity, nor outside the socio-economic matrix of contemporary society.

Overall, in the sphere of education and health, the intercultural emerges as a vehicle for bringing social welfare and higher education programmes to the indigenous population generously defined, tailoring those programmes to their needs, and for broadening indigenous participation in political institutions, in the process opening a niche in the state for indigenous people and their leaders, sometimes in corporatist fashion.

Legal provisions are supposed to endure, independently of political changes, enshrined as collective rights and backed up by the national judicial system. We saw in the Colombian example the difficulties that arise in adjudicating cases in which they are called on to decide what is and what is not in keeping with *usos y costumbres* unless definitions and procedures are defined in terms which satisfy standard rational-legal criteria. It has to be admitted that once those definitions and criteria are adopted, then the hegemonic culture can be said to prevail and some might argue that the principle of recognition is weakened. But at least one can speak of rights protected by law.

Repeatedly, we see convergence between the indigenous and the society-wide approaches to social justice, to respect for human rights and to the law, so it is not surprising that Aída Hernández criticizes the idea that the indigenous peoples of today are 'different, pre-modern or opposed to the values of progress' (Hernández Castillo 2008a: 264, 2008b). It is perfectly possible to place material inequalities and universalist criteria of welfare in the forefront while by no means underemphasizing the ways in which cultural difference accentuates material inequality and deepens its wounds.

We can conclude by taking this inversion further, briefly turning attention away from the improvements brought by indigenous movements to their followers' livelihoods and to the respect accorded to them in society and towards their wider democratizing impact on society as a whole. I have not been able to explore this question, and it might seem premature at a time when democracy in the region is frequently said to be in retreat – or, in the striking quip of Jean Grugel and Lorenza Fontana, 'stable but stale' (Fontana and Grugel 2016: 249). It remains the case that ILO Convention 169 has been ratified by all Latin America except Cuba and by hardly any other nations at all. The indigenous territorial demarcation in Brazil remains in the Constitution despite the brazen hostility of the current administration. The Zapatistas brought a widespread democratic awakening in Mexico, which they unfortunately dissipated by staying outside the system and retreating to behind their Chiapas bastion. Evo Morales's campaigns went under an indigenous banner, but his governments had democratizing effects in poverty reduction and in breaking down the domination of a white oligarchy until his constitutional manipulations brought the country into crisis. We should be thinking not only of what indigenous movements and the state can do for their own people but also of what they do for society as a whole, and especially for social justice.

3

Religion and Culture:
Popular, Indigenous and Hegemonic

Indigenous religion is also popular Catholicism

Why have decolonial theorists focused so much on the colonial attack on indigenous science when we have a historical record of mammoth proportions overflowing with evidence of the colonial attack on indigenous religion and on indigenous people to impose the very non-scientific Catholic faith? If they did bring anything in the way of texts or knowledge, the conquerors brought the Roman Catholic liturgy and with it the Trinity, the Virgin Mary and the saints, not Descartes. (Not even the Gospel, because lay people were not supposed to have access to sacred texts – that came later with Protestantism.) Although Bartolomé de las Casas, in his denunciation of the violence perpetrated by the conquerors, described the rituals and sacrifices of native peoples as their way of worshipping the one true God according to their own traditions (Gutiérrez 1993 [1992]), the colonial system and its religious missionaries ignored his pleas to treat Indians as humans and proceeded in its campaign of destruction of the artefacts, the symbols and the priests, shamans and royalty charged with the population's relationship with their gods and spirits. It is ironic that one of the inspirations of the theoretical apparatus of the decolonial approach is a product of Catholic theology, namely, the Theology of Liberation, of which the young Enrique Dussel was a prominent exponent (Dussel 1973).

It was not only in the field of religious ritual and celebration that we observe the commingling of European and indigenous cultural traits and habits. One example is architecture and house building, a field where the Incas were in the habit of borrowing from local traditions as they extended their short-lived empire through the Andes. When the Conquest brought a new power with similar aspirations of control, the

121

builders incorporated both Spanish and Inca building techniques and design motifs, as can be seen in the streets of Cuzco and as detailed in the description of houses in Chinchero, a town near to Cuzco, by an architectural historian (Nair 2007). Nair argues on the basis of the design of the buildings that the notion of a radical break between Inca and Spanish architecture and design which has underpinned scholarly and popular understanding is not sustainable. Different styles should not be packaged in homogeneous compartments with different ethnicities, different political powers or even different social classes. The 'indigenous inhabitants' of Chinchero in the early colonial period 'incorporated the Spanish arches into their own Andean houses; the arches cannot be a reflection of Spanish ethnicity'. Inca architecture used niches where Spanish style would use openings and doorways under arches, so the use of both within a single structure 'reveals the problem with seeing the two styles as always existing in opposition. The arches in the colonial indigenous homes remind us that the meaning of architectural styles and iconography is not set but rather changes over time and across space, depending on the context' (Nair 2007: 57). In architecture as in religion, colonial imposition of clear-cut and exclusive 'before-and-after' categorizations, perpetuated in ready-made scholarly narratives, tend to dissolve on close inspection. The extirpation of idolatry, for all its violence and despite the epidemics that decimated indigenous populations, did not eradicate indigenous religion (Gruzinski 1988; Wachtel 1977). Over the subsequent centuries, indigenous religion gradually transformed into what we now know as popular Catholicism, another topic ignored by decolonial theory.

Popular Catholicism can be associated with uprisings, with resistance and also with enduring patterns of oppression and repression: banners carrying images of the Virgin of Guadalupe were carried by the insurgents during Mexico's independence wars and in support of the liberal cause during the country's civil wars of the mid-nineteenth century. The same pattern was repeated during the revolutionary wars of 1910–1917 and during the Cristero revolt of the 1920s, this time against the post-revolutionary state (Brading 2001; Meyer 1973–4; Poole 1995). The story of the appearance of the Virgin of Guadalupe, dated 1531 in the immediate aftermath of the conquest, albeit only 'recorded' a century later, reiterates a perennial theme in popular Catholicism worldwide: a humble Indian peasant's innocent faith is pitted against the authority of the powerful bishop who eventually has to bow down before him, and forever after the story becomes a fable of indigenous inclusion in the community of the faithful.

In Brazil, popular revolts or movements in late nineteenth- and early twentieth-century Brazil, inspired by millenarian hopes and Catholic autonomy, were highly localized but gained nationwide notoriety: one of these, in the commune-like town of Canudos in Bahia state, was led by popular preacher (*beato*) Antonio Conselheiro, whose ruthless destruction at the third attempt by an expeditionary force in 1897 was documented in Euclides da Cunha's classic work of history and literature *Os Sertões* (da Cunha 1995 [1902]; Galvão 1974; Levine 1992; Pereira de Queiroz 1976). Another Brazilian example is the still enduring cult around the figure of Padre Cicero (1844–1934) in the north-eastern state of Ceará in which the church hierarchy failed to suppress the celebration of a purported miracle, and also failed to undermine the authority of the priest who became the standard-bearer of resistance while at the same time enjoying support from a variety of local and national notables (della Cava 1970). The third Brazilian example is the case of the 'Contestado' (1912–1916) (Diacon 1991; Teixeira Monteiro 1974; Vinhas de Queiroz 1981), a region so called because it was disputed between the southern states of Parana and Santa Catarina at the time. The armed uprising, in protest at the expropriation of land for the purposes of building a railway, combined visions of a popular saint ('João Maria') with a small-scale military organization derived from stories of Charlemagne and the Knight Roland (cf. the *Chanson de Roland*, which was and still is widely popularized in north-eastern Brazil in a style derived from medieval romances of chivalry through chapbooks known as *literatura de cordel*; Slater 1982).[1]

These revolts are localized and unusual. More pervasive is the incorporation of indigenous rituals in popular Catholicism, especially in Meso-America and the Andes. Few have disentangled these *mestizajes* better than Antoinette Molinié in her description of the joining of the Corpus Christi ritual with the veneration of the Colquepunku glacier, at 5000 m altitude, in the shadow of the Ausangate mountain not far from Cuzco. In it, we see people in the role of *ukuku*, disguised as mountain bears (the 'spectacled bears'[2]) from the intermediate zone between the highlands and the tropical lowlands, perform a series of dangerous and haunting rituals. The *ukuku* climb up to a glacier where they create a candle-lit chapel, dance away and detach pieces of ice, watched from below by crowds from surrounding communities (Molinié 2005). They then carry the blocks of ice down to be offered at the chapel's altar in celebration of the host as the body of Christ on Corpus Christi. The ritual is replete with Andean imaginary. The *ukuku* represent an intermediate category between the highest and lowest ecological niche (*pisos ecológicos* in the anthropologists' terminology[3]), between male and female, between nature and culture and between human and animal. The snow-covered peaks are divinities to whom the people make offerings and pray through their shamans. The journey of the ice blocks continues: after being placed on the chapel altar, they will be taken to the communities where they will dissolve into water valued for its healing properties. The *ukuku* consume the God of the Mountain by cutting off ice, and they consume the Christian God in the form of the host. It is a perilous venture: quite often they fall to their death from the glacier and are left buried 'in the embrace of their God', whence, it is sometimes said, they will bring good fortune to their communities.

The ritual dates back to a miraculous apparition in 1870, when a young shepherd, Mariano Mayta, sent by his father to look after their alpaca, encountered a white child in magnificent clothes, just like the effigies in local churches. The bishop sent a group of priests to investigate and on arrival they were blinded by a white light. As they approached, the white child was transformed into an effigy of Christ crucified; Mariano was overcome and, believing that his new friend had been killed, died of a broken heart. He is buried in the same spot, overlooked today by a fresco of Christ, and a sanctuary was built for the altar where the ice-bearing *ukukus* complete their task. As in Mexico's Guadalupe myth, a humble young Indian is the bearer of a divine message, and the church dignitaries have to go down on their knees in recognition of his vision.

Various aspects of the ritual point to the convergence between the Eucharist – the white disc of the host – and the Apu ('Lord') Colquepunku, whence shines forth the great white disc of the solstice sun (coinciding with the feast of Corpus Christi). The lives sacrificed in the ritual performances on the glacier converge with the sacrifice of Christ represented by the host.

Molinié's interpretation revolves around the Christianization of the glacier and the 'Andeanization' of Christ. The faces of the two divine beings transform one another into a 'dual divinity' as they domesticate and 'contaminate' each other, creating a monstrance (*custodia*) – the repository of the host: the monstrance always faces two ways, so in this ceremony it has an Andean and a Christian face (ibid.: 7).

A decolonial perspective has little to say about the religious *mestizaje* which is a pervasive feature of the cultures of Mexico, Central America and the Andes. Nor does it account for the equally pervasive, and creative, tension between popular and erudite (Catholic) religion, sometimes beholden to established authority, sometimes in rebellion against it. The previous examples showed Catholic symbols and faith mobilized against the established order as evidence that popular sectors can 'inject' them with agendas beyond the Catholic symbols of the life and death of Christ without a murmur of dissent from local priests or bishops. A decolonial narrative might answer that the true indigenous meaning of the rituals has been distorted by a colonial church – but the reverse, that the church has lost control to indigenous appropriation, could also be claimed. Alternatively, the decolonial interpretation could be that this is a case of resistance to colonial religiosity, in which case how has it come about that communities and their shamans readily incorporate the Catholic imaginary and paraphernalia into their sacred spaces like the glacier?

The dialectic of the erudite and the popular

'Lo popular' is a ubiquitous underlying presence in the dissident discourses that pervade art and scholarship on the region. There is a dialectic relationship between popular and erudite religion within Latin America's Catholic culture, and in a similar pattern erudite art, literature, cinema and music take up themes from the popular and elaborate them in a parallel dialectic. Examples come in many forms, from Brazil's Música Popular Brasileira (MPB), which made samba into a high art form, to Violeta Parra who set her poetry to music derived from Chilean folk music; Frida Kahlo's variations on motifs drawn from Mexican popular religion; Elena Poniatowska's *Hasta no verte Jesús Mío* (1969), channelling the inner thoughts of a young Mexican in the idiom of popular language; and Manuel Puig's elaborations on the culture of Hollywood as transmitted through the fantasies of young women and gay men in *Boquitas Pintadas* (1969), *La Traición de Rita Hayworth* (1968) and the more political *Beso de la Mujer Araña* (1976) – transferred with great success to the screen as *The Kiss of the Spiderwoman* (dir. Hector Babenco, 1985). This interweaving of genres perhaps reaches its apex in the dystopian burlesque of the films of Alejandro Jodorowsky (*El Topo*, 1973: *La Danza de la Realidad*, 2013). The anthropologist Nestor García Canclini enumerated many instances of construction of the popular by the state or by the intelligentsia in *Culturas Populares en el Capitalismo* and *Culturas Hibridas* (García Canclini 1989, 2002) and we shall return to his ideas.

The distinctive place of terms like 'lo popular', 'cultura popular' and 'religiosidad popular' in the language of Latin American social and academic commentary lies in the self-conscious blurring of the lines between the cultures of different social strata. The terms are inherently contestable because social strata cannot be said to control cultural practices or complexes, nor can lines be clearly drawn between high and low culture. Yet at the same time social life is replete with habits of speech, of dress, even of gait, signalling differences of status, prestige and wealth, sometimes deep and wide, sometimes mere hints of the 'tyranny of small differences', which are readily recognized by those involved, encapsulated in the rarely spoken but frequently implied interpellation: 'Você sabe com quem está falando?' (Portuguese for 'Do you realize who you are speaking to?').

In his landmark *Popular Culture in Early Modern Europe*, Peter Burke showed that there have been periods in Europe when intellectuals from the erudite classes expressed positive appreciation of popular cultures, but whether the disposition was one of constructing barriers or overcoming them, the assumption of separateness and difference was clear (Burke 1978). The three points which in his words encapsulate the conceptions of folklore by the late eighteenth-century romantics the Brothers Grimm (of 'Grimm's Fairy Tales') and the philosopher Johann Gottfried Herder were 'primitivism, communalism and purism'. When starting a long engagement with Brazil in the 1980s, Burke wrote a paper about Carnival, he noted many similarities over the long history of the region, but after observing how the latest incarnations of carnival in that country and elsewhere in the Americas were incorporating African themes, he concluded that 'what makes American Carnivals different from European ones is above all the mixture and interaction of cultures which they put on public display' (Burke 1997). To this I would add that there is a subtle and even tricky reflexivity at play in the ways in which the erudite secular culture interacts with 'lo popular' in Latin America, and the plurality of cultures exists across classes and regions as well. The *locus classicus* of this dance is found in the essay by the Brazilian modernist intellectual Antonio Cândido, entitled 'Dialética da Malandragem' ('Dialectics of the Rogue's Life'). The essay was about the picaresque-like work of Manuel Antônio de Almeida, describing urban life among the popular classes in the early nineteenth century, and Cândido argued that bad behaviour of a folkloric and also transgressive sort is built in to the social order of urban Brazil (i.e. Rio de Janeiro) (Cândido 1970). It is not precisely dissident, it is certainly not political: it describes a consecrated way of life on the borderline between legality and illegality, lived with an abundance of roguish charm. As another instance of the dialectic, Chico Buarque, the celebrated poet, composer and singer of the 1970s and since, troubadour of MPB, created a work derived from *The Beggar's Opera* (1728) and Brecht and Weill's *Threepenny Opera* (*Dreigroschenoper*) entitled *Opera do Malandro* (*The Rogue's Opera*) (1979), which weaves Weill's music in and out of samba rhythms. Chico and his fellow MPB artists were hardly members of the popular classes, but their use of modes and rhythms from the samba and from Brazil's north-east had an undoubted dissident or resistant tone and content in the context of the military regime which also marked the period of their greatest success.[4] In their book about the place of memory in popular culture, William Rowe and Vivian von Schelling are particularly alert to the dissident political messages in inter-class borrowings from popular culture. Their main theme is the ambiguity of inter-class and inter-genre borrowing, and in arguing that 'the popular cannot mean purity', they also make a point of including the mass media, contesting the idea that the culture industry brings a loss of purity (Rowe and von Schelling 1991: 96).

The dialectics of *malandragem* is a fitting expression for the ways in which Latin American high culture has incorporated the popular in a manner that is artistically seamless yet still preserves, or echoes, the social distance – the 'abyss' – separating the educated classes from the *povo* or *pueblo*. This is the dominant theme in Canclini's *Culturas Híbridas* (García Canclini 1989, 1995, 2001, 2005), a book which can be read both as a polemic and as a meditation. Canclini starts out with a plea for an end to the academic division between 'lo culto' (high culture and the art exhibited on museum walls) and 'folklore', mentioning the unique fusion of genres by the Argentinian Astor Piazzola (who studied with Nadia Boulanger), the Brazilian MPB singer and composer Caetano Velloso and the Panamanian salsa-jazz musician Rubén Blades. We need, he says, 'nomadic social sciences able to tread the staircases separating these floors, or even to redesign the building and place the floors on the same level' (García Canclini 1989: 14–15).[5] At the end of the book, he returns to the theme of hybridity, now incorporating the mass media and welcoming official recognition of folk art as representative of a country's artistic achievements. He notes that for all its transgressive challenges designed to shock elites and establishments, modern art (as celebrated worldwide) remained a world apart, a rarefied taste, and he deplores the efforts of the high priests and priestesses who rule over the different fields to preserve the frontiers even in the face of overwhelming evidence that the opposition between the erudite and the popular in art is unsustainable. The dividing lines in terms of style, meaning, message and subject matter cannot justify this kind of classification (García Canclini 1989: 337, 339).

In analysing the relationship between the state and the popular, Canclini focuses on Mexico, a state which has gone further than any other in the Americas in sponsoring monuments and monumental art memorializing indigenous heritage and also in supporting *artesanía* (crafts). But this also means that the state draws a line between art as folklore and professional or aesthetic art – art for art's sake. Museums and anthropologists (at least, he might have said, those in the service of the state) have sacralized, nationalized, essentialized and stereotyped the country's Indian populations, ignoring their diversity and also ignoring the pervasive presence among them of all the artefacts of modern living.

That much is widely recognized but, using Bourdieu's model of the field of art and its autonomy, Canclini is also disappointed by the material underdevelopment of the artistic field in Latin America, its lack of institutionalization: artists are too dependent on the state and on the conservative tastes of private patrons. Nonetheless, the leading figures of modernism in the interwar period overcame the twin risks of provincialism and folklorization, finding inspiration outside the art world. Returning, as so many of them did, from time spent in Europe, or in some cases arriving as immigrants from Europe (like Lazar Segall in Brazil), they were able to establish independent modes of expression and communication in confrontation with the problems of their own societies (García Canclini 1989: 77).

Thus Brazilian modernists (the generation of Antonio Cândido) tended to adapt Cubist techniques – though some might contest that. He encapsulates their problem by noting that when Picasso finds inspiration in African art, it occurs to no one to wonder whether he is faithful to the source, whereas in Latin America to use indigenous motifs as inspiration is assumed to have a political force and unavoidably provokes those questions about authenticity.

The absence in Canclini of sustained treatment of the indigenous peoples, their artistic output and their access to the field (that is, to museums, academies and publications, to vernissages, curators and gallerists) would be unthinkable today. But reflecting the intellectual climate of the time, he does not draw a dividing line between the popular and the indigenous in the cultural sphere. He also recognizes the collapsing boundaries in the field of art, which include the line dividing art from *artesanía*: the academic study of art had long since derided these categories as constructions, no longer defined by an 'a priori essence' (ibid.: 18). But the 'subaltern sectors' were still left to construct their own positions and remained outside the sphere of professional artistic education. In his view, it would be better to encourage and support people from those sectors by enabling them to attend art school than to patronize crafts made for sale on tourist markets.

At the end of his book, Canclini confronts the collapse of boundaries within the art forms themselves, writing of 'procesos ambiguos de interpenetración y mezcla' and 'hibridización intercultural' (ibid.: 254, 264). In a long section on the border town of Tijuana, he laments that the simulacrum – comparable to kitsch – has become a 'central category of culture' (ibid.: 301). Few places, or few spectacles, could be more visually expressive of the contemporary colonial condition than the US–Mexican border, but it is culturally and artistically representative hybridity. Authenticity is artistically irrelevant save in the sense that artists must convince their public that they are true to themselves.

Canclini uses the word 'intercultural' in a different sense from that which it acquired in later years. In the 2001 introduction to a new edition, he takes the (slightly extreme) position that the intercultural abstract features of an original lead to an absolutist notion of identity and, by marginalizing heterodox modes of language and music, deny the possibility of changing culture or politics. He then adds a cautionary note about hegemonic groups who select elements from various periods and fashion them into a coherent narrative.[6] In defining his concept more carefully, he performs a high-wire balancing act (or maybe tiptoes through a minefield): he guards against excessively comforting versions of *mestizaje* and defines the study of hybridity less as a state than as an approach to *processes* of hybridization, enabling *multiculturalidad* to discard its elements of segregation and open the way to *interculturalidad*. My own interpretation of why Latin American intellectuals, social scientists and policy makers have opted for *interculturalidad* follows in his footsteps (García Canclini 2001: 17). If I prefer, marginally, to speak of the dialectic of the popular and the erudite to speaking of hybridity, it is because of the element of projection, or self-consciousness: the 'hall of mirrors'.

Unlike many other anthropologists, Canclini does not privilege ethnicity, framing it as one of many facets of the intercultural and hybrid subaltern. Since he wrote that book, *interculturalidad* has become a banner and a set of government policies operating around the relationship between ethnic cultures and languages and the hegemonic culture. The spokespeople of ethnic recognition underplay hybridity, as they must, to support their claims to recognition and to intercultural educational and health programmes. Expressions of popular culture, in Canclini's view, have fallen victim to commercialization, to state co-optation and to the tourist market. They have been extracted from the rhythms and rituals of social life that function as the guarantors of their authenticity and placed on display in museums, craft markets and academia (García Canclini 1989: 18). Postmodernism, however, has rescued heritage by removing it from the museum (*decolección* – his italics), disembedding (*desterritorialización*) and reconverting knowledge and customs, readying them for hybridization.

Dividing lines are almost impossible to define in these discussions, as he himself recognizes in delineating 'authenticity' and the idea of a palpable frontier between what is in a museum and what is in a street market. The point is illustrated by an anecdote of a visit to an artisan's workshop in

129

Oaxaca where he was surprised to see tapestries with motifs and images from Picasso, Klee and Miró. He was even more surprised to learn that visitors from New York's Museum of Modern Art had proposed to renew the designs for him. Canclini says this was the moment when he realized that the artisan in question was untroubled by his concern for the decline of local artistic traditions and moved effortlessly between English and Spanish and between the culture of his own ethnic group, the world of art criticism and mass culture (García Canclini 1989: 224).

Authenticity may routinely be recognized to be a constructed term, but it is nevertheless very difficult to escape the intuitive, possibly sub-conscious reflexes which draw even the most sceptical postmodernist to a certain sort of artefact, alerting us to a people, their traditions and deep roots of nationhood or of the popular, especially if the reaction is triggered by a context like a church, a fiesta or a street market. As the critique of authenticity implies, there is no defining feature of popular creative practices which would inoculate them against a degree of what Canclini calls 'teatralización': that is, being put on display, disembedded from their 'natural' or 'original' context. If authenticity is constructed, so is the lack of authenticity.

Bolivia: a crucible for the intellectual, anthropological and political intersections of ethnicity and authenticity

The following sections explore further the interweaving of ethnicity, performance and intellectual disagreements about ethnic boundaries. The context is the Bolivia that produced Evo Morales, where the strands intersect and also where some of the most interesting anthropological writing is to be found.

The authentic Indian, the Oruro Carnival and Pachamama: positioning the observer

A highly successful ethnography of authenticity and its performance is that of the late Thomas Abercrombie observing festivities at Oruro, a highland Bolivian town whose carnival has been elevated to nationwide prominence as an embodiment of Bolivia's nationhood and to world-wide recognition from UNESCO's *Representative List of the Intangible Cultural Heritage of Humanity*. Together with that elevation has come the 'takeover' or even 'gentrification' of the carnival: once controlled by associations of workers, Indians and *cholos*, and performed in the face of elite disapproval, this and other carnivals are now dominated by newer elites composed not, as in the past, of landowning families but of state employees and businesspeople (Abercrombie 1992: 281). That summary view, as Abercrombie shows, distracts from the mixed and cross-cutting messages that are being conveyed by the different types of dance, of dress and of processions that occur during the carnival, which coincides with the Festival of Corpus Christi – and not, as is usual, with the days preceding the start of Lent.

Abercrombie published three sparkling papers with interpretations of the Oruro Carnival: in 1991 in English, in 1992 in Spanish, and again, with further developments, in English ten years later (Abercrombie 1991, 2003). His multi-levelled interpretation starts with the successive rearrangements of local government over three centuries of colonial rule and culminates with Bolivia's post-1952 nationalism. The following sentence gives an oversimplified version of the concluding phase: 'Urban non-Indians also enjoy "playing" Indians as well as appropriating for themselves (and for the nationalist projects) a generalized indigenous ancestry' (Abercrombie 1991: 111).

But Abercrombie also pursues the mutual projection to the point in his concluding paragraph where the images that the 'Indians' (his quotes), who are purportedly represented in rites such as the Oruro Carnival, increasingly adopt 'the Other's Other as their internal demon' (ibid.: 123). The Indian as imagined by the elites (their Other) crosses paths with the actually existing Indians, again as in a hall of mirrors.

The 1991 paper starts by saying he hopes to show 'that rural/"Indian" and urban/"non-Indian" cultural formations' are jointly implicated 'as parts of a "colonial situation," while remaining distinct analytic arenas, as experientially "real" mutual hypostatizations constituted by each Other's gaze in a discourse of power and identity' (Abercrombie 1991: 100). (Note the use of quotation marks and slashes in his text.)

That is, in the colonial relationship, the Spanish authorities tried to shape indigenous society but in the process the institutions they tried to impose were also shaped by the indigenous and their own authorities, and the worldview of the indigenous was transformed but not eradicated. As an example, his interpretation of a civic ceremony in an *ayllu* concludes that in the eyes of the participant Indians, the mummified corpses within pre-Columbian tombs are 'essentially pre-human'; 'the founding time is the Spanish Conquest and the colonial discourse is made into a first principle' (ibid.: 110). Maybe he means to say that the Conquest was a big success in the annals of evangelization.

His description of the interaction of pre-colonial and colonial institutions and belief systems undermines the idea of a rejection of the latter or return to the former, at least until a few twenty-first-century intellectuals were attracted to the fantasy of an Inca restoration. Prevailing late twentieth-century urban notions, he says, 'romanticise Indians, stripping them of the complex understandings of history and power relations and projecting them as living fossils' of a pre-colonial past, 'thus taking a version of one half of the rural dwellers' own ambivalent identity sources for their own' (ibid.: 111). In other words, they airbrush out the Spanish elements of indigenous culture. Even in modern Oruro's pre-Conquest myth of origin, the Virgin of the Mineshaft (the Virgen del Socavón) is likened to the pre-conquest Inca princess who defeated an invasion of 'evil Indian "antigods"': that is, the Virgin was there to protect Indians even before the colonial invasion.

The contemporary binary of Indian and *mestizo* (the category of white barely exists in modern Bolivia) was undermined early in the colonial period as 'the "reduced" Indians[7] took control of the institutions of *doctrina* (rural parish) and *cabildo* (town council)', and 'Christ was equated with the Sun; the Virgin with the moon; saints with atmospheric mediating powers (such as lightning) . . .' (ibid.: 105).

By the eighteenth century, the colonial systems were losing control of labour for the mines and of the silver that was extracted from them, and 'interstitial kinds of people' appeared in large numbers in mining towns – people escaping labour obligations (the *mita*), joining guilds of mulattoes and Creole Indians and even Spaniards who did not fit into the official Spanish categories, working in or running clandestine ore mills and foundries – these interstitial people were precursors of today's *cholos* (ibid.: 111).

For Abercrombie and many others, Bolivia's 1952 Revolution empowered *mestizo-cholo* elites drawn from the trade unions and the bureaucracy who, in contrast to the European orientation of the pre-existing mining and landowning oligarchies, welcomed a narrative connecting them to the country's pre-colonial past. He describes it as a 'tragic romance of their very particular love of their fatherland': 'el trágico romance de su particular *amor patrio*' (Abercrombie 1992: 312; emphasis in the original). In the 2003 paper, 'tragic' is replaced by 'transgressive', reflecting that paper's greater emphasis on the lifting of sexual taboos with which Carnival is associated: '[C]reole elite ambivalence toward cross-class, cross-race (and one might add, cross-gender) cultural alters (intimate others) found expression in public performance in venues such as Oruro's carnival' (Abercrombie 2003: 177). Dressed in *indio*-style clothes and rehearsed to perform large-scale *comparsa* dances (masquerades), the protagonists enact seemingly indigenous or quasi-shamanic ceremonies which Abercrombie sees as part of their domestication of the spirits of *indio* cosmology, culminating in a

Catholic mass dedicated to the Virgen del Socavón. If only because it is superimposed on Corpus Christi, this is not a Brazilian-style Rabelaisian carnival 'turning the world upside down'.

Likewise, the elites have turned the imagined cult of Pachamama inside out and have made themselves into 'their own indios' (Abercrombie 1992: 285). Quoting Olivia Harris, Abercrombie writes that in rural Indian communities, female divinities are seen to occupy a dangerous and sometimes diabolic space in the underworld, and he describes them as 'consorts' of the gods incarnated in the mountains and hillsides, counterposed to the 'Vírgenes de Arriba' (Virgins from Above), for example, the 'Madre Luna' (Mother Moon) (ibid.: 309). This is not the protective Pachamama imagined by political indigenism.

This interpretation shows that ceremonies in homage to the Pachamama which proliferated to mark Evo Morales's political rituals are as much a simulacrum of Christian ceremonials as an enactment of pre-Columbian or indigenous ones. Harris also explained that the Pachamama figure in the indigenous cosmology rather resembles inconstant or fickle Fortune on whom the fertility of the land and its mineral wealth depend. Like Abercrombie, she tells how indigenist intellectuals throughout the twentieth century have adopted a Christianized version, portraying the Pachamama as an earth mother, a protectress like the Virgin Mary. 'Once this kind of step is taken the Pachamama is rapidly loosed from her Andean moorings and drifts off into a haze of *criollo* and European mysticism' (Harris 2000: 213).

In 2021, after three periods of Morales as president and the decisive electoral victory of his protegé Luis Arce in late 2020, the ecological writer and anti-mining advocate Eduardo Gudynas wrote of the use and abuse of what now had become *pachamamismo*, to such an extent that Arce described a gas extraction plant he was inaugurating as a 'gift from our Pachamama'.[8] Pachamama had become an all-purpose banner, used by some to refer to anything indigenist or environmentalist, and by others to denote a mystical Andean concept inspired by or even covering for capitalist ideology and politics.

Abercrombie interpreted the rearrangement of the indigenous pantheon as a response of Bolivian elites to their paradoxical postcolonial position and to their changing ethnic and occupational composition: they inherited a social order derived from colonial conquest via a nineteenth-century Republican refoundation and a nationalist revolution, and now they were distilling from the life-worlds of the *indios* they so long despised a basis for their own 'chthonic' or 'telluric' legitimacy. Their writers and spokespeople reformulated the vocabulary of social hierarchy, discarding the pejorative word *indio* in favour of the more romantic *indígena* (Abercrombie 1992: 298). Where once the carnival was divided between the refined strata's European-style festivities and the *indios*' offerings to the mountain deities, now the trade unionists and state officials adopted Indian modes of dress and, rather than dancing in couples, enacted *comparsas* organized under the auspices of the miners' unions or butchers' corporations.

The hint of mockery in Abercrombie's 2003 English article, conveyed by expressions such as 'ancestral warrants' (p. 178), 'surrogation' (p. 180), and 'pageant romance' (p. 183), is again reinforced by a forest of quotation marks:

> by eliding cultural differences between rural "Indian" and urban "cholo" cultures, by relabeling "cholo" belief systems (such as those involving the earth mother Pachamama and the tíos [devil idols] of the mines) as authentically ancient and "Indian" ones, and by Indianizing both the provenance of urban dance-dramas and their representational content, the predominantly urban mestizo-cholo dance-drama and religious complex could be made to stand in for that of the rural "Indian." (Abercrombie 1983: 201)

These Indian practices have been adopted 'for nationalist purposes', even while the *cholos* and *cholitas* (who are 'below' the *mestizo-cholo* elites in the social hierarchy) have themselves been 'marginalized from the patriotic and devotional core of the spectacle' (p. 203). The same slightly patronizing tone can be found in his allusion to 'stylized piquant cholita dress' in the context of remarks about urban migrants who once wanted to distance themselves from *indio* status but now find it suits their purpose in advertising their adherence to the 'new populist politics' (p. 206).

The intellectual honesty, as well as the boundless erudition, of the 2003 paper in grappling with the hall of mirrors is noteworthy. Each example of customs and ceremonial practices being exchanged across the divisions of class, of neighbourhood, of city and countryside and of race (skin colour) and ethnicity (culture, dress, language or accent) is balanced by an observation reminding us of the underlying pattern of inequality and prejudice:

> Even when the egalitarian principles of republican popular sovereignty erased racial language from censuses and voting rights laws, Creoles remained white and culturally figured Indianness remained the principal criterion for the exclusion of Indians from the rights of citizenship. This was possible through a crucial trick, by which enactments of status are taken as indices of essential difference . . . the workshop for learning this trick, and for forgetting its basis in artifice, was (in Joseph Roach's term) the process of surrogation in festive play. (Abercrombie 2003: 180)

RELIGION AND CULTURE

And yet the paper has many examples of 'rural people called "Indians"' (a circumlocution he uses three times), finding a way to circumvent or to capitalize on the barriers set up by those essential features.

Convergence or mutual appropriation is mentioned frequently: 'wealthier folks dance in costumes of cultural alters' from the outskirts to the centre – 'that is . . . from the places of underworld gods into the Christian temple' (Abercrombie 2003: 191); 'Indian participation in 16th century performances [. . .] confirmed the victory of Christianity over the devil and also Christianity's role in saving the Inca from devilish threats' (ibid.: 195); 'a Satan imprisoned on the outskirts of Potosí is brought under control by "magical practices" – the very practices that Satan is meant to encourage or embody!' (ibid.: 196); 'as the urban appetite for "Indian" customs waxes, drawing the rural people called "Indians" into their pageants as once they only invited them into their markets (and, as maids, into their homes), so does the rural "Indian" appropriation of urban folkloric Indianness, which from the countryside looks like cosmopolitan progress' (ibid.: 209). In placing the word 'Indian' in double quotes and adding the phrase 'people called', he distances himself from any hint of essentialism, even implying a question as to whether the term is at all justifiable, while also signalling that it denotes divisions of class as well as those of race and lifestyle.

Decades ago, I was told that his publications had caused uproar in Oruro and if that was true, one can understand why. In Abercrombie's Oruro, much ingenuity, organization and handiwork is expended by people disguising themselves as their Indian 'others' in order to exhibit their own superior urban *mestizo-cholo* status.

Xavier Albó, in a down-to-earth contribution to the review symposium that accompanied Abercrombie's 1992 article in the *Revista Andina*, pointed out a similar pattern in the La Paz *Fiesta del Gran Poder*, while reminding readers indirectly that innumerable other people living in Oruro and La Paz are probably not in the least troubled by these racial or ethnic differences. Young middle-class women, he said, who dress up for a festive event in the multi-layered skirts associated with indigenous womanhood, and with the prosperity of women market traders,[9] probably do not give a moment's thought to mimicking or mockery, looking rather to display prestige and socio-economic status (Albó 1992: 328).[10]

Sian Lazar's description of fiestas more than a decade later in the 'rebel city' of El Alto overlooking La Paz makes hardly any allusion to borrowed, mimicked or memorialized identities. In her interpretation, ethnicity *intersects* class, age and gender, and the fiestas appear as celebrations of citizenship in El Alto's 'independent republic' (my words). The words *chola* and *mestiza* denote class and social status

135

RELIGION AND CULTURE

(respectability) as much as heritage or tradition, let alone physiognomy, and the important effect of participation in the fiesta organization and in competition for prominent roles is to strengthen feelings of citizenship in that independent republic. Lazar uses the words *cholo* and *mestizo* in a direct way without quotation marks, recognizing their ethnic connotations, but without getting entangled in their multiple possible meanings or in moralizing undercurrents

> The Morenada [dance] ... expresses something about adulthood, dignity, and appropriate gendered behaviour ... When younger people dance the Morenada in the Oruro Carnival or the Entrada Universitaria, the boys' movements are much more athletic than the older men's, involving more elaborate jumping and twisting, while the girls dance in flirty mini-*polleras* instead of the full *pollera* worn by the older women, a fact commented upon with disapproval by one of my (younger) friends. The issue of dignity addressed here is not only about women of different ages wearing different clothes, but also about the ethnicity of the dancers. With her snorts of disapproval at the short skirts, my friend expressed a view that mestiza women are more flirtatious and less dignified than stately chola women, who move in a more measured fashion and wear more demure clothes. (Lazar 2008: 136)

Lazar and Xavier Albó both adopt what could be called a 'matter-of-fact' approach to these performances, somewhat at odds with, though not necessarily better than, Abercrombie's and others' tip-toeing through the identitarian minefield. I only wonder whether the tip-toeing is not an artefact or even a transplant of Anglo-Saxon hypersensitivity around naming race. As a further contrast, I look to another practitioner of the 'matter-of-fact' approach, Ana Mariella Bacigalupo, describing the cultural and supernatural dimensions of Chile's Mapuche movement. The ethno-cultural dialectic which Abercrombie describes is different in Southern Chile, to the extent that one might ask whether it existed at all until recently. Mapuche ceremonial activity has no history of crossed boundaries or performative borrowings as we saw in Oruro: it has only recently appeared for example in the recourse to Mapuche medicinal treatments by non-Mapuche under the auspices, as we saw, of the National Health Service. Indeed, Bacigalupo describes shamans travelling the world to administer cures untroubled by a lack of ceremonials in far-off places. They have commodified their practices 'using and defying folkloric stereotypes ... setting up offices in major cities ... treating spiritual illnesses' affecting Mapuche and 'stress, depression and insomnia' suffered by non-Mapuche (Bacigalupo 2004: 521–2). Shamans, as she describes them, have little patience with the political loyalties of indigenist politics: they 'have always mediated between the human and spirit worlds. They now use those skills, perspectives, knowledge, and imagery in the realm of interethnic politics and in mediating relations with the state'. The 'politicizing of indigenous shamans and the shamanization of indigenous politics' has opened opportunities for them to negotiate as they see fit and female *machi* in particular resist Chilean national notions of power associated with partisan political authority – that is, with the formal organizations that represent the Mapuche demand for land and territory (ibid.: 530). This description can lead to two conclusions: either the Mapuche struggle is far less about culture than indigenist demands elsewhere or Bacigalupo is adopting a less reverential posture towards cultural and religious practices than some of her Andeanist colleagues.

Once Benedict Anderson's *Imagined Communities* and Hobsbawm and Ranger's *Invention of Tradition*, borne on the wings of postmodernism, had launched the era of identity construction and deconstruction, social scientists found themselves drawn into a difficult conundrum: how to describe identity-driven movements without questioning the authenticity of the sentiments of their followers or the sincerity of their leaders? Am I entitled to advance an interpretation which states that a particular group is borrowing the identity markers of another group to which they do not really belong or that they are claiming an identity which I believe not to be theirs? And what is the force of the word 'really' in that context? In matters of identity can my statements be ever more than just an opinion?

Evo Morales: divisive but also a unifier

Bolivia's 1952 Revolution, led by a coalition of military and civilian figures, expropriated the highland landed estates which held the Indian population in quasi-serfdom, created *campesino* unions (*sindicatos campesinos*), and by nationalizing the tin mines placed the highly politicized miners' unions in a position of power within the state. For Silvia Rivera Cusicanqui, it was more like an assault on the culture and institutions of the indigenous population: in the countryside, the Agrarian Reform removed the very word *indio* and marginalized the ethnic authorities who wanted the revolution to support indigenous forms of territorial control ('formas indígenas de ocupación territorial'). In the late nineteenth century, the state had removed colonial protections from the highland *ayllus* – the autonomous communal authorities overseeing land allocation among households – and now indigenous leaders and communities hoped the revolution would restore that recognition and their authority. But nationalist revolutionaries at mid-century, like the Peruvian military reformers who seized power 16 years later in 1968[11] saw the term *indio* as a pejorative, racist word, whose abandonment was a progressive gesture.

The revolutionary leaders' Agrarian Reform and the *sindicatos campesinos* (peasant unions) they created as beneficiaries of the redistribution and as their rural base ran contrary to the *ayllu* leaders' hopes (Rivera Cusicanqui 2010b: 96–7). When the military overthrew the revolutionaries' government, they drew up a 'pact' – the *pacto militar-campesino* – with the *sindicatos* – a most unusual move for the Latin American military.[12]

In an earlier article, using her intimate knowledge of North Potosí (and the studies of Olivia Harris and Tristan Platt), Rivera explains the 'fundamental colonial contradiction between the world views and cultures of the *mestizo*/Creole urban elites and the indigenous ayllus' (Rivera Cusicanqui 1990: 98), and how it materialized in the 1952 revolution, in the proselytizing of the rural unions thereafter and in the policies of the NGOs of the 1980s. The contradiction was not only cultural: the land tenure and development programmes of those periods were based on private land ownership, whereas in North Potosí the *ayllu* was 'a whole articulated system of posts which the various families are to occupy throughout their life cycle, in ascending order, as part of the services and duties they are to render to the collective' (ibid.: 101). The 'leftist political parties and NGOs' misinterpret the system as 'rigid, hierarchical and inegalitarian' (ibid.: 102), whereas behind these appearances lay a balance of access to land and pasture with family size and the domestic cycle. Such a system was essential in an environment where a livelihood has to be assembled through access to several ecological niches at different altitudes. The appearances also mask a 'richly democratic communal life' in which positions are filled not by a single periodic electoral event but by constant consultation and rotation: even if Rivera may present them in the most favourable light, glossing over conflicts and tensions, and not mentioning the importance of migrant labour as people move between agriculture and mining, or between their community and the city, it can be seen that people brought up in the midst of this system of kinship, land tenure and governance would resist the 'formalisms of union activity'. Nonetheless, Rivera allows that in other regions an 'articulation between direct and representative democracy' has been achieved (ibid.: 109).

The postcolonial *mestizo* nationalism born out of the revolution rested on an assumption of *indio* subordination: to change their social position, *indios* had to go to town and dress differently, and the attention paid to them by urban or regional 'elites' – a narrowly based social class defined, as we saw in Oruro, more by its proximity to the state than by its control of capital – rested on an assumption of superiority. Elite women may have dressed up as *indios* at their festivals but they hardly wanted to *be*

138

indios. For Indians, social inclusion meant a degree of distancing from the cultural markers of their home communities, their parents and grandparents. The indigenist intellectuals quoted by Abercrombie rhapsodized over the indigenous people as the origin of the nation, but marked them out for their 'telluric' qualities, not for the lettered sophistication which might open their way to positions of national leadership.

The revolution of 1952 sank under the weight of economic crisis and successive and ruthlessly repressive military dictatorships, with a brief and tragically doomed military progressive interlude in 1970–1,[13] and a succession of guerrilla campaigns, culminating in the sanguinary rule of a cocaine mafia headed by García Meza in 1980–1. The subsequent civilian-elected governments in the 1980s brought ruthless austerity programmes followed in the 1990s by a government combining decentralization and a degree of recognition of indigenous communities with free-market policies – 'neo-liberal multiculturalism' again (Dangl 2019). Mine closures and privatization of utilities (water and gas) plus the prospect of concessions to Chile to settle the two countries' ancient conflict over Bolivia's access to the sea provoked repeated popular uprisings and forced the resignation of two presidents until the election of Evo Morales in 2006. The US presence, front and back of stage, was a matter of constant discord, involving deep penetration of the military ever since the murder of Che Guevara in 1967, and innumerable 'monetarist' or 'neo-liberal' stabilization programmes inspired variously or jointly by the US government and the IMF.

The community institutions of the *ayllu* nevertheless survived through networks of local leaders and long-standing practices of rotation in office behind the facade of the *sindicatos* (Platt 1982a, 1982b). In the 1980s, the new arrangements for recognition of indigenous land and decentralized capital budgets (the LPP – Ley de Participación Popular) encouraged local highland organizations to rebrand, or perhaps reveal, themselves as *ayllus*.

This period marked the arrival in force of international NGOs. In 1978, the German anthropologist Jurgen Riester founded a 'Casa del Campesino' for lowland Ayorea Indians living in La Paz, raising funds from Danida and various NGOs, OXFAM America, Cultural Survival and Hivos, to found what eventually became CIDOB (Confederación de Pueblos Indígenas del Oriente, Chaco y Amazonía de Bolivia) (Fontana 2014). With significant input of resources and perhaps ideas from OXFAM America and the Danish NGO IBIS, a national council of *ayllus* (CONAMAQ – Consejo Nacional de Ayllus y Markas de Qullasuyu[14]) began to come together, converging with the oral history and participatory ethnography of indigenous anthropologists in the Taller de Historia

Oral Andino (Andean Oral History Workshop – THOA), founded by Carlos Mamami and Rivera Cusicanqui (Burman 2014).[15] Describing this effervescent ecosystem of scholarship and commitment, the historian Brooke Larson writes that 'nowhere else in the Andes did anthropologists and grassroots political activists seem to be so impactful as in Bolivia' (Larson 2019).

The Taller founded a new history of Bolivia in which the indigenous population was recovered from the marginal role previously ascribed to them as much by liberals as by Marxists. Enlivened by the voices of the *indios* and of *indio* anthropologists, THOA challenged the standard formulae according to which, like the rest of Latin America, the country's history had been shaped by its elites (colonial, republican and *mestizo*-nationalist) in treacherous conjunction with foreign powers (first colonialism and then American imperialism) (Dangl 2019). The Taller gathered oral history in rural communities, and its research strengthened indigenous organizations (which in Bolivia means popular organizations in general) and fed a successful campaign to regain legal recognition of the *ayllus* and indigenous forms of governance, 'at least on paper', in the 1990s. It produced a highly successful 1986 radio series consisting of 90 episodes recounting the life of a 'legendary Aymara leader' (Stephenson 2002: 111–12). Tensions between a top-down and a grass-roots way of doing both scholarship and politics were becoming visible, and a 'counterpublic sphere' (to use Stephenson's word) was preparing the way for Morales to inscribe indigenism in the place of nationalism on the banner of the nation's identity.[16]

Another crack – more an abyss than a crack – in the country's fragile unity escaped Evo's broad canopy, namely the regional divisions separating highland, Yungas and Chapare regions from the lowland east – the crescent moon, or 'media luna', as the provinces of Tarija, Pando, Beni and Santa Cruz are known. In that vast region, a quite different society of ranchers, wealthier and with little in common culturally or indeed racially with the highland and Yungas populations, or with their own neighbouring Indian population, formed a bitter and sometimes violent opposition to his government, while its lowland Indian populations also came to oppose his neo-developmentalist strategy based on oil, gas and infrastructure. A second regional conflict also pitted the old capital of Sucre, where the independence of Bolivia had been proclaimed in 1825, against La Paz: the Sucre elites fought for recognition as the country's capital against Morales during the Constitutional Assembly, as vividly described by Goodale (2019).

Beginning in the early 1990s, long before reaching power, Morales and his movement pioneered a change in the framing of Bolivia's nationhood in public discourse. Indigenous identity was shifted out of the 'telluric' and the foundational to legitimize a new inclusive modern nationalism, echoing the 1952 revolution. First, he united six federations of farmers and *cocaleros* (coca growers) – many of whom were former mineworkers – in the semi-tropical Chapare region in 1994 and then together they constructed a hierarchical organization and undertook a quasi-military (unarmed) campaign against coca eradication and its accompanying violence. Although the *cocaleros*, like the majority of Bolivians, came from an *indio* background, this was distinct from the *ayllu*-based highland Indian mobilization (CONAMAQ) that was already under way. Like the Zapatistas and other Latin American *campesino* movements, they were migrant farmers opening up new lands for cultivation. Coca growers undertook 'spectacular acts to draw public attention to their plight, including hunger strikes, self-crucifixion, and sewing their mouths closed' (Grisaffi 2019: 39) and, as Morales, suffered arrest, beating and torture (ibid.: 45). Morales formed the MAS (Movimiento al Socialismo) as the 'political instrument' of the coca growers' union and its support grew in reaction against the US government and military involvement in the coca eradication campaign and against the aggressive pursuit of free-market and privatization policies by twice-elected President Gonzalo Sanchez de Losada (1993–7 and 2002–3). Sanchez de Lozada's relatively uncontroversial LPP decentralization programme brought him little political benefit, and he was eventually forced out by popular revolts marked by dozens of deaths. However, by opening the way for the first time in Bolivian history to the election of municipal authorities, it was an opportunity for the MAS and others to set down roots in communities and neighbourhoods (Dangl 2019: 163).

During the period 2000–2005, Bolivia was in a state of permanent quasi-revolution: privatization of water rights and gas distribution; attempts to regulate rural land tenure and to maintain foreign direct investment in oil and gas were blocked or reversed by mass demonstrations; and repeated highway blockages that sometimes cut off La Paz, Cochabamba and Sucre. The notorious coca eradication campaign, in which the US military had a direct role, was also suspended. These revolts frequently met violent repression, such as the death of 63 inhabitants of El Alto when the government tried to force the transport of gas out of a neighbouring refinery and also brought violence from demonstrators and organized local communities, whose anger reached the extremes of setting fire to municipal buildings and warehouses, and the sporadic lynching and kidnapping of military officers and soldiers. Seen in retrospect, it is remarkable that the Bolivian state did not collapse, and we can see the reasons for this resilience in Raquel Gutiérrez's invaluable chronicle (Gutiérrez Aguilar 2008, 2014).

Gutiérrez's engrossing style reflects her engagement with the cause while avoiding the moralism and partisan language which could otherwise undermine her credibility. Her book's structure, both chronological and analytic, brings out a few consistent themes: defence of community control of land and water; the need for that control to defend livelihoods, assuring the ability to plant and harvest crops in a system adapted to the local environment and community (*ayllu*) institutions, and, for the *cocaleros*, to produce coca; the sensitivity of the price of gas for urban communities, especially the rebellious town of El Alto above La Paz, itself an embodiment of popular self-management and distrust of the state (Lazar 2008). Beyond those immediate concerns was the defence of *comunario* autonomy at the local level and dignity and sovereignty for the nation as a whole. When foreign soldiers come to spray herbicide on your crops, national sovereignty is more than a theoretical concern, and when a multinational raises the price of your water by a multiple, then it is not surprising that demands for expropriation and cancellation of contracts ensue. Nonetheless, the Bolivian popular response was much broader based and drew on more enduring communal bonds than, say, the response in Chile when the Pinochet government restructured Mapuche land tenure and privatized irrigation water and the canals along which it flowed. The reasons for the difference are many, not least Pinochet's disposition to unleash violent repression, but the difference does highlight the rebellious political culture among Bolivia's subaltern classes and their *mestizo* and *criollo* allies at that time.

The two leading figures in this series of episodes were Felipe Quispe and Evo Morales. An indefatigable grass-roots campaigner, and known as the Mallku ('condor'), Quispe was the leading Indianist politician and had been in prison between 1992 and 1997 after leading the Tupak Katari guerrilla movement. He sometimes advocated an '*ayllu* socialism' and sometimes a structure in which there would be self-determination for each *nación originaria*, overlaid by a federated state (Gutiérrez Aguilar 2008: 117–18). He oscillated between insurrectionary rhetoric and combative negotiation, reaching accommodations, for example, with former General Hugo Banzer who, after a sanguinary tenure as military dictator in the 1970s, re-emerged successfully in electoral politics in the late 1990s. He was outmanoeuvred by Evo, who at one stage joined with him but then went to the 2002 elections on his own, and with great success.

Whereas successive presidents – even Banzer – failed to master a rebellious populace in constant evolution, with limitless capacity for self-reproduction as one dispute followed another, Evo Morales emerged from 2002 like an acrobat weaving between subversion and negotiation, gathering support from the '*mestizo* and *criollo* left' and, perhaps crucially, armed with a strong international brand and NGO support.[17] He outmanoeuvred Quispe again in 2002, leaving him alone leading a blockade of the highways while he negotiated an end to the coca and water disputes with the Quiroga government, who gave in on all counts except the removal of Evo from the Congress – a face-saver for the sake of the United States (Gutiérrez Aguilar 2008: 197, 206). Although he did not win that year's election, he knitted alliances with various groups, achieved an electoral earthquake and entered Congress with 27 deputies and eight senators, followed by many further crises and uprisings, culminating in the occupation of La Paz by the enraged people of El Alto and others, and the 60,000 in Cochabamba in September 2003 (ibid: 242), paving the way to his victory in the 2005 presidential elections. If the Bolivian state did not collapse, or go in the direction of Venezuela or Guatemala or Honduras, it was surely thanks in no small part to Evo Morales and also to the extraordinary capacity for popular self-management exhibited by its *indio* population, urban and rural. The MAS's arrival in Congress in 2002 had placed a lot of patronage in the hands of its members and that also seems to have had a calming effect (ibid: 216).

These popular revolts were more than movements for they involved physical and even on some occasions armed confrontations with the state, which, as Gutiérrez writes, the Mallku did not know how to convert into revolution and Evo, for all his inclination to spectacular theatrics (his 2002 hunger strike, his ejection from Congress), channelled into institutional change – namely, a telescoped electoral calendar and his own election followed by a Constitutional Assembly. The word '*pachakuti*' in Gutiérrez's title is variously interpreted as the 'alternation of opposites' or 'turning time or space upside down' (ibid: 143–4),[18] but she herself is distrustful of facile transpositions of its meaning into the jargon of left-wing politics and the 'seizure of power', looking instead to a democracy of the grass roots 'nesting amidst all its contradictions within the internal horizon of the fabric of community life', and to Aymara values of 'agreements' and 'equilibrium' (ibid: 174).[19]

Finally, it has to be asked in what sense this, the most torrid uprising of indigenous people in recent times, was truly an indigenous uprising? To be sure, the shock troops, the demonstrators, the people who activated the grass-roots support were all indigenous, but the only foregrounding of cultural belonging was the *cocaleros*' coca leaf emblem. The protest against reform of land tenure in the first wave was a demand for the protection of community oversight in accordance with the self-governing institutions of indigenous communities. But for the most part the protests

143

were against oppressive and abusive exercise of political authority and state violence, and against privatizations that reduced the supply or mercilessly raised the prices of basic necessities of life (water and gas). In addition to the nationalist sentiment fuelled by the involvement of multinational corporations or the US government, this was a classic popular revolt in which the decolonial emphasis on cultural recognition played little part.

As Morales the international celebrity became Evo, he distanced himself from indigenist intellectuals and the post-1952 intelligentsia. The refashioning of the coca leaf, symbol of the coca growers' particular demands, as a sacred emblem of Andean culture, was a masterly exercise in branding amidst growing international recognition of the injustices suffered by indigenous peoples. His top-down approach to organization may have been necessary to the success of the MAS but also led to division and breakaways in indigenous organizations.

Evo promoted a new constitution, ratified by referendum in 2009, which is a masterpiece of inclusive verbosity. The document describes Bolivia as an 'Estado Unitario Social de Derecho Plurinacional Comunitario' ('Unitary Social State under Plurinational Community Law'), recognizing the languages and judicial institutions of its different 'naciones y pueblos indígena originario campesinos' and further defined as 'each and every human collectivity that shares cultural identity, language, historical tradition, territorial institutions and worldview, and whose existence predates the Spanish colonial invasion' (Art. 30). That phrase has been translated by Nancy Postero as 'indigenous, originary, and peasant nations and peoples' and by Andrew Canessa as 'native, peasant, indigenous' (Canessa 2016; Postero 2015). I would opt for a translation closer to what appears to be the intended meaning of the original: 'indigenous and founding nations and peoples and the peasant nation' since it makes no sense to speak of the peasantry (*campesinos*) as 'a people'. The nearest English equivalent to '*originario*' – the Canadian term 'First Nations' – would be even more awkward. Gabriela Zamorano simply says the notion of a Plurinational Unitary State is 'contradictory' (Zamorano Villarreal 2020: 153). The wording shows that the authors were conscious of the fluidity of these categories and the risks of defining them too tightly, referring to plurinationalism as a 'transterritorial articulatory process', and also adding models of autonomous sub-national entities, or *autonomías*.

RELIGION AND CULTURE

MAS and gender equality: tensions and intersections

More radical perhaps than indigenous recognition and ascension was the Morales government's opening to organizations of indigenous women, which started in the lowlands among women from Aymara and Quechua-speaking colonizing populations who had migrated from the highlands in search of land. A women's organization began to emerge within the *campesino/cocalero/*miners' union (CSUTCB) in the 1980s and was recognized and institutionalized in the 1990s, becoming known as the 'Bartolinas', after Bartolina Sisa, leader of revolts against Spanish rule and wife of Tupac Katari, who was subjected to a cruel and exemplary execution (hung, drawn and quartered) in 1782 (Rousseau and Morales Hudon 2018). In the 1990s, women were at the forefront of the gas and water 'wars', and already in 1999 (seven years before Evo's election) parties were obliged by law to reserve 30 per cent of the places on their candidate lists for women. The 2010 Constitution stipulated that 50 per cent of all elected offices were to be filled by women (Rousseau and Morales Hudon 2018: ch. 2) and at one stage half of Morales's cabinet were women. And yet gender played out *intersectionally* in ways that illustrate the non-correlation between feminism, indigenism and social justice.

The Bartolinas assembled a very broad appeal to *campesino* and indigenous women and to aspirations of sovereignty in territory and food. They presented a proposal to the Constituent Assembly in 2006 'focused on political participation, land rights, education, and domestic violence'. They demanded '50 percent female representation in Congress, in parties, and in policy-making bodies; women's equal right in land titling and land re-distribution; and women's right to participate in bodies regulating land tenure ... free public education, sanctions for violent spouses, and the creation of women's shelters' (Rousseau 2011: 18). By the 2020 election, women made up a *majority* of the members of the Legislature.

In this political field, however, discourses are multi-vocal. So as against Rousseau's assessment, we have that of Andrew Canessa who tells us, based on personal communication from an insider, that, unlike their male counterparts, 'behind the public face of gender equality prominent women struggle to maintain an independent voice within [Evo's] cabinet and privately complain of having their decisions controlled and approved by the president, vice-president, or other cabinet members in ways that [do] not happen for their male counterparts' (Canessa 2010: 176).[20]

There are other dimensions. For example, while Rousseau describes the Bartolinas' undying political fealty to Evo, Goodale reports Patricia Choque, who had come from her *ayllu* and was elected national executive

145

secretary of the Bartolinas in 2006, aged 32, expressing her doubts as to the authenticity of his indigenous lifestyle:

> You need to understand something important – Evo Morales is neither indigenous nor a peasant, and neither is he a miner as far as I know. . . . he doesn't speak Aymara or Quechua, and frankly he doesn't speak Spanish perfectly either, right? . . . But there is something else that is even more difficult for us to accept, the fact that he is not married, he is not *chachawarmi*. (Goodale 2019: 214)

Yet Morales did not hesitate to invoke the race-based rhetoric of one of the country's most prominent advocates of *indianidad*, Fausto Reinaga (1906–1994). At the peak of his career as prophet of irredentist racial resurgence and dominance, when he was involved in the formation of the Partido Indio de Bolivia, forerunner of the 1973 Manifesto of Tiahuanaco and Felipe Quispe's Movimiento Revolucionario Tupac Katari (the *kataristas*), Reinaga was proclaiming the following:

> The politics of *cholaje* ['cholo-ness'] are a deadly pestilence for the Indian. They are the cholera, leprosy, that which flays his virginal humanity. For the Indian, Bolivia's political parties are a poison: they kill him like a dog. For this, the Indian doesn't have any other remedy but to form his own party, a party . . . that heralds to the entire world from the summit of Illimani, with the thunder of the pututu and the waving of the wiphala, the coming of the Indian Revolution in America. (Reinaga 2007 [1970]), quoted in Goodale 2019: 221)

Morales wove these sentiments with other threads of ethnic, racial and nationalist discourse, combining this language with his modernizing agenda and the demands of his *cocaleros*, with the *ayllus*' demand for land and legal status, and demands from the country's many ethno-linguistic groups for legal recognition of cultural rights and a modern constitution. As Goodale emphasizes, they understood, as did he, that it was not enough to proclaim mystical communion with a historical destiny: recognition and rights had to be enshrined in law. And so the *kataristas*, who had pioneered Indianist politics, were eventually marginalized in the name of a modernization through law.

One could also see the Bartolinas as highlanders on a mission to modernize the country. They seemed to be ferociously loyal to Morales and, as predominantly of highland origin and in some cases as colonists in the lowlands, they were not at all supportive of the lowland indigenous peoples who found themselves in a relationship of subordination to those indigenous colonists. The colonization of indigenous lowland areas by Aymara from the highlands created a pattern of unequal labour and kinship relationships under which migrant men establish a second family, taking local women as wives and employing others to cultivate lands they were appropriating (Canessa 2016). Vice-President García Liñera was in the habit of referring to those lowland Indians as living like '*animalitos*' and a prominent leader of the Bartolinas also spoke of them as living like animals in need of modernization through education and infrastructure.

Populism with an indigenist face

Were Evo's performative politics really inauthentic or out of tune with the indigenist cultures themselves? His quasi-coronations at the ancient ceremonial site of Tihuanaco, his appearances at international gatherings in his trade mark horizontally striped sweater or in ceremonial dress, his recognition as spokesperson for the indigenous peoples of the world, their languages and their threatened environment could be described patronizingly as 'folklorization', but who is entitled to make that a criticism when the folklorizer is himself seen as representative by millions – though not all – of his country's indigenous people? We may look with disdain at the Museo de la Revolución Democrática y Cultural (the Museum of the Cultural and Democratic Revolution) which opened its doors in his birthplace, Orinoca in 2017, but at least still then his followers seemed untroubled. Even his blatant disregard for his own environmentalist pronouncements, as evidenced by reliance on oil and gas to achieve high rates of economic growth and the construction of an international highway to Brazil through the TIPNIS region reserved for indigenous habitation and environmental conservation in the lowland Amazon (Andreucci and Radhuber 2017), does not appear to have dented his popularity. (After the violent repression of the 60-day protest march against it in 2011, construction of the highway was suspended, only to be reinstated in 2017.) Morales and the MAS were not exemplary liberal democrats, and numerous 'hyphenated' concepts of democracy have been marshalled to categorize their regime. A highly partisan account lists numerous abuses also found in other members of the Chavista axis: the electoral authority was made 'subservient to the MAS, while the freedom of electoral processes was compromised by the repeated truncation of the supply of electoral candidates, at all levels of government' (Sánchez-Sibony 2021: 138). There were 'enormous disparities in access to resources . . . via the extensive patrimonialization of the state' and on occasion victorious candidates from the opposition were simply 'removed from power'.

> The MAS . . . weaponized the legislature, utilizing the supermajority it enjoyed in both chambers after 2009 to churn out legislation that

helped it repress civil society, the media, and the political opposition. The MAS neutralized the judiciary as an institution of horizontal accountability by dismantling the Constitutional Tribunal and capturing the Supreme Court, thus enabling the onset of abusive constitutionalism. (2021: 138).

In the end it was not the intricacies of ethnic boundaries and solidarities but his monopolization of power in his own person, his disregard of a referendum he himself had called (and lost) on whether he could stand for a fourth term, and his abuse of the electoral tribunal and the electoral system that were Evo's undoing.[21]

In an interview for the online publication *desInforménonos* (19 August 2019), Silvia Rivera Cusicanqui denounces Evo's indigenism as a 'façade of the *indio*', and describes him as in thrall to a cholo mentality – military, colonised, anti-Indian, acculturated, machista, brutal, irrational and ecocidal.

Over a period of 25 years, Morales has performed in a range of guises: sometimes against the state and sometimes at its head; sometimes as victim of the military and sometimes as a president ordering the military into action to repress protests; he managed to present himself to the world as a defender of the environment; he figured on the international stage as no previous leader of his country; he presided over the increased visibility of an entrepreneurial *burguesía criolla*, a 'Creole' or home-grown bourgeoisie, even at the same time as he invented what Andrew Canessa calls a new unifying political subject – the 'indigenous *originario* peasant' – in place of rival versions of multiculturalism.

For Nancy Postero, the MAS has sought to centralize power at the expense of the recognition and autonomy of the country's multiple ethnic and regional groups, to 'gain control of the state, so as to be able to restructure the national development model and then redistribute the benefits of Bolivian patrimony to the Bolivian people' without touching the interests of agribusiness and cattle breeders of the 'media luna'. This despite their ferocious opposition to him, which culminated in his removal after the 2019 election (Postero 2015). But the growth of that patrimony has been unprecedented: GDP per capita, which had only grown from US$700 to US$900 between 1988 and 2002 (29 per cent in 14 years), shot up almost fourfold to US$3,500 by 2018[22] and, according to the UN, was accompanied by the highest rate of poverty reduction in Latin America (Dangl 2019: 164).

The ethnic-racial hierarchy has also changed. During the Morales presidency, the 'line' separating the indigenous from the *mestizo* strata of urban society shifted upwards in the socio-economic hierarchy, and people who once would not have dreamt of identifying themselves or being identified as indigenous, despite the indigenous ancestry they share with almost the entire population, have 'gone back' to take pride in that ancestry. The visibly female *burguesía criolla* readily proclaim, through their presentation of self, their dress and their habits of speech, that theirs is an indigeneity shorn of subaltern connotations.

The Morales years brought the recasting of the country's nationhood in a way that affirms both its indigenous character and national unity – as opposed to earlier versions in which the indigenous was present, intermittently cherished, but socially excluded. For Canessa, following Postero and others, the 'new national culture based on indigenous principles' is more an incantation than a guide, especially since they minimize linguistic and territorial differences between the country's ethnic groups. Nancy Postero speaks of the 'descolonizado permitido': according to this new dispensation, the multicultural conditional acceptance of Indians into the polis (as in the phrase *indio permitido*, or 'tolerated Indian', coined by Charles Hale) is replaced by a developmental state 'to endorse a specific kind of indígena: the patriotic indígena, the loyal Bolivian indígena, the nationalist trade union indígena' and also – in Burman's view – the 'exotic', spectacular, multiculturalist *indígena* that we know from the 1990s (Burman 2014: 259; Postero 2017). But, like Abercrombie, do these observers, writing from their bases in the present (and former) imperialist North, display a hypersensitivity vis-à-vis a colonized corner of the global South?

It is easy to patronize Evo's ventures in indigenist flamboyance: his visits to the Tiwanaku archaeological site to enact presidential rituals or welcome the 'Aymara New Year' at the winter solstice. It is also easy to criticize his reliance on oil and gas to promote economic growth. Yet he created a political force representing the country's popular classes and much of the middle class which flourished during his governments. Would those who criticize his generic but mercurial indigenism prefer an *authentic* indigenism, attracting in its turn pejorative epithets such as 'essentialist' or 'folkloric'?

Evo's charisma was undoubtedly accompanied by abuses of power. The quotes from women leaders have already shown that there was resistance among indigenous organizations to his personalistic leadership. His personality cult extended beyond indigenous symbolism to, for example, the mass marriage ceremony, where the president in person acted as a sponsor of 'a radical process of depatriarchalization of the colonial, liberal and neo-liberal family' (Canessa 2016: 80).[23] Like Perón, he moulded a broad-based political force that outlasted his own deposition, as was seen when the MAS leader Luis Arce secured a

149

first-round victory in the 2020 election. It remains to be seen whether he and the MAS will remain satisfied with his background role. Like the Zapatistas, he pursued a modern agenda of social inclusion under the banner of indigenism. An appeal to indigenous identity is not usually described as populist because populist discourse emphasizes sameness while indigenism emphasizes difference, but in Bolivia, unlike other countries, the indigenous are the majority, coterminous with the 'people'. Latin American populism is often taken to denote a multi-class alliance and as Maxine Molyneux and Thomas Osborne have forcefully argued, populism is 'generically hybrid and parasitic' (Molyneux and Osborne 2017): in Bolivia it has been grafted, perhaps for the first time in the region, onto an indigenist discourse.

Conclusion

In this chapter, I have interwoven two threads: one of them recognizes mixture and the other disentangles mixture. In the example of popular religion, the Andean ritual interweaves with the Catholic ritual but the two do not fold into one: the Catholic ritual terminates at the ice chapel, while the Andean one continues down to the community where the ice melts into the water with its curative properties.

In García Canclini's analysis of the relationship between popular and erudite culture, the erudite struggles with a notion of authenticity while the popular seems serenely indifferent to that issue. Canclini would like the art that is sold in local markets and the art that hangs on the walls of museums to enjoy equality of esteem, or at least to operate in the same sphere. But the very act of patronizing popular art creates a relationship of superiority or dependence.

The mimetic American-style urban fabric of Tijuana, the seething border town in northern Mexico, might seem out of keeping and in bad taste to the educated classes, but it is perfectly authentic in its context. Northern Mexico has fashioned its own version of the suburban southern United States.

The Oruro Carnival offered a veritable feast of representations of others and others' others. The anthropologists showed us how the idealization of the *indio* as an incarnation of Bolivia's deep roots went together with the *indio* as a patronized other. Silvia Rivera, for her part, traced the dress codes of urban Indian women to a tactic for 'passing' that was then adopted by middle-class women as a way of looking like Indian women at the carnival, before the carnival dress underwent further tweaks.

RELIGION AND CULTURE

Like populism, indigenism can be attached to many causes and interests and, like populism, it draws on and encourages sentiments of belonging, of victimhood and of collective identity. We have also seen how Evo Morales succeeded in overcoming the tortuousness of identity debates by gathering all of Bolivia into the big tent of indigeneity, as if he had read Bonfil's *México Profundo*.

The next chapter explores how a radically different and, to many, unsettling, cultural trend has developed in Latin America over the past half-century, which has set aside the hybridities, the exchanges, the reflections and the intercultural and inter-ethnic *métissages*. I refer to the rise of evangelical Christianity, which has been so unsettling that the decolonials have simply ignored it. But they have done so at their peril, as the evangelical tide threatens to undermine the intellectual edifice they inhabit.

151

4

From Popular Culture to the Cultures of the People: Evangelical Christianity as a Challenge to the Decolonial

Pentecostalism and neo-Pentecostalism

The test case for a decolonial approach must be evangelical Christianity, an umbrella term used in Latin America to cover Pentecostalism and neo-Pentecostalism. ('Evangelical' in English-speaking cultures has different connotations referring to a more fundamentalist, more text-centred version of Christianity.[1]) Pentecostalism, with its openness to globalization, free markets and entrepreneurship, is surely ripe for decolonial dissection, but the leading exponents of the decolonial do not mention the subject, nor indeed do they say much about religion in general. Even Enrique Dussel, despite his training as a theologian, his early contributions to liberation theology and his role as general director of the multi-volume history of the church in Latin America (Dussel 1983–1994), has apparently put that behind him and devotes himself to secular philosophical and political subjects.

By 'test case', I mean that although Pentecostalism has many of the demographic features of a social movement, such as its vast social base among low-income groups, its multiracial inclusiveness, its organizational capacity and ability to produce grass-roots leaders, and its success among indigenous peoples, its values stand in open confrontation with politicized movements for social change and with decolonialism's contestatory culture. Pentecostalism and neo-Pentecostalism stand for entrepreneurship, for individualism, for a respectable middle-class life-style, for aspiration and self-realization, and for conventional morality, and they profess an admiration for the United States, a veneration for the State of Israel and a disinterest in blaming external historical forces like colonialism for their countries' ills – at least until about 2016 when campaigns began to whip up fear of 'cultural Marxism'. To these values must be added the energy that drives evangelicals to express a strong collective consciousness and their confidence in the supernatural inspiration of their faith.

And yet, despite the evident challenge posed by Pentecostalism to the ideas promulgated by it, the only decolonial mention I have found is in an appearance by Rita Segato at the CLACSO[2] Congress in 2018, when she said that the two great threats to Latin American democracy, described by her as conspiracies, were the drugs traffic and the Pentecostal churches.[3]

Although Pentecostal Christianity is a region-wide Latin American phenomenon, I shall focus almost exclusively on Brazil, where I have studied it since the early 1990s, and which is the world centre of the neo-Pentecostal variant that has turned the religious field inside out throughout the region and also in Africa.

The main religious features of Pentecostalism are:

- an ecstatic, uninhibited form of prayer in which imploring and imprecation are directed towards the Almighty in formulae expressing immediate fears and desires;
- an interactive ('call and response') style of preaching which invites congregants to respond with cries of 'Amen', 'Hallelujah!', or 'God be Blessed';
- an absence of liturgy in the sense of a consecrated sequence of words, gestures and rites repeated on regular weekly and annual occasions;
- a radically monotheistic trust in God to whom the faithful can turn without intermediaries such as priests, saints and mediums.

There is little professional training of a clerical cadre: preachers and pastors emerge from the congregations. Pastors seeking to study formally for the ministry attend mainstream Protestant seminaries. Nonetheless, the absence of a written theological dogma has not hindered the development of a distinctive ethos among Pentecostal churches.

The following can be considered core elements of that ethos:

- the unity of God;
- the inerrant truth of the Christian Bible;
- the idea that a traumatic conversion, like a bolt of lightning, often accompanied by supernaturally induced recovery from illness, is a turning point in the life of a believer;
- the idea that 'the devil' or forces of evil intervene in people's lives, especially ruining family relationships;
- a church is a context in which the Holy Spirit can alleviate, or heal, physical and psychological suffering through the mediation of a pastor.

EVANGELICAL CHRISTIANITY

In this ethos, certain elements of Catholicism are significantly missing:

- almost no mention of the Trinity or of the Virgin Mary;
- little attention paid to Easter;
- no effigies, often no cross, no saints, no altar in the sense of the place where a Eucharistic sacrifice is offered;
- no consecration or ordination of a pastor in the sense of the conferral of a charisma by a hierarchical superior who has themselves received the charisma.

Classic Pentecostalism demands that its followers adopt a sober biblical lifestyle, namely:

- a respectable and faithful marriage;
- sex life strictly within marriage;
- no smoking or drinking;
- regular contribution to a church (tithing);
- clear differentiation of roles of men and women in the family.

If they 'fall by the wayside', congregants may suffer sanctions in the form of exclusion from church services or from participation in the distribution of a wafer and a thimble of grape juice known as the 'the Lord's Supper' (Portuguese: *santa ceia*).[4]

As communities, Pentecostal churches allocate roles to many followers in order to sustain their premises and their services and to strengthen the ties binding members and their families to each other and to their church, for example:

- choirs and bands;
- teaching children and leading Bible study;
- children's activities such as enacting scenes from the Bible;
- visiting sick members.

The habitus of worship are pervasive hallmarks of Pentecostal prayer meetings across the world:

- *always* a microphone, no matter how small the meeting place;
- *always* an electronic keyboard and percussion;
- the dominant role of the preacher or pastor and the central place of his (occasionally her) preaching;

Other familiar aspects of Pentecostalism are not defining features but, rather, widely observed sociological correlates:

154

- the independence of each church, even if affiliated to a large organization like the Assemblies of God or the Four-Square Church (Igreja Quadrangular);
- an affinity for entrepreneurship;
- a broadly conservative – but not extreme – political outlook;
- the availability of many opportunities for women to take prominent roles in church, albeit only rarely leadership positions;
- the multiracial composition of their following (except in the United States, where congregations are more 'mono-racial');
- the disproportionate presence of low-income groups among the followers.

These are the features of what has come to be known as classic Pentecostalism in the light of the upheaval brought by the more recent rise of neo-Pentecostalism (Fernandes et al. 1998; Lehmann 1996; Mariz 1993; Oro and Seman 2001; Oro and Tadvald 2015).

Starting in the 1980s, the Pentecostal field and the religious field as a whole were disrupted by a radically new style of worship, a new ethos and a new mode of organization. This variant has acquired such a high profile that although quantitatively it accounts for a minority of Pentecostals, it has become synonymous with Pentecostalism in the public sphere. The variant was pioneered by Brazil's Universal Church of the Kingdom of God (henceforth IURD – Igreja Universal do Reino de Deus), and its model has been followed by others in Brazil, in Latin America and in Africa. Latin American and African neo-Pentecostal churches have also established branches in Europe and beyond.

The Universal Church operates a centralized and global model in which pastors and preachers are rotated between local churches nationally and internationally, and form part of a hierarchy of 'church assistants' (obreiros), pastors and bishops. The pastors and bishops are encouraged to marry and to make their spouses part of their pastoral work, but they are discouraged from having children or even real property of their own. These are radical departures from the classic model.

Although neo-Pentecostal pastors propagate a similar core ethos to that preached by Pentecostal pastors, there are crucial differences of emphasis:

- limited use of biblical text, and more for moral exhortation than for narrative and recounting of miracles;
- more and more spectacular emphasis on the presence of diabolic forces in the lives of followers, with public exorcisms and excoriation of spirits from the feared possession cults, or African-derived cultos;

- much greater and more literal emphasis on healing in the sense of 'cure' going beyond alleviation;
- devoting a much greater portion of services to the call for contributions.

The culture of neo-Pentecostalism complements the sober ideal of a good biblical life with an emphasis on financial success and the pursuit of high levels of consumption, and is often described as following prosperity theology. It links those aspirations to contributions to the church, persuading congregants that the more they contribute, the nearer they will come to fulfilling their desire for material comfort, and this message is supported by the choreography of donation. Just as the forces of evil are managed in a spectacular fashion compared with the discretion observed in classic Pentecostal churches, so the call for donations becomes a summons to walk to the front of the church and donate sums of money.

To speak of the culture of neo-Pentecostalism is to speak not of the culture of a community of faithful but of the culture of the church as an organization. The title of one of the few in-depth ethnographies of the secretive IURD, undertaken in South Africa, where it has a strong presence, describes it as 'a 'community of strangers' (van Wyck 2008). In the place of choirs and bands forming ties of cooperation between members, the Universal Church offers services, for example, workshops in business management and child care for children while their parents attend church. It has created associated organizations in a variety of areas and has claimed volunteers numbering 257,000 who support people in occupations ranging from the police, the military and the fire protection services to truck drivers and prostitutes, with services ranging from legal advice to haircuts and manicures.[5] In February 2018, the website of R7, a radio station belonging to the church's founder and leader Edir Macedo, claimed that three million drug addicts had been cured by the church's own treatment, but it looked as if the treatment consisted neither of therapy nor of a magic cure, but simply of church attendance.[6] We shall return to churches' problematic involvement in addiction recovery.

The IURD promotes a stable family but does so in a framework of rational decision making and a distinctive type of feminism. The leader Edir Macedo's daughter, Cristiane Cardoso, and her husband have developed a system of support directed entirely at women for the building of a lasting 'armour-plated' marriage – *matrimonio blindado*. This network of closed discussion groups known as a 'sisterhood' (the English word is used) under the leadership of 'big sister' Cristiane, in which membership is subjected to a careful vetting process, has spawned a much bigger and more open offshoot, Godllywood, easily reachable on Facebook. Godllywood even has a signature greeting: women recognize each other holding the back of their hands against their cheeks. Godllywood has further offshoots including 'Love School' and 'Love Walk'. The carefully balanced feminism of its leaders avoids undermining the position of husbands and boyfriends, emphasizing the ways women can realize their own potential in accordance with Macedo's advice that a rational choice is a more durable basis for marriage than passionate love.[7] This embrace of a certain sort of feminism, plus the IURD's distance from campaigns on themes of personal morality in favour of themes of personal success and self-realization, tells us that it inclines towards the middle or lower-middle classes and that its public is less concentrated among the poorest than other churches. There is also some evidence that its members were less hostile to the Workers' Party in the 2010 and 2014 elections than members of other churches (Araujo 2019: 73).

No other neo-Pentecostal church in Brazil can match the diversity and professionalism of the Universal Church. Others may be more charismatic preachers than Edir Macedo, but they tend to keep to one particular theme – for example, Valdemiro Santiago, who also has a vast network of churches (the Igreja Mundial do Poder de Deus – Worldwide Church of the Power of God), broadcasts services on cable television and the internet, as well as conducting services in person, but keeps to the theme of healing, exhibiting in public cases of people he or his pastors have cured of their ailments. Macedo in contrast has built up TV Record, the country's second biggest free-to-air television network. The station is owned by him personally, and its programming is mostly secular, but it relies on fees paid by the church for airing its night-time religious programmes and is widely identified with him and his political interests. Valdemiro Santiago is a former bishop of Macedo's church, as is R.R. Soares (also Macedo's brother-in-law), who appears daily on the cable channel of his Igreja Internacional da Graça de Deus (International Church of the Grace of God) and also has a network of church buildings.

Apart from the television station, the IURD has three other 'legs': the churches and the portfolio of services and voluntary organizations which take religion out of church and into society and politics. The churches are all over Brazil but tend to be in highly visible locations where they make the church look more like an institution, rather than in the narrow streets of low-income neighbourhoods or in rural locations. The most spectacular are the Catedral da Fé in Rio de Janeiro (Gomes 2011) and the grandiose 'Temple of Solomon' in São Paulo, with seating for 10,000 people, inaugurated in 2014, as a statement of the church's claim to a Jewish genealogy going back to the Old Testament, as its headquarters and as the residence and eventually (it is believed) the mausoleum of its leader.

The third 'leg' is politics, where the IURD seems to care little for ideology but much for influence. It supported Cardoso against Lula in the 1990s and then Lula and Dilma Rousseff twice each. Its own Republicanos party has established a college of higher education (Faculdade Republicana Brasileira), concentrating on social and political science, in Brasilia.[8] Bishop Marcelo Crivella, nephew of Edir Macedo and formerly a senior member of the church hierarchy who had led its implantation in Mozambique, Angola and South Africa, was elected mayor of Rio de Janeiro, now a majority evangelical city, in 2016, having previously served two terms as senator. After failing to be re-elected in 2020, he was indicted for corruption.

In 2018, Macedo supported Bolsonaro in a polarized campaign fired by conspiracy theories and fake news. On 1 September 2019, in front of 9,500 worshippers at the Temple of Solomon, Bolsonaro went down on his knees and Macedo anointed him with oil, saying 'I use all my authority to bless this man and give him wisdom . . . that the country be transformed and that he enjoy determination, good health and vigour' (O Globo, 1 September 2019).[9]

Pentecostals elected to the Constituent Assembly in 1986 numbered 33, mostly from the Assemblies of God, and aimed to resist liberal provisions concerning family and sex. They suffered a reversal in the 1990s due to involvement in corruption scandals, but in 1998 membership in the Congressional evangelical *bancada* (caucus) rose to 51, and in 2020 to 195 deputies and eight senators (Rodrigues-Silveira and Urizzi Cervi 2019: 562). Strictly, only 93 of them describe themselves as evangelical Christians. The IURD tends to keep its distance from other pastor-politicians and from their concern with laws governing marriage, family and sex, reducing the age of criminal responsibility and the freedom to possess firearms.

The depth of the Pentecostal penetration in grass-roots politics (*capilaridade* in Araujo's felicitous expression) enables pastors to coordinate their efforts to support one or another candidate at the local level independently of the political parties. Since party identities and ideologies are mostly ill defined, what counts is the position of the individual candidate, so pastors can create in effect a closed-list system prioritizing candidates who fit their moral agenda, irrespective of party affiliation (Araujo 2019; Figueiredo Netto and Speck 2017: 65; Rodrigues-Silveira and Urizzi Cervi 2019). This analysis leads to the question whether people do not choose to become pastors as a path to fulfilling their political ambitions rather than the other way round, a hypothesis reinforced by their involvement in corruption: for example, the pastor who baptised Bolsonaro in the River Jordan in 2016, Everaldo Dias Pereira, leader of the evangelical caucus, was in 2020 arraigned on corruption charges in the state of Rio de Janeiro and sent to prison while awaiting trial (*Correio Braziliense*, 28 August 2020).

In an interview with the *Folha de São Paulo* (1 January 2021), the sociologist Ricardo Mariano commented on the impressive results achieved by the Universal Church's Republicanos party in the 2020 municipal elections, increasing its number of mayors from 106 to 211 (out of a total of 5,565), and electing 2,604 municipal councillors (out of 56,810). The Social Christian Party, which is linked to the Assemblies of God, a less centralized body but with far more followers than the IURD, only raised their number from 86 to 115 – a relatively poor performance due perhaps to the scandal surrounding Everaldo. But even more striking is the finding by the Instituto Superior de Estudos da Religião (ISER) that almost 13,000 local government candidacies were registered with a religious title (cf. 'Pastor') – 24 per cent more than in the previous elections, although only 679 were elected.[10] Mariano said he did not regard the evangelical faithful as a docile voting flock and, although not strictly comparable, it does not appear that they weighed as heavily in these local elections as they had done in the 2018 presidential election. The reason for that may be that local elections do not bring moral 'wedge' issues, like same-sex marriage and 'gender ideology', to the fore.

Araujo shows that Pentecostals have been unsympathetic to the PT for decades, but in the period after 2010 the distrust in the party's ideological stance sharpened on account of disputes over same-sex marriage and gender rights. As has happened elsewhere in Latin America, for example during the 2016 Colombian referendum on the agreement with the FARC, these issues became the subject of fake news and alarmist rumours turbo-charged by social media and WhatsApp, laying the way for Bolsonaro's victory and for continuing representation of evangelicals in Congress at the expense of the PT and also of centrist politicians.

Data on Pentecostals for Latin America as a whole are not convincingly assembled in one place and, since different censuses use different approaches to religion, regional estimates are vague. Overall, it is recognized that Pentecostalism is growing throughout the region. Guatemala has for a long time been a majority evangelical country; Brazil has the second-highest proportion, reaching 17.6 per cent of the population aged 10 years and more in the 2010 Census,[11] but rising to 31 per cent in a survey by the Datafolha research company in January 2020. This survey shows evangelicals to be darker-skinned and to have a lower percentage of people with higher education than the average, but unlike other sources does not show a difference in income levels between evangelicals and Catholics. Inclusion of traditional (or 'historic') Protestants (such as

Lutherans, Methodists and Anglicans who tend to be more middle class), among the evangelicals by Datafolha means that these indicators underestimate social exclusion.[12] Like other sources, Datafolha also shows that women form an extremely disproportionate share of evangelicals (58 per cent). Separate research by the Brazilian Electoral Survey in 2010 also showed evangelicals are less likely than others to listen to news programmes or read newspapers and had a markedly lower level of support for the Workers' Party (PT). The effect of evangelical religious affiliation on voting in presidential elections was strong even when controlled for the obvious correlated socio-economic variables such as education, age and social class. Araujo uses this observation to support his theory that, at least in Brazil, Pentecostalism, capitalizing on the attachment of its poorer and poorly informed followers to conservative personal morality, at least reinforces the negative association between income inequality and support among low-income groups for a politics of redistribution (Araujo 2019: 35, 106). It is, nonetheless, possible that those voters tend to think that parties or politicians other than the PT would undertake redistributive policies, but rather in the form of targeted, clientelistic programmes.

More concentrated qualitative and quantitative research in the Minas Gerais town of Juiz de Fora coincides with Araujo's findings on moral issues, and concludes that evangelicals are becoming separated from other citizens, and that their views on sexuality, family issues and homosexuality are increasingly homogeneous and, importantly, that they have developed 'the most active repertoires of political engagement' (Smith 2019: 129). That fits with their 'below average willingness to extend civil liberties to groups they dislike' (ibid.: 145). But they are not right-wing in other senses: their views on economics, poverty and anti-racism were found to be compatible with a social democratic or liberal democratic outlook.

These indicators could give rise to an extensive discussion of the world of Brazil's urban poor, those living on the other side of Santos's abyss amidst unstable family relationships, violence and insecurity, surrounded by images of a world of conspicuous consumption and comfortable nuclear families which few of them could ever attain by legitimate means – a complex of pressures and enticements to which evangelical churches offer one kind of response, as Oosterbaan has well described (Oosterbaan 2017). Our discussion of the decolonial, however, is more narrowly focused, and for that it is enough to emphasize the characteristics shared by Pentecostalism with a model of social movements: its responsiveness, its flexibility and its capacity for developing leadership at the grass roots.

Beyond a formula for organizing, Pentecostalism represents a profound cultural change, though not the sunny individualist uplands heralded by sociologists David Martin and Peter Berger when they welcomed it in the 1980s and 1990s (Berger 1999; Martin 1990). It is in that field – of culture and the imaginary – that the decolonial faces the more serious questions.

The break with popular culture

The mould-breaking goes back a long way. Classic Pentecostal churches had already been taking Brazilian religious culture in a new direction for many decades, away from the limelight of politics and the media, but with great success in rural and low-income urban areas. They drew a thick frontier separating themselves from the African-derived *cultos*, and from indigenous supernatural beliefs, thought to be vehicles for the forces of evil. The contrast in the social and ritual relationship between pastor and congregation as compared with the Catholic priest was visible; the music and the very act of praying substituted spontaneity for controlled solemnity. Already classic Pentecostalism undertook a radical break from the music, the dance and the religious *métissages* which go to make up popular culture. The one continuity was with the pervasive prayer groups gathering in small towns and villages around lay people, mostly women, known for their special relationships with saints, sought out to lead people in the recital of their rosary, to offer blessings or for their healing gifts (*rezadores*, *benzedeiras* and *curandeiras*). Carlos Rodriguez Brandão described this world at length in *Os Deuses do Povo*, based on research in a township in the interior of São Paulo in the 1970s. In a place sharply divided between the people who live (and pray) in the upper and lower parts of town, with their erudite and popular versions of religious observance, Brandão describes a world of intimate neighbourhoods and lives permeated by public prayer, only rarely in the presence of a priest (Brandão 2007 [1980]). Brandão uses distinctive expressions like 'especialistas autônomos dos sortilégios populares de cura' (independent specialists in popular healing spells) (2007 [1980]: 118) and writes vividly of people like the woman who 'circulates through the world of popular religion between the things in which she believes, those that she accepts and those that she abominates, depending what is happening in her life and on invitations she gets from celebrants of different persuasions' (2007 [1980]: 263).[13]

In this way, he captures a fluid religious field in which people transit freely between nominally different religious institutions, while retaining an intimate relationship with the supernatural entities that oversee their lives. The constant in these accounts is that intimacy, in implicit contrast with the formalities of Catholic ritual.

Already at that time, Pentecostal chapels were proliferating, but although they did not lack followers, leadership was localized and not always very stable. By the time I came to study Pentecostalism in the early 1990s, regional and national federated bodies like the Assemblies of God contributed to the consolidation of leadership in the chapels, and the IURD and other similar neo-Pentecostal ventures were breaking through into the public square and the mediascape. Neo-Pentecostals challenged the conventions of religious decorum: they noisily attacked the possession cults and their healing ceremonies, defied laws against charlatanism – the unqualified practice of medicine – and branded the Catholic Church the 'great whore of Babylon' (Revelation 17: 1–18) (Birman and Lehmann 1999).

The *malandragem* to which I referred in the previous chapter may have been dissident, but it was not a challenge to the established order. In contrast, when neo-Pentecostalism irrupted onto the public stage in the 1990s, it placed the hegemony of polite behaviour, elite thinking and elite taste, including respect for the intelligentsia and its left-wing culture, on the defensive. The theology of liberation was ridiculed: as their leaders saw it, the poor did not want to be told by priests and theologians, who had attended universities that were far beyond their reach, that thanks to their poverty they were God's chosen: they were fascinated by wealth and wanted some themselves, and Macedo spoke of theology itself as the work of the devil designed to sow confusion in the people's minds.

Eventually this socio-cultural dissent would translate into something like political ideology, contradicting assumptions that the themes of personal morality that so dominate evangelicalism in English-speaking countries would not find fertile ground in Brazil. Towards the beginning of the second decade of the century, a new brand of political pastors appeared on the national stage with strident speeches against the spectre of same-sex marriage and 'gender ideology', and in support of extreme right-wing stances on race and Amazonian Indians. In 2010–11, a scare was propagated that the Ministry of Education was to prescribe a sex education booklet, labelled *kit gay*, to shape children's sexuality and encourage them to become homosexual (Carranza and Vital Da Cunha 2018: 490–2). By the time of the 2018 election campaign, these ideas had put down deep roots among the evangelical public, laying the way for Bolsonaro's victory over the PT candidate. In a survey conducted shortly before the election itself, 56 per cent of those questioned said they would vote for Bolsonaro – almost exactly the percentage he obtained in the election itself – but he got support from 69 per cent of the *evangélicos* (Lehmann 2021).[14]

Although it is necessary to mention the political consequences of Pentecostalism, which is receiving much attention from political scientists and others, my main purpose is to underline the radical nature of Pentecostalism and neo-Pentecostalism's effects on Brazilian popular culture. It has propelled the small-town religiosity described by Brandão into a global charismatic maelstrom. It has cast aside those elements of Brazilian popular culture most prized by the intelligentsia and associated internationally with the country's brand – carnival, samba, *umbanda* and Candomblé, and *saudade*, as conveyed in the *bossa nova* fusion of samba and jazz. Those elements evoke a shared heritage, composed or enacted against a background of assumed social inequality but creating a complicity between the elite and the popular. Candomblé is associated with black and slave heritage but draws practitioners and followers from all social classes, and populates its pantheon with Catholic saints like Santa Barbara. Carnival is a grandiose ritual of the world turned upside down: in Rio seamstresses, designers, dancers and musicians labour for months to produce a show when the masses invade the privileged neighbourhoods like Copacabana and Ipanema. Those few days of permissiveness allow the classes to mingle: blacks appear as whites, men as women, and the rich try to act like the people, who for this brief period are the heart of the city freed of their stigma as the dangerous classes (Agier 2000; da Matta 1983, 1992; Pereira de Queiroz 1985, 1992a, 1992b). Although more boisterous in appearance than the Bolivian versions, the Rio Carnival is also a product of elaborate organization and entrepreneurial initiative, as well as municipal finance (until it was reduced by the evangelical Mayor Crivella).

Pentecostalism is a rejection of all this, and also of the social hierarchy that underlies that music and dance. The pastors propagate an ideology of self-sufficiency and individual responsibility, beginning with the individual's personal relationship to the divine and the centrality of the conversion experience. The churches also fulfil an ambiguous role in the lives of women who constitute the majority of their followers: women tell that after conversion their lives have been transformed and they speak as if empowered over the men whose violence and bad habits make their lives so difficult. But the words 'as if' are important: we saw how the Universal Church has institutionalized a female following under the motto of empowerment, yet like other churches it endorses the role of men as decision makers in the family, and the upper reaches of its hierarchy of pastors and bishops are exclusively male.

There remains one aspect that does not quite fit that total rejection, namely the ambiguous relation created, especially in neo-Pentecostalism, with the possession cults. As Véronique Boyer has explained, like the adepts of the cults, Pentecostals represent the world as a competitive place riddled with envy, where individuals need the support of higher powers to counter the spells cast upon them by their enemies or rivals. Classic Pentecostal churches deal with exorcism in a discrete way because their pastors seem to truly fear the risks of handling the powers of ethereal, mysterious and disembodied spirits, or entities, operating without intentionality.

In contrast, the IURD 'concretizes', materializes and almost personalizes those spirits. In high-pitched and menacing tones, pastors warn congregations of the harm that the devil, in the form of the spirits of the *cultos*, can wreak on their lives and their families. Whereas the *mães* and *pais de santo* of the *cultos* submit in a trance to possession by their governing spirits, the IURD pastors summon the evil spirits to manifest themselves so as to expel them (Boyer 1996: 258). Individuals emit sounds as if from a force independent of them yet residing within their bodies. Pentecostals did not dare do this before the IURD came on the scene and made *libertação* – the deliverance of followers from the demons that possess them – a central feature of its services. In Patricia Birman's view, a 'culture of possession' is diffused throughout Brazilian society and the church has operated a profound change in the manipulation of those supernatural forces. Yet, as ever when the supernatural is invited into everyday life, the consequences are double-edged: for people in the church, having a past as a medium in the *cultos* is a mark of distinction, however much those same people claim to have broken with that past (Birman 1996, 1998: 189, 196).

These examples offer a particularly striking case of neo-Pentecostalism's recomposition of the signifiers of popular culture, and of the dissolution of its popular–erudite dialectic. In addition, we have also seen how it has penetrated a range of institutions and fields, reconfiguring the boundaries of the religious field.

Pentecostalism and Indian populations

Evangelical Christianity has shown that, despite beliefs and practices that vary little across cultural and geographical frontiers, it is able to penetrate the most varied cultural contexts across the world. In Latin America, it has established itself among indigenous populations ranging from the highland Andes to southern Chile and to the deepest Amazon. This flexibility is illustrated by Aparecida Vilaça's description of the alternating adoptions by the Wari' Indians of north-west Amazonia of both Protestantism and Catholicism. Protestant missionaries – as she calls them, but they more resemble evangelicals – are much more sensitive to the Wari' ritual life than stereotypes would lead us to believe: they brought cannibalism to an end by organizing shared collective meals – as Vilaça remarks, 'you don't eat people with whom you share a meal'. The Wari' had moulded the Protestant creed to their culture and the missionaries seemed not to mind so long as they declared their belief in God (Vilaça 2002). Their Catholic counterparts were too concerned with getting the theology right, firstly by trying to change their beliefs and later, in a complete about-turn with the arrival of liberation theology, by treating them with an excess of respect. This attitude provoked a crisis when a child died after a priest refused to baptise it: he thought he was respecting their culture by refraining from imposing a Catholic rite, but the parents blamed him for the tragedy. When eventually the Indians adopted baptism, the missionaries thought they had taught them its proper significance, only to discover that parents' motivation was the acquisition of influential godparents for their children – rather like *compadrazgo* in the Andes and Meso-America. Ten years later Vilaça returned and found that most of the Wari' had lost interest in Catholicism and were now *crentes* (evangelicals) again, but with pastors drawn from among their own (Vilaça 2002: 65). Protestantism had 'gone native'.

Other examples, among many, in Guatemala and Mexico, relate to entrepreneurship and the disruption of what some would call age-old popular traditions and other entrenched local hierarchies. In the Guatemalan town of Almolonga, converts put the burdensome rituals of popular Catholicism behind them, and the last stage of the Protestant shift was marked during the early 1970s by exorcisms including 'being thrown across the room by the exiting demons', or 'spewing up blood and bile as Satan departed from their bodies'. These lightning conversions opened the way to economic success, borne along by clean living and a readiness to take risks. This is chronicled by Virginia Garrard, who says that the farmers' economic success has the ingredients of a Weberian narrative, except that they have preserved a strong local and Mayan identity and the K'iche' language, and continue to ascribe sacred power to the mountain spirits. The difference, as in the IURD, is that they now see that power as a malign influence which has to be resisted with the weapons of Christianity: as in Brazil, 'the particular appeal of Pentecostalism in Almolonga is not its rupture with traditional culture, but rather its resonance with it' (Garrard 2020).

Another story of economic success, but without the mountain or other spirits, comes from the Ecuadorian province of Chimborazo, noted for secular stagnation and extreme forms of servile dependency, where Pentecostals brought modernizing/capitalistic change, an aptitude for business, cooperation in pursuit of profit and institution building, and not least churches. An austere version of Protestantism was introduced originally by American missionaries, but as local pastors took over leadership roles, they shifted to a Pentecostal style, guiding their followers towards more oral, more charismatic, more musical celebrations and restoring the indigenous language in services and on a local radio station (Andrade 2004; Muratorio 1980). They also incorporated habits intrinsic to autochthonous conceptions of the supernatural, such as the interpretation of dreams, did away with the segregation of men and women at prayer, and discarded imported hymns in favour of their own songs and instruments. From the 1970s, churches multiplied, with deacons and, unusually, elected pastors. They claimed that they had turned their back on wife beating and drunkenness and had convinced villagers that worshipping saints' images constituted idolatry. Followers started to migrate, nationally and internationally, as small business people and traders, establishing churches as far afield as Caracas. The migration brought a higher standard of living, but the temptations of the city brought so many difficulties that some pastors instituted bilingual schooling in their new environment, reminding children of their roots. In Caracas, their sense of difference, both ethnic and religious, led some to speak of themselves as the 'chosen people'.

In Mexico, the Summer Institute of Linguistics, and Cameron Townsend its founder, much admired by the integrationist President Cárdenas in the 1930s, established projects of modernization in conjunction with propagation of the Christian Bible in indigenous languages. They have been accused of destroying indigenous culture, but others, like Christian Gros (whom we have previously met as a chronicler of Colombia's CRIC), have written of the ways in which the SIL provided an escape from the petty exploitations of village life, notably the debts incurred by sponsors of fiestas celebrating local patron saints, and from occasional violence against Protestants (Gros 1999). In some places in Oaxaca (Gross 2003) and elsewhere in Mexico, Protestants refused to join in *faenas* and *tequios* (communal labour obligations) because of the alcohol consumption required of participants. This self-ostracism became highly conflictive in Chiapas where evangelicals were expelled from the village of San Juan Chamula and elsewhere in the midst of complex internal conflicts (Uribe Cortez and Martínez Velasco 2012).[15]

These examples cannot support a generalization about evangelical interactions with indigenous cultures, for they show the enormous variety of both, but if they illustrate Pentecostalism's penetrative capacity in situations where it has no history, they also show its missionaries as outsiders setting a process in motion and eventually losing control, and perhaps not intending to keep control. Almolonga is something of an

166

exception because the missionaries came from the town itself and have retained a prominent role, and in any case not all commentators agree that the lightning conversion of its inhabitants explains its economic boom, but the contrast drawn by Garrard with nearby towns and villages show that it did take off on a path all of its own.

The cases should serve as a counter to the black legend of Protestant missions to Indian peoples as agents of the United States sent to Latin America to pre-empt or detect revolutionary uprisings. But we should recall from Brazilian neo-Pentecostalism's involvement in politics and encroachment on the limits of the law that evangelical movements can operate in a grey area. The association between certain evangelicals and the dictator Efraín Ríos Montt, who was convicted of genocide and crimes against humanity, as also chronicled by Virginia Garrard, should not be forgotten (Garrard 2010). The next section therefore pursues this darker side to the evangelical *capilaridade* mentioned earlier.

Pentecostalism on the edge of the 'abyss': prisons and the drugs traffic

Latin American prison systems are too often demoralized and desperately overcrowded, and such safety as exists is preserved by tacit or explicit agreements between the official administration and the gang leaders and enforcers among the inmates. In Argentina's prison system, the Catholic Church enjoys special status that entitles its chaplains to receive an official rank and a salary, but they appear to take no responsibility for the collective life of the facility. Pentecostals do not enjoy the same status, but they find other, unofficial, ways to gain access and influence.

Algranti describes an arrangement between a pastor-officer and the prison administration which facilitated the formation of a network of inmate preachers and in effect ran the establishment. The pastor-officer negotiated improved conditions for evangelical prisoners, namely 'their own spaces and resources in return for governability and pacification of daily life within the penal context . . . Our mission', he explained 'is to have a church within the Evangelical prison and not religious convicts.' The fully staffed prison-church was established in 2002 and was still in operation around 2017 (Algranti 2018: 7–9).

Another study, undertaken in two prisons in the state of São Paulo, begins by describing how evangelicals again succeeded in establishing an enclave of their own. Evangelical prisoners spoke enthusiastically to the researcher about their conversion, and it appears that they were able to keep a distance from gang rule and *omertá*. But then in the latter part of her paper, the author reveals that the evangelical enclave is a refuge for prisoners who have fallen foul of crime bosses, and that they are more or less forced to abide by rigid evangelical norms because the other prisoners taunt them if they fall short. They say that evangelical norms prohibit their participation in football or in open-air exercise, but it turns out that they also fear being beaten up if they join in (Dias 2006). A similar phenomenon has been reported to me in Guatemala, where traffickers 'allow' henchmen to exit from the business so long as they join an evangelical church: it seems that they rely on the pastors to ensure they do not try to set themselves up in competition.

These instances of evangelicals growing their following through relationships formed on the borderlines of legality or by using their political muscle are replicated in the field of addiction recovery. In Brazil, Catholic and evangelical churches are licensed and contracted by the state to provide therapeutic communities, but they are not allowed to oblige 'patients' to attend religious services. In 2011, as a result of political pressure in the Congress from deputies representing both evangelical and Catholic interests, the prohibition was lifted, and by 2015 the number of projects funded had grown to 371 across the country, with 8,000 places (Vital da Cunha, Lopes and Lui 2017: 58). The convention governing the separation of secular and religious domains had been broken again.

There is also plenty of evidence of evangelical pastors trying to distance their followers from the traffic (Oosterbaan 2017). An earlier study from the 1990s by an anthropologist-psychiatrist in Puerto Rico offers a convincing picture of a recovery centre operated by a Pentecostal pastor under agreement with and funded by the country's health authorities, and makes the case that the churches do achieve a degree of success with some people by adopting an approach which is the opposite of that of psychiatrists, for whom addicts are mere 'cases'. For the churches, they are human beings to be touched and handled and almost compelled to renounce their addiction even through the most terrible pain of withdrawal. For the ethnographer, this is not exactly 'faith healing', even if retrospective narratives of her informants, replete with hallucinations, visions, dreams and intimate conversations with God, do make it sound like that. But successes are few, and if they are to recover in the long term, addicts need the support of a surrogate family, which may be the church or what remains of their former network (Hansen 2017).

The relationship with the drugs traffic may be even deeper: apart from visible relationships between traffickers and churches, such as those described by Christina Vital da Cunha (Vital da Cunha 2015), preachers repeatedly, almost as a ready-made narrative, recount (not least to researchers) their history of recovery from former double lives as both perpetrators and victims: according to Hansen, ministers involved in recovery rate their successes by the numbers who graduate to a life as church workers or preachers. Church workers are expected to evangelize and they addictively repeat their stories to any who might listen. Where once they dedicated their hustling skills to the manipulation needed to access their drugs, they now dedicate them to managing congregations and to controlling people in recovery. As with the former mediums, or *pais* and *mães de santo* in Brazil, being an ex-addict or dealer can become a mark of distinction for a preacher, but one may also wonder whether, like the ex-mediums in the IURD, the tie has really been definitively cut.

And so we return to the abyss, so central to Santos's description of the colonial condition: the churches hover at the edge of the abyss, or maybe succeed in straddling it: an extreme example is that of Pentecostal recovery ministries in Guatemala City, of which there are apparently some two hundred, for in the case described in depth by O'Neill the ministry was an unregistered and unsupervised for-profit prison: the pastor would pick addicts off the street, incarcerate them in his recovery centre and charge their families for the service. The inmates could not leave, and their supposed treatment consisted of several hours of preaching per day, a brutal separation from drugs and subjection to violence on the slightest pretext. When O'Neill reported the situation to the police, he was told if he submitted a formal report they could indeed enter the premises and free the inmates – but where would the inmates go once released (O'Neill 2019)?

In reporting this literature, it has to be said that these cases only apply to a minority of the region's myriad Pentecostal churches. In a less sensationalist account of the efforts of men and women evangelicals to reach out to gang members in neighbouring El Salvador, Robert Brenneman, reporting on intensive and risky field research, wrestles with both practical and ethical questions: he worries that pastors have good motives but lack the professional skills to support ex-gang members and help them avoid returning, whether voluntarily or not. The only professional future they can offer them is as preachers. But Brenneman also wonders whether pastors are not sometimes manipulated by criminals and describes one telling encounter in a luxury prison cell (Brenneman 2012: 191–234).

All this evidence amounts to a realization that evangelical churches are very often operating in what Guillermo O'Donnell called the 'brown areas' where legal and institutional norms are in question (O'Donnell 1993, 1999). Pentecostalism lends itself to abuse – by traffickers who see in them a convenient channel for money laundering or a convenient cover for their re-emergence as 'reformed characters'; by pseudo-pastoral operations such as the Guatemalan 'recovery' centre; by people with political ambitions; or in the co-optation of prison governance. Even the more institutionalized large-scale neo-Pentecostal churches, with their media businesses, their blatant political involvement in violation of their non-profit status, their murky finances and their claims to cure people of infirmities, inhabit those same brown areas. In Guatemala in 2007, Brenneman reports, 'in a televised interview for his Christian talkshow', the then director of the National Police, Erwin Sperisen, 'defended the practice of social cleansing and openly admitted to the existence of "death squadrons" while confirming that evangelical police personnel had been active in them' (Brenneman 2012: 215). In 2019, he was sentenced to 15 years in prison in Switzerland.[16]

Conclusion

So we return to Santos's abyss, which in his description is an impassable divide. Yet Pentecostalism, like so many political intermediaries, seems well placed to negotiate and to perpetuate it. This form of religion, which turns the region's tradition of popular culture on its head, is able by straddling the abyss to provide sustenance to the established political order, from which the churches draw more advantage than might appear.

The difficulty for the decolonial is that Pentecostalism has established itself in the very field which decolonials believe to be at the core of the injustices suffered by the region's populations – the cultural field. It has also mobilized those social classes and ethnic groups who might be expected to join the anti-colonial struggle. The absence of this phenomenon from their writings illustrates the failure of decolonial theory to ground its ideas in actually existing social processes and the danger that its intellectual contribution will be perpetually confined in the prison of academia.

Conclusion: Democratizing Democracy

Since about 1992, Latin Americanists have focused heavily on race and ethnicity and have distanced themselves from the prominence accorded to social class by the 'marxisant', or broadly Marxist, approaches that had dominated the subject since the late 1960s. To be sure, the concept of class has not been discarded, but the change of emphasis has been palpable, and it has been accompanied by a shift towards a concept of social justice that places strong emphasis on demands for collective recognition. Those demands are grounded in all too real histories of cultural marginalization, social exclusion and discrimination which are the dominant concern of the decolonial, but a condition for a universalistic response to those demands is a confrontation with inequalities of class and gender

The injustices of gender are universal because they transcend injustices of race, exhibiting common patterns across cultural and geographical frontiers. Feminist approaches still need to be foregrounded, so that instead of talking of women in indigenous or anti-racist movements, we talk of a spirit of gender justice spreading across the frontiers of law, politics and culture.

The decolonial

Decolonial thinking draws on an interpretation of the region's woes in terms of an idea of the colonial which is applied from the Iberian conquest up to the continuing colonial character of contemporary society. The word 'colonial' has broadened its meaning from foreign conquest and occupation to a way of describing the close interweaving of modernity with forms of oppression that penetrate indigenous societies and racially defined subcultures, rendering them functional for the capitalist order. In

CONCLUSION

its most radical expressions, it has gone together with the casting of all that can be traced to western modernity, whether free markets, capital, legal institutions, liberal democracy or ideas about women's rights, as harmful to the people, to their environment and to their culture. As an illustration of this dismissive attitude to the institutions of democracy, in a recent 'open letter to two young indigenous Ecuadorians' on the subject of the country's 2021 elections, Boaventura de Souza Santos dismissed the corruption cases against the politicians of the 'pink tide', such as the country's former President Correa, as 'lawfare', trumped up for political reasons, and made no mention of human rights and civic freedom. On lawfare, he was half right, but that is not a reason to empty democracy of civic freedom and clean government.[1]

Even the international human rights regime has been denigrated for its colonial connotations and its focus on individual rights which are associated with neo-liberalism. For example, in an 'Afterword' to one of his books (Mignolo 2011), Walter Mignolo ridicules the concept of freedom with sarcasms and distractions, pointing to the atrocities perpetrated by European powers and the United States while brushing aside violations of freedom in China, referring, as if in compensation, to that country's success in poverty reduction. Accusations of famine are bandied about in the same chapter as Amartya Sen is denounced for propagating universal liberal ideas, in ignorance of Sen's work on famines in both China and India and also of his concept of capabilities which departs from a liberal concept of freedom as developed by John Rawls, for example.[2] That is, Mignolo does not deal with the issue, avoids conceptual or philosophical discussion of freedom or democracy, preferring instead to indulge in mockery or innuendo. In tandem with the decolonial, the word 'neo-liberalism' has become a catch-all term of abuse used to denigrate anything distasteful to an author: it was originally coined to describe the Pinochet regime's adoption of radical free-market policies inspired by Hayek, as well as the programmes of structural adjustment, privatization and fiscal austerity imposed by World Bank and IMF conditionality on governments seeking bail-outs from the debt crisis of the 1980s, known as the Washington Consensus. But by now it has come to denote almost any type of governance arrangement, including multiculturalism, the requirement to consult communities affected by mining projects and international NGO funding of initiatives in the field of gender and race equality and indigenous development (Venugopal 2015). It has even been blamed for the expansion of evangelical churches. Behind this variegated use of the term lies the need to recognize that the damage caused by aggressive and sudden shifts away from the statist or *dirigiste* development policies of the post-war period should not hide the unequal

CONCLUSION

pattern of development that had prevailed under those policies. The reactivation of *dirigisme* under the neo-developmentalist policies of the post-2000 'pink tide' did indeed contribute to a reduced incidence of poverty, notably in Bolivia, and to a short-lived reduction of inequality in Brazil, but regrettably in too many of the cases the progress was not sustained. The decolonial use of neo-liberalism is grounded in false dichotomies.

In the preceding chapters, I have criticized the theoretical and empirical foundations for the decolonial perspective, dissenting especially from its binarisms of race and of global history, and discovering that neither the authors of empirical research inspired by the decolonial nor the leaders of social movements acclaimed by its spokespeople give reason to decry or discredit universal liberal values of freedom, human rights and impartiality in the administration of justice. In addition, the movements for indigenous recognition and racial equality are at one and the same time movements for the democratization of society as a whole and, unlike revolutionary Marxists of an earlier generation, are rarely found to issue diatribes against those liberal ideas.

The analysis of Latin American race relations regimes requires a different framework from those used in countries where the modern study of racial inequality first developed. Stated summarily, this is because despite pervasive race mixture (*mestizaje* or *métissage*), race continues to be a major – though not the only – cause of persistent social inequality, and race and ethnicity feature prominently in patterns of everyday and police violence as well as violence perpetrated by traffickers of all kinds, land speculators and illegal miners against indigenous communities and their leaders.

None of this is in serious dispute, but like the leading figures in decolonial theory, my main focus has been on the cultural dimension of race and ethnicity. In contrast to their thesis of 'epistemicide', according to which colonial rule and violence instantly deleted indigenous knowledge and culture, I point to a centuries-old interplay between elite cultural practices and those of indigenous peoples, of the popular classes and of black, or Afro-descendant, populations. The interplay can be described as a dialectic, an interaction or a feedback loop between stylized conceptions of hierarchically ordered socio-economic groups and ethnic/linguistic groups or racially identified populations. This dialectic is found in a host of fields, most notably religion, but also in music, dance, food, the visual and plastic arts, highbrow literature and public displays like carnivals. In developing the idea of a dialectic, I have proceeded as if on tiptoe, wary of overtones of reductionism or essentialism, and of objectification or reification of particular collectivities or the subject matter under discussion.

173

CONCLUSION

The counterpart to the dialectic could be the concept of *intersectionality* which conveys relationships of inequality in a more univocal and material manner than the dialectic of hegemonic and subordinate cultures: in its standard usage, the term assumes that a host of variables all operate as if correlated to accentuate patterns of inequality in its different forms. We see this in the cumulative correlated effects of race and class inequality. But drawing on the original formulation of the concept by Kimberle Crenshaw (Crenshaw 1989), it is important to leave the conclusion open and to allow that intersection does not necessarily mean correlation and that the different variables can operate in different directions. One example is the intersection of gender, race and education, especially in Latin America. Another was already present in Crenshaw's explanation that the application of laws on sexual violence in the US legal and police system could harm black women more than black male perpetrators. Silvia Rivera Cusicanqui's summary of the social history of Bolivia is another example in which we saw indigenous women becoming *cholas* as pioneers of early urban migration and the consequent upward mobility, and the counter-intuitive performative correlates in the dress codes adopted for different occasions by *cholas* and elite women (Rivera Cusicanqui 2010 [1997]).

Aside from questions of historical interpretation, my divergence from the decolonial starts with its denigration of European philosophy (except phenomenology) and its branding of Cartesian philosophy as the initiator of the idea of a universal western epistemology that disqualifies all other forms of knowledge and modes of being. I also dissent from their misuse of the works of Fanon and Levinas. Although they shared a heritage in the sense that Levinas was a philosopher in the phenomenological lineage of Husserl and Heidegger, and Fanon read Merleau-Ponty and had great admiration for Sartre, a comparison of their work shows little in common in either style or substance. There is a chasm between Levinas's very difficult style and Fanon's directness, but if there is something in common between the two it is a universalism to which the decolonial is so hostile. The attempt to make Levinas into a *tercermundista* is, to say the least, seriously misguided, and the depiction of Fanon as a prophet of blackness, as distinct from a prophet of a non-racialized society, is also misleading.

A central element in the decolonial worldview is Santos's word the 'abyss'. This is inspired by the idea that colonialism consigned indigenous people to a state of nature and claimed the right to govern them without laws. This is misleading: though the conquerors most certainly acted lawlessly, they also took much trouble to impose laws on their subjects, for example, (in what is now Bolivia) establishing a system

174

CONCLUSION

of parallel Indian and colonial authorities (Abercrombie 1991: 102). Santos's claim does not fit what we know about the colonial system. However, the notion of an abyss does convey well the modern division between formal and informal sectors of economic activity, and between areas where the law and the state do (more or less) govern and those where gangsters, traffickers, criminal networks and militias hold sway. The abyss is not only a division between neighbourhoods of cities like Rio de Janeiro: it is global, even passing through the heart of financial centres – for the abyss is part and parcel of the capitalist system and also of the system of public security: just as money is laundered through financial centres, so police and traffickers work together and so also politicians do deals with criminals. We also saw that churches can bridge the abyss as well.

The decolonial, therefore, is mistaken to depict a world of binaries built on race and ethnicity in which neither racial nor cultural *métissage* has a place, and that worldview has been subjected to coruscating criticisms by Silvia Rivera Cusicanqui, who uses the Aymara word '*ch'ixi*' to denote a mixture which is still not a suppression of its component parts. I hope to have built on her polemics by assembling examples of misleading binarisms from a wealth of creative Andean and Brazilian ethnography.

Gender has found a place, but almost as a separate branch of the decolonial school. The 'gurus' of the decolonial hardly mention it at all, but there is a thriving decolonial, or autonomous, feminism with different (female) gurus, different meetings and a diverse agenda. The title 'autonomous feminists' may express a will to independence vis-à-vis the gurus of the decolonial, but their hostility to the European 'neo-liberal feminists of the NGOs' who want to work with (and fund) women's projects and movements shows they share those gurus' suspicion of universalism: their hostility derives also from a resistance to involvement with NGOs and their suffocating bureaucratic embrace and their revindication of a distinctive Latin American, or occasionally black, feminism. At the grass roots, however, it is not hard to find women exercising autonomy and carving out independent roles like the Mapuche *machi* – healer-priestesses of Southern Chile – who have figured prominently as emblematic political prisoners incarcerated because of their participation in protest marches or in alleged acts of violence. As shamans who 'have always mediated between the human and spirit worlds ... [t]hey ... use those skills, perspectives, knowledge, and imagery in the realm of interethnic politics and in mediating relations with the state'. Despite the 'politicizing of indigenous shamans and the shamanization of indigenous politics', they retain substantial independence of action and, unlike many of their male counterparts (shamans and also community leaders

175

CONCLUSION

or *longko*), they tend to resist clientelistic or party-political ties which would constrain their freedom of action (Bacigalupo 2004: 520, 531).

One aspect of the autonomy of autonomous feminists is that several of their most prominent figures lead lives outside academia, and their writings are more directly engaged in movement politics and street demonstrations than the writings of their male counterparts: words by leading figure Rita Segato found their way into the sung dance routine 'Un violador en tu camino', devised in Valparaíso, Chile, by Las Tesis and enacted in thousands-strong events in many capitals in 2019. This stands in contrast with the oracular, often impenetrable language of the decolonials, especially Mignolo, Dussel and Maldonado-Torres, when they are writing in philosophical mode. That style does capture one central feature of the decolonial – the coexistence of a fervent political ideology with an entirely intra-academic life and audience. They are not known for membership of political parties or for standing for office: for the decolonial, the world of learning is itself a field of political struggle and not at all an ethereal one. There are tens of thousands of professors distributed through the Americas and millions of students, and competition for resources in higher education and research is fierce. Academia is no longer the protected, self-reproducing, inward-looking world portrayed for France by Bourdieu in his *Homo Academicus* (Bourdieu 1990). Bourdieu himself pointed to the forces that were undermining that world post-1968, and today, forty or more years after the research reported in that book, we can see that the humanities and the social sciences are importing the confrontations and insecurities of society as a whole, and contributing to public debate – as I described in *The Prism of Race* for the development of affirmative actions ('race quotas') in Brazil. But the academic world, thanks to the protections of tenure (for some), remains the decolonials' primary arena throughout the hemisphere.

A discrete universalism

Although the decolonial and allied schools oppose liberalism as well as neo-liberalism, when we step 'down' from the oracular philosophical discourse to research done by their followers, it is hard to find a deep contradiction between their underlying positions and basic liberal democratic tenets. When I turned to the (mainly Mexican) ethnographies broadly inspired by decolonial concerns and a commitment to racial equality and ethnic recognition (Hernández Castillo 2016; Sieder 2017; Sierra 2009, 2013), I found that their message is one of universal rights, especially where gender and the law are concerned. Because Mexican anthropology

CONCLUSION

generally and feminist anthropology in particular have devoted so much of their attention to rural indigenous communities (though most indigenous people now live in cities and in the United States), much attention has been paid in public academic exchange to the exclusions and violence suffered by indigenous women. Nonetheless, despite this indigenist inspiration, the merits of indigenous judicial practices highlighted in Sieder's anthology have been precisely the merits one would look for in any judicial arrangement – namely, equity, openness and impartiality. These are precisely the merits not found in the application in Mexico of indigenous *usos y costumbres* under the aegis of an unreformed state judiciary and bureaucracy. We saw the risks in the town of Cherán in Michoacán (Román Burgos 2019; Vázquez León 2010, 2016).

It would be inconsistent to point the finger at undemocratic practices and the abuse or marginalization of women in indigenous contexts without reminding ourselves firstly that they are widespread in society as a whole and secondly that women are at the forefront not only of indigenous women's movements but also of the broader indigenous movements themselves – as we saw in Bolivia. (Women became the majority of members of the Bolivian Plurinational Assembly after the 2020 elections, making up 55 per cent of senators and 47 per cent of deputies.) These are not restorationist movements or even movements of cultural recovery: they are movements for basic rights to which all citizens are entitled. If we then combine that observation with the generalization that ethnic and identity-driven movements have displaced class-based movements from front of stage of contemporary Latin America, we realize that indigenous movements are leading forces in the struggle to 'democratize democracy'. By this I mean the institutionalization of basic protections against abuse of power, against corruption, against the impunity of sexual abusers, and thus the defence of human rights, in short the institutional apparatus of liberal democracy, the weakness or absence of which was long ago lamented by Guillermo O'Donnell at a time when it was assumed by some that a transition to 'free and fair' electoral competition would solve the problems inherited from military governments (O'Donnell 1996).

Civil society movements cannot be the whole picture: many of these are indigenous and Afro-descendant movements making demands of the state, and states have responded in various ways. One type of response, not covered in the preceding chapters, is through the judicial system, by applying laws against racial discrimination and punishing individuals and corporations accordingly. This is essential because of the universalism of the law, but it is not an adequate way to dismantle deeply ingrained and often subconscious habits. Judicial remedies are particularly important

177

CONCLUSION

for Afro-descendant populations and black people generally because only in a few cases does their situation and history fit the model of collective rights designed for indigenous peoples as constructed under colonial rule (Hooker 2005). Judicial application of laws against racial discrimination tends to receive little attention because it gains few votes and has a low profile. Yet those are the gains which survive the inconstancies of politics (at least until a dictator comes to undo them . . .).

Being so often slave descendants, black people can only rarely demand the restoration of usurped land or of their own institutions of self-government. Some governments and social movements have fashioned remedies at least for rural black populations that mimic remedies for indigenous peoples. The Colombian solution has been to recognize that certain regions with predominantly black populations are entitled to special representation in Congress like indigenous peoples (Paschel 2016).

The Brazilian solution is found in laws and institutions for the restoration of land formerly controlled by escaped slave settlements (*quilombos*) to their *quilombola* descendants; the artifice of a *quilombo* history – in circumstances where, of their very nature, fugitive slave settlements are hardly documented at all – led to a loosening of the criteria such that applicants for *quilombola* recognition were only required to constitute a community of some sort and so *quilombola* status in effect became a matter of choice (Boyer 2014; Lehmann 2018: 33). Official recognition of anthropologists as experts in assessing these communities has helped, but the slowness of the bureaucracy has limited the translation of recognition of *quilombola* status into grants of land. These grants have been hindered by the bureaucracy's imaginary, which has codified a *quilombo* community living and working collectively on land held in common – a conception which bears little if any relation to the communities' lives.

Another type of state response is reparation of the injustices perpetrated during the colonial period and in the Republican period when colonial protection of Indian territory was withdrawn and indigenous land seized – a process known as *reducción* in Chile – sometimes accompanied by massacres and near-genocide (Bayer 1972; Bello 2011; Bengoa 1985; Platt 1984; Richards 2013). These programmes take the form of land restoration, of initiatives in intercultural education and medicine, and of official recognition of language, of indigenous belief systems and religious practices. They also include the establishment of Secretariats and Departments of Indigenous Affairs to take care of indigenous issues and in which indigenous people can find employment.

The exercise of the rights arising from such initiatives depends on administrative discretion and political sponsorship: the access to land

178

depends on the will and speed of the relevant agency; agencies may endure but not their budgets. Because of prolonged legal and bureaucratic procedures, they are unlikely to benefit more than a minority of the potential pool of beneficiaries and may be subject to clientelistic manipulation.

Evo Morales seems to have understood these lessons well, and therefore his administration devoted strenuous efforts to enshrining their plurinational ideal in legal texts, although in the end they ran up against the difficulty of reconciling oral traditions of customary law with the positive legal requirements of a modern system of law (Goodale 2019).

We saw both in Brazil (the *quilombolas*) and in Chile (Mapuche land 'restitution') that governments can try hard to apply positive law by opening a path to land ownership through the recognition of communal structures that have evolved under customary arrangements; the outcome has the merit of being based in law but is extremely bureaucratic and far removed from a strengthening of communal ties or the communal attachment to ancestral title or territory, and the number eventually benefiting in proportion to the incidence of poverty and landlessness among the potential beneficiaries is paltry (Mallon 2005).

A third path to reparation is affirmative actions, as they are called in Brazil. According to the country's 2012 affirmative action law, this obliges federal universities to set aside 50 per cent of undergraduate places for students from state schools[3] and within that number for a proportion of black, brown and indigenous candidates equivalent to their proportion in the population of the relevant state. This is not affirmative action as understood in the United States, where quotas were ruled illegal by the Supreme Court. Quotas continue to be in force throughout Brazil's federal university system and, under a separate 2014 law, in the federal civil service, in spite of a president who regards such measures with contempt and takes little care to disguise his prejudice against blacks and indigenous people. The colour of the student body in prestige universities has been transformed. At the Federal University of Minas Gerais, for example, one of the 'top' universities in the country to which entry has been highly competitive, the proportion of 'self-declared' black and brown students almost doubled in ten years from 27 per cent in 2008 to 49 per cent in 2018.[4] Many of those will have entered as *cuotistas* through the separate competition for low-income and black students.

The advantage of this system is that it does not enable politicians to allocate the resources in clientelistic fashion. Thus, although Dilma Roussef and her successors have withdrawn funding to support black and low-income students' living and studying costs, the law remains in force.

The difference between affirmative action and discretionary support is that if the federal government had limited itself to handing out scholarships or maintenance grants to black students, far fewer students would have benefited and the programme would have been subject to withdrawal at the whim of another government. That more expensive option would have been less effective in increasing the proportion of black students.

In a chromatic race regime like Brazil's, it was soon asked where and how to 'draw the colour line'. That question has been changed into a legal question with the introduction of procedures – or verification committees – for third-party identification (*heteroidentificação* as opposed to *autoidentificação*). Although such procedures would probably be unacceptable in Europe or North America, they have encountered little resistance in Brazil where ultimately judges may be called on to resolve disputes or appeals.

Not only does the socio-economic criterion in Brazil's affirmative action model ensure a universalist element in the allocation of university places – but also the proportion of 'negros' (i.e. '*pretos*' and '*pardos*') in the Brazilian population does not cease to grow, to the point where now it is a matter of common agreement that they constitute half the population, thus accentuating the egalitarian thrust of the system and reducing differences in opportunities between black and white state school graduates.

In comparison with these legal and institutional measures, the multicultural initiatives, particularly in education, instituted in most Spanish-American states are principally a contribution to the formation of indigenous leadership, and their reliance on the ups and downs of politics and patronage. The standout exception is in Colombia's Cauca Valley, where multiculturalism has come from 'below' and a web of institutions of self-government and education has grown up and spawned a local elite of indigenous intellectuals. This might be what the Zapatistas aspire to even without knowing it. The Cauca Valley CRIC is exemplary as a case of democratization more even than of cultural renewal, for the freedom of the institutions it has created in justice and self-government is exercised in the framework of the Colombian state.

Gender

One way in which ethnic and race-based mobilizations contribute to democratizing democracy is by the visible involvement of women in their leadership and the demonstration effect this can have on the rest

CONCLUSION

of society. If the movements were to make it a rule that women occupy half of all positions, the result would be more attention paid to health, to education, to reducing violence and to transparency in the affairs of their organizations, as well as to women's rights themselves. For anthropologists and the Zapatista women whose activism they describe, Zapatismo was a movement for recognition of indigenous rights and territory, but it could equally be said that those women were advocating change in their relations with their men and opportunities for their children as Mexican citizens (Speed, Hernández Castillo, and Stephen 2006). The Zapatista leadership had already included women when they came to the Lacandonian jungle, and their representative when they addressed the Mexican National Congress on 28 March 2001 was Comandanta Esther. In the process leading up to the Bolivian Constituent Assembly in 2006 and 2007, indigenous women's organizations came together and drew up very radical egalitarian proposals on gender relating to 'political participation, land rights, education, and domestic violence', provision of women's shelters and the right to decide how many children they would have (Rousseau 2011: 21). These rights were for all women, not only the indigenous among them. In the Ecuadorian Constituent Assembly of 2007–8, a campaign by a group of women forced the inclusion of clauses protecting internationally agreed women's rights within provisions on indigenous legal institutions and taking precedence over indigenous customary law (Lavinas Picq 2016). Their campaign was motivated by life in indigenous society, but it applied to the country as a whole.

Joanne Rappaport offers a more tempered (and perhaps more realistic) account of women who became office-holders and, through education, indigenous intellectuals in the Nasa area of Colombia. They attended university away from the area, and even had to work as domestic servants to finance their studies: on top of the subordination they would have experienced on their home ground, they now experienced discrimination as Indians. They regarded that period of their lives as a 'step in their reindianization', for their experience of university sharpened their commitment to their cultural background. But on their return they were intellectuals, and thus an 'inappropriate (woman) other' because to be an intellectual did not fit the gender values of their communities of origin (Rappaport 2005: 52–3). Nonetheless, some were gaining positions of prestige, being elected, for example, as presidents of *cabildos*.

These experiences tell us that to formulate a scholarly domain, or indeed a political field, under the heading 'indigenous women' or even 'black women' is unnecessarily restrictive. Of course, Kimberle Crenshaw was right to point out the perverse effects of universalist legislation on

181

CONCLUSION

the lives of black women in the United States and on unjust treatment at the hands of the police and the justice system. But that is because the universalism is distorted by prejudice, not because they seek another kind of justice. When in Spanish America indigenous women organize, they demand equal rights – they do not demand to be treated in accordance with the traditions of their peoples. The Brazilian black feminist writer Djamila Ribeiro says that a black woman speaks from a different place. The phrase 'lugar de fala' in the title of her book could mean authorized speech, or the 'feminist standpoint' (Ribeiro 2017). White feminists should think about the way their thinking is influenced and limited by their situation of privilege, just as black women's thinking is imprinted with the pain they experience on account of their bodies and those of the generations that came before them. In Brazil, black women are in the forefront of social movements, especially movements in defence of black people, of *quilombolas* and of people living in *favelas*. (Women are rare, although not entirely unknown, among evangelical leaders.) Their activism and leadership stretches beyond the defence of specifically women's rights.

Ribeiro's discussion is conducted in terms of essentialisms, if not stereotypes, with little recognition of the diversity of locations of black women across the class structure and other hierarchies of status or distinction. She does not imagine an escape from colour, unlike Fanon, who imagines a society in which skin colour has no relevance at all to relationships of superiority and inferiority. However, by focusing on the multidimensionality of oppression afflicting black women, Ribeiro opens the way to the universality of women's movements and their demands. Just as black women's oppression is multidimensional, so to combat that oppression is to create social justice for all women and all people.

Women in religion and social movements

At a CLACSO Congress in 2018,[5] Rita Segato spoke before a very large audience in almost lurid terms of the 'conspiracy' (*complot* in Spanish) against an 'effective democracy' in Latin America: firstly, she spoke of a parastatal sphere of control over life ('la esfera paraestatal de control de la vida') to describe the penetration of the state, politics and business by pervasive criminality and organized unofficial violence. In writings on which her speech was based, she characterizes this as *dueñidad* ('lordship') traceable back to a 'mandate of masculinity' ('el mandato de masculinidad'), or regime of male entitlement, which predates the structures of capitalism (Segato 2016: 17–18; 2018: 199).[6] Patriarchy is the source

182

CONCLUSION

of power in all its forms and the prime victims of the reign of violence in the region are women.

She sees the advance of 'religious fundamentalism' as an integral part of this assault on women, linked to a moral panic driven by an alliance of political interests and pastor-politicians going back to about 2010, fanning fears of 'gender ideology', gay marriage and child sexuality, and campaigns to remove 'political bias' – that is, liberal ideas – from the schoolroom. She foresaw the rise of fascism through elected majorities governing unshackled from the institutional restraints of pluralist democracy. A few months later, Bolsonaro was elected in Brazil with 55 per cent of the second-round votes.

The political involvement of pastors in politics at all levels is so widespread now in Brazil that people with political ambitions may be setting up churches of their own – something easier and cheaper to do than setting up a café[7] – because they see the potential of an 'available mass' of churchgoers. Cases of pastors involved in corruption add credence to the hypothesis. There remains the question of how they succeed in whipping up electoral mobilization driven by moral panics, and part of the answer may simply be that they are expert at navigating the fluctuating alliances of local politics. In Guatemala, too, there is a pattern of evangelical support for politicians accused of corruption (Dary 2018).

The main purpose of including a chapter on the churches was to show that the decolonial approach, as contained in the writings of Santos, Mignolo and Quijano, had little to say about this very profound change in the sphere that interests them most – the region's culture. How can they ignore an increasingly politicized mass-based phenomenon which exhibits little interest in social or racial injustice, and for whose leaders greater injustice comes from feminism than from low wages? Yet I remain reluctant to accept Segato's conspiracy explanation. To denounce the evangelical phenomenon as an extraneous implantation wrenching people away from their own culture is to deny them the possibility of agency.

Women have told me in the course of fieldwork in Bahia how membership of a church strengthens them in the face of violence in the home – but I also heard a pastor advise them to 'turn the other cheek . . . your assailant will calm down'. (He did not say 'go to the women's unit of the local police station', as he might have done, for such units exist.) Some folk sociology would like to see in the churches a refuge from the breakdown of social constraints in low-income urban neighbourhoods, but this may be an artefact of women's agency: Christina Vital's detailed ethnography of a suburban neighbourhood of Rio de Janeiro indicates that if Pentecostalism does protect or discourage people – especially young

183

CONCLUSION

people – from involvement in 'bad things', that is most likely because the relationship with a church is mediated by mothers, sisters and girlfriends (Vital da Cunha 2015). They must compete, however, with the harsh reality of a labour market in which young men can earn five times as much from dealing than from the dreary and often humiliating legal jobs on offer. Segato would see the efforts of these women as at best damage limitation and would also note that the churches preach an ideology that protects and perpetuates 'el mandato de masculinidad'.

Seeing no hope within the frameworks available at present, Segato ends with a yearning for the time when domestic space and its forms of interpersonal contact had not been closed off by coloniality and modernity: colonialism gave rise to a male-dominated public sphere with its bureaucracy and enforced distancing of social relationships. Her imagined future will bring a restoration of the ethnic and of community through feminine political practice – a practice to be valued in itself whatever outcome it may pursue (Segato 2016: 31). Once again, in this utopian vision, we see feminism coming to the resue of society as a whole.

In response to growing political involvement, feminism and gender politics have, as we have seen, become a field for at times murderous attack – as illustrated by the exemplary killing on the open street in March 2018 of the Rio de Janeiro municipal councillor Marielle Franco, who has become a martyr recognized throughout the hemisphere. Maxine Molyneux and her co-authors have described a 'fourth generation', or fourth wave, marking a further development in the world feminist movement, of which Marielle was herself perfectly representative (Molyneux et al. 2020). This generation is characterized by higher levels of education than its predecessors, by its diversity, by the leading role of youth in its public demonstrations, but also by a severe crisis of unemployment among young people: in Latin America, the unemployment rate for those aged 15–24 years was nearly 20 per cent in 2016 (ILO 2017). That was before the pandemic which raised the incidence of poverty in the region from 33.7 per cent to 37.2 per cent.[8]

Segato is not alone in her deep pessimism. A recent book by two veterans of the generation of 1968, Fernando Calderón and Manuel Castells, diagnosing the condition of the region with a completely different approach from the decolonial, is only marginally less pessimistic. They do not ignore the ethnic and gender issues, but their priority is political economy and macro-sociology. Despite an apparently optimistic title, The New Latin America offers a bleak diagnosis centred on the penetration of the state by criminal organizations and corrupt networks binding politicians to big business (Calderón and Castells 2020). There are weaker and stronger states, and different degrees of penetration, but the

184

egregious examples of the region's two most populous countries, Mexico and Brazil, give cause for extreme concern. A few decades ago, those authors would have laid the blame on external forces and US imperialism, but no longer. The diagnosis applies as much to governments labelled 'neo-liberal' as to those in the 'pink tide', labelled 'neo-developmentalist' ('populist' according to some, even 'left-wing' according to others). Like so many Latin Americanists in recent decades, they only see a ray of hope in social movements and grass-roots mobilization borne on the shoulders of women, of young people, of environmental campaigns and of indigenous and Afro-descendant peoples – that is, outside the institutionalized political field. The prominence of women in social movements can be traced back at least to the human rights mobilizations in Argentina in the late 1970s (the mothers and grandmothers of disappeared persons who gathered weekly and proceeded to walk in silence, wearing their white headscarves, around the Plaza de Mayo in front of the cathedral in Buenos Aires) and, after the country suffered another economic collapse in 2001, women were protagonists in the grass-roots mobilizations that proliferated across the country (Kotler 2008; Longa 2017; Tabbush and Caminotti 2015). Under military regimes and often with encouragement from priests and nuns inspired by liberation theology, women were prominent across the region in Christian Base Communities (Comunidades de Base) (Theije 1998) and Mothers' Clubs in low-income urban neighbourhoods. In those cases of what I call urban self-management, they were extending the scope of their role as heads of households to the wider community (Lehmann 1990). But now their involvement and autonomy has gone much further. Calderón and Castells quote a 'series of quantitative indices of objective, subjective and democratic agency' from a UN Report on the MERCOSUR countries of the Southern Cone which indicate that 'in almost all national cases, as well as in all social and generational contexts, among young people of different ages, women were found to have significant capacity for action' (Calderón and Castells 2020: 161). Surveys undertaken in 2008 in four major cities (sample size 1,500 in Buenos Aires and Rio de Janeiro, and 800 in Asunción and Montevideo) showed that women had a higher disposition to civic action (*agencia ciudadana*) than men (50% vs. 45%). Women over the age of 21 tended to favour causes related to income inequality and participation, while younger women tended to see injustice in terms of race, ethnicity, gender and sexual orientation (Programa de las Naciones Unidas para el Desarrollo 2009: 257).

Even before COVID, the region was facing very difficult challenges, and now they are more difficult than at any time in living memory, yet few advocate socialist or revolutionary solutions, not only because their

CONCLUSION

outcomes have been at best disappointing and at worst catastrophic, but also because the faith in the state that characterized progressive projects until the last quarter of the twentieth century has faded. Segato calls for thinking 'outside the res publica', which means putting our trust in social movements again.

After the decolonial

The decolonial has cloistered itself behind the protective walls of academe and has addressed almost exclusively an audience of students and professors. Having produced the most comprehensive denunciation ever of the region's condition, we might have been entitled to expect at least an attempt to chart a path to the future, but it has not been forthcoming.

The previous paragraphs show how despair has overtaken one of its most popular feminist standard-bearers. While the male branch emits oracular pronouncements, the feminists both in everyday life and in public debate confront the most basic of challenges: how to stay alive. That was before COVID. The desolation now afflicting the region, with rare exceptions, is providing material for uncounted tragedies and among social scientists, it is to be hoped, much soul-searching. We now face the consequences of COVID and must ask some difficult questions. As for me, my conclusion is that after the decolonial, the feminists' revolution must continue because it exhibits the diversity which is required and because it seems to have more of the groundedness and the rootedness of the liberation theologians' ideal of a *teologia pé-no-chão*.[9]

Notes

Introduction

1 I say 'Anglo-Saxon' because in Latin languages *la science* or *ciencia*, like the German *Wissenschaft*, refers to a body of knowledge in general, not only to knowledge based on experimentation and numerical precision.
2 *Cholo* is widely used in Peru and Bolivia to refer to people located in between the *indios* and the more elite *mestizos* in the social hierarchy. It can also be used as a term of endearment (cf. 'Hola cholito!'). *Blanco* is rarely used. Outsiders tend to assume that *mestizo* is also a term used to refer to people of mixed race or 'light brown' complexion, but in daily parlance it often refers simply to elites, local or national, and includes people who in Europe would count as white.
3 Consulting indigenous healers is a worldwide practice, but usually those healers appear as practitioners of 'alternative' or 'homeopathic' medicine and are detached from their 'home base', nor do they usually receive patients or clients in public hospitals.
4 The use of the word *criolla* is interesting because it seems to have gained popularity by not using the word *indígena*. 'Criollo' was used in Hispanophone countries in the colonial period to refer to elite people – not Indians or indigenous – born in the colonies, as distinct from those born in Spain. Perhaps the phrase is putting a slight distance between those entrepreneurs – whose presentation of self would appear undoubtedly Indian to an outsider – and the Indian masses.

Chapter 1 The Latin American Decolonial

1 'En efecto, si se observan las lineas principales de la explotación y de la dominación social a escala global . . . es imposible no ver que la vasta mayoría de los explotados, de los dominados, de los discriminados, son exactamente los miembros de las "razas", de las "etnias", o de las "naciones" en que fueron categorizadas las poblaciones colonizadas, . . . desde la conquista de America en adelante.' This much-quoted article was first published in Peru in 1992, and was later reprinted and translated widely.

NOTES TO PP. 23–29

2 I refer to the notorious Turkish-Greek population 'exchange' of 1923–6, agreed at the Treaty of Lausanne and consummated at the cost of hundreds of thousands of lives of people who were massacred, deported, conscripted as forced labour and so on. Estimates refer to 350,000 'Greek Muslims' and 190,000 'Turkish nationals of the Greek Orthodox Religion' being forcibly deported. Michael Barutciski, 'Lausanne Revisited: Population Exchanges in International Law and Policy', in Renée Hirschon (ed.), *Crossing the Aegean: An Appraisal of the 1923 Compulsory Population Exchange between Greece and Turkey* (New York: Berghahn Books, 2003), p. 28. See Juliet Davis, 'The Greek-Turkish Population Transfers in 1923–1924: A Discussion', ms. https://www.researchgate.net/profile/JulietDavis4

3 Everything written here about Fanon owes an enormous debt to David Macey's biography with its wealth of detail and historical background (Macey 2000).

4 My translation of 'le dos au mur, le couteau sur la gorge ou, pour être plus precis, l'électrode sur les parties génitales, le colonisé va être sommé *de ne plus se raconter des histoires*'. In the La Découverte edition, the powerful phrase *tourmentes oniriques* appears as a reference to the trance, translatable perhaps as 'dreamlike storm'. *Le couteau sur la gorge* is a figurative expression meaning a decision cannot be delayed any longer, but here is used in a dual reference to torture (with thanks to Jean Khalfa).

5 'The colonized subject also manages to lose sight of the colonist through religion. Fatalism relieves the oppressor of all responsibility since the cause of wrongdoing, poverty, and the inevitable can be attributed to God. The individual thus accepts the devastation decreed by God, grovels in front of the colonist, bows to the hand of fate, and mentally readjusts to acquire the serenity of stone' (Fanon 2004: 18).

6 Macey writes as follows of Fanon's time as a psychiatrist in Blida in Algeria: 'As at Blida, Fanon's goal was to create a therapeutic 'neo-society' in which patients could establish a multiplicity of social bonds, fulfil a variety of functions and act out a variety of roles. The symptomatology to be observed in the traditional hospital – the appearance of 'pure' or desocialized symptoms at the physical level – began to change.' He then quotes from an article by Fanon written with Jacques Azoulay entitled 'L'Hospitalisation de jour en psychiatrie: valeur et limites', *Tunisie médicale* 37(10) (1959): 689–732; reprinted in *Information psychiatrique* 59(10) (1975): 1117–30: 'Social therapy wrenches the patient away from his fantasies and forces him to confront reality on a new basis. Occupational therapy and forms of psychodrama were introduced to further the creation of the neo-society, whilst visits to the cinema or even a café helped the outside to filter back into the hospital.' See also McCulloch (1983).

7 Philcox's translation. 'Tout est permis car, en réalité, l'on ne se réunit que pour laisser la libido accumulée, l'agressivité empêchée, sourdre volcaniquement. Mises à mort symboliques, chevauchées figuratives, meurtres multiples imaginaires, il faut que tout cela sorte. Les mauvaises humeurs s'écoulent, bruyantes telles des coulées de lave' (Fanon 2014: 467–8). Jean Khalfa notes that Fanon observed such trances when accompanying his student and co-author Azoulay in his research.

8 The word was coined by Léopold Sédar Senghor, the Senegalese leader, in the 1930s, together with the poet Aimé Césaire as a motto for black awareness

NOTES TO PP. 29–48

and protest – later it became a slogan for post-Independence regimes, including Senghor's own in Sénégal.

9 I have modified Markman's dreadful translation (Fanon 1986). 'Le Noir veut être Blanc. Le Blanc s'acharne à réaliser une condition d'homme./ . . . Le Blanc est enfermé dans sa blancheur./Le Noir dans sa noirceur . . .'

10 'C'est un fait: des Blancs s'estiment supérieurs aux Noirs./C'est encore un fait: des Noirs veulent démontrer aux Blancs coûte que coûte la richesse de leur pensée, l'égale puissance de leur esprit./Comment s'en sortir?'

11 'Aussi pénible que puisse être pour nous cette constatation, nous sommes obligés de la faire: pour le Noir, il n'y a qu'un destin. Et il est blanc' (Fanon 1952: 27–8, 2011: 251).

12 Variously translated as 'Anti-Semite and Jew' or 'Portrait of the Anti-Semite' (Sartre 1946, 1948a, 1948b). There seems to have been resistance among English and American publishers to using the phrase 'Jewish question', as there would be today.

13 My translation. Here is the original: 'Je n'ai pas le droit, moi homme de couleur, de souhaiter la cristallisation chez le Blanc d'une culpabilité envers le passé de ma race.'

14 My translation. Here is the original: 'Le nègre n'est pas. Pas plus que le Blanc. Tous deux ont à s'écarter des voix inhumaines qui furent celles de leurs ancêtres respectifs afin que naisse une authentique communication.'

15 The article was published in English in *Cultural Studies* in 2007 (Quijano 2007).

16 *Imperialismo y 'marginalidad' en América Latina*, Lima: Mosca Azul 1977; and *Crisis imperialista y obrera*, Lima, 1974.

17 The only government of those he mentions which has not ended badly – if we count Dilma Roussef as the continuation of Lula – was that of Mujica in Uruguay, which was the closest to a European social democratic model and had nothing in common with Chavez or Correa.

18 The original is as follows: 'los movimientos latinoamericanos construyen sus luchas basándose en conocimientos ancestrales, populares y espirituales que siempre fueron ajenos al cientismo propio de la teoría crítica eurocéntrica.'

19 *Milestones* is widely available on the internet in English.

20 Thanks are due to Raphael Lehmann for bringing this article to my attention.

21 Those who were 'out to get him' even questioned his Palestinian belonging.

22 '. . . construyen sus luchas basándose en conocimientos ancestrales, populares, espirituales que siempre fueron ajenos al cientismo propio de la teoría crítica eurocéntrica . . . sus concepciones ontológicas sobre el ser y la vida son muy distintas del presentismo y del individualismo occidentales. Los seres son comunidades de seres antes que individuos, en estas comunidades están presentes y vivos los antepasados así como los animales y la Madre Tierra. Estamos ante cosmovisiones no occidentales que obligan a un trabajo de traducción intercultural para poder ser entendidas y valoradas.'

23 My translation is from Levinas. The published translation is by Richard Cohen (Levinas 1984).

24 '. . . j'analyse la relation interhumaine comme si, dans la proximité avec autrui – par-delà l'image que je me fais de l'autre homme – son visage, l'expressif en autrui (et tout le corps humain est, en ce sens, plus au moins, visage), était ce que m'*ordonne* de le servir' (Levinas 1982: 94).

25 '. . . objetos de conocimiento y control' and 'la búsqueda del conocimiento

189

NOTES TO PP. 48–50

como una tarea ascética que busca distanciarse de lo subjetivo/corporal' and the elevation of 'escepticismo misantrópico y las evidencias racistas ... al nivel de filosofía primera y de fundamento mismo de las ciencias'. I take it that 'evidencias' is meant in this ironic sense of that which common sense believes to be 'evident' and that *ciencias* refers to knowledge in general, not only the natural sciences.

26 One *locus classicus* is Schwarz (1992a, 1992b).

27 'El plano del ser, cuando es tomado como fundamento último, plantea la eliminación de las *huellas* de aquello que lo funda y lo disturba, la relación trans-ontológica ... Esto hace que los ideales de libertad e igualdad se ganen a expensa de la muerte omnipresente de la fraternidad o, mas bien, de la altericidad ...'

28 '"[E]l ser es" resume toda la ontología. Ante el ser no hay sino contemplarlo, especularlo, extasiarse ante él, afirmarlo y trágicamente permanecer en la pasiva autenticidad (*Eigentlichkeit*) favorable para el dominador; mortal para el dominado' (Dussel 2013: 71).

29 Like the translator of his two master works, I translate *autrui* as an other and *Autrui* as the Other.

30 Maybe in this last sentence Dussel is recalling Fanon, who evokes at several points in *Peau Noire* his memory of a small child pointing at him and exclaiming: 'Tiens, un nègre!' The original is as follows: 'Al otro en tiempo de peligro se lo transforma gracias a las ideologías en "el enemigo". En tiempo de paz, aunque siempre se le tenga por peligroso potencial (causas de la angustia fundamental de todo sistema totalizado o esquizoide), al rostro del otro se lo manipula como mera cosa sin trascendencia ni misterio, se lo constituye como instrumento. El rostro se lo cambia por una máscara, fea, usada, por los climas, rústica. La máscara ya no es rostro; ya no interpela; es un mueble más del entorno. Se pasa junto al otro y simplemente se dice: "¡Un obrero!", o: "¡Un indígena!", o: "¡Un negro!", o: "¡Un pakistaní desnutrido!"' (Dussel 2013: 75).

31 'Responsable por el otro en y ante el sistema es la anterioridad a toda anterioridad; pasividad que es casi actividad metafísica (más activa que el respeto pero todavía más pasiva que la praxis de liberación). Es anterioridad metafísica del orden nuevo o realmente futuro. Es anterioridad a la apertura ontológica al mundo, por cuanto la hace posible, en su a priori real. Responsable por el hijo indefenso es la madre, como el maestro es responsable por su discípulo, el gobernante por su pueblo.'

32 Levinas, during the interview, is providing a guide to *Totalité et Infini*: 'La proximité d'autrui est présentée dans le livre comme le faire qu'autrui n'est pas simplement proche de moi dans l'espace, ou proche comme un parent, mais s'approche essentiellement de moi en tant que je me sens – en tant que je suis – responsable de lui. C'est une structure qui ne ressemble nullement alors relation intentionnelle qui nous rattache, dans la connaissance, à l'objet – de quelque objet qu'il s'agisse, fût-ce un objet humain. La proximité ne revient pas à cette intentionnalité; en particulier Elle ne revient pas au fait qu'autrui me soit connu.'

33 'Ce sont là des formules extremes ... beaucoup d'autres considerations interviennent et exigent la justice même pour moi ... Mais la justice n'a de sens que si elle conserve l'esprit de desintéressement qui anime l'idée de la responsabilité pour l'autre homme.'

NOTES TO PP. 51–54

34 My translation from Levinas. Here is the passage from Constance Garnett's translation of Dostoevsky. 'Every one of us is undoubtedly responsible for all men – and everything on earth, not merely through the general sinfulness of creation, but each one personally for all mankind and every individual man. This knowledge is the crown of life for the monk and for every man. For monks are not a special sort of men, but only what all men ought to be' (Garnett translation, Book IV, ch. 1. The translation of 'responsibility' is a matter of discussion among the experts.).

35 See his Talmudic lectures delivered annually to the Congrès des Intellectuels Juifs de Langue Française (Levinas 1994a, 1994b).

36 In fact, in the original French Cherki describes Fanon's opposition between the ideal life – 'épanouissement ou développement d'une fécondité essentielle' – and the reality of the life of the excluded as 'lutte permanente contre une mort atmosphérique' (Alice Cherki: Préface à l'édition de 2002, p. 13) (Fanon 2002).

37 The word for 'one' in Hebrew is composed of three letters. In Hebrew, as in Latin, letters double as numbers, and the three letters of the word for 'one' add up to thirteen.

38 'Hay una profundización de la cultura de la muerte y el dominio; se sigue haciendo de las mujeres el más redituable botín de los señores de la guerra que, en la atávica seducción por la muerte, arrastran a pueblos enteros en luchas de etnías, lenguas y territorios, honras, odios, memorias de ultraje, religiones y delirios ante la mirada impávida del llamado moderno orden internacional. Con gobiernos, instituciones y hasta movimientos sociales deshaciéndose en la corrupción y en la colusión con el submundo de la droga, no sienten como máxima expression de su modelo de democracia, la posibilidad de elegir, pero elegir siempre en el menor de estos males peores.'

39 'Una declaración feminista autónoma: hacer comunidad en la casa de las diferencias' http://feministasautonomasenlucha.blogspot.com

40 '. . . votando como en la falacia de las democracias burguesas, ocultan lógicas patriarcales, niegan las reflexiones que reconocen las diferencias en las ideas.' Posicionamiento Politico ante XI EFLAC: 'A las feministas niñas, mujeres y lesbianas de America Latina y el Caribe', 9 March 2009. http://feministasautonomasenlucha.blogspot.com/2009/03/posicionamiento-politico-ante-el-xi.html

41 '. . . formas innumerables e interconexas de subordinación y colonización de nuestros cuerpos y subjetividades;' from the Declaration of Mujeres Autonomas, Mexico City, 9 May 2009.
'Una declaración feminista autónoma: hacer comunidad en la casa de las diferencias'.

42 'En nuestra genealogía recogemos todas las formas de resistencia activa de nuestras ancestras indígenas y afrodecendientes; el legado del feminismo radical de los años setenta; las experiencias tempranas de los grupos de autoconciencia; . . .; el feminismo situado, descentrado y antirracista del movimiento de mujeres latinas, chicanas y de color en los EEUU que ha tenido su continuidad en Latinoamérica y el Caribe; los aportes de las lesbianas feministas en lucha contra el régimen de la heterosexualidad obligatoria opresiva para todas las mujeres; el reconocimiento de las mujeres como categoría política y no natural tal cual nos lo enseñaron las feministas materialistas; . . .'

NOTES TO PP. 54–62

43 '. . . orgasmo, resistencia, locura, juguetes sexuales, sexo casual, solidaridad, complicidad, vulva, rebeldía, movimiento'. https://www.youtube.com/watch ?v=NOup TvhL34&feature=related

44 'Nuestra autonomía feminista es una postura ante el mundo más que un legajo unívoco de preceptos. La autonomía no se alimenta de dogmas ni mandatos, porque ella escapa a toda regulación y a todo intento de sustraernos de nuestra singularidad y responsabilidad como sujetas históricas comprometidas con otras formas del hacer y del estar en lo íntimo, lo privado y lo público . . .'

45 Esta agenda de derechos mutila en cualquier sujeto su potencial transformador y su fuerza subversiva.' The quotation is from a chapter which is a summary version of Galindo (2013).

46 'Quijano entiende al sexo como atributos biológicos que llegan a ser elaborados como categorías sociales.' The article was originally published in *Tabula Rasa* 9 (2008): 73–101.

47 'Esta cruza es realmente fatal, porque un idioma que era jerárquico, en contacto con el discurso igualitario de la modernidad, se transforma en un orden super jerárquico y [desarraigado], debido a los factores que examinaré. a seguir: la superinflación de los hombres en el ambiente comunitario, en su papel de intermediarios con el mundo exterior, es decir, con la administración del blanco; la emasculación de los hombres en el ambiente extra-comunitario, frente al poder de los administradores blancos; la superinflación y universalización de la esfera pública, habitada ancestralmente por los hombres, con el derrumbe y privatización de la esfera doméstica; y la binarización de la dualidad, resultante de la universalización de uno de sus dos términos cuando constituido como público, en oposición a otro, constituido como privado' (Segato 2014: 78).

48 For example, https://pacifista.tv/notas/mujeres-lideres-colombia-asesinatos-informe/

49 '. . . explotados como productores, pero al mismo tiempo oprimidos colonialmente como sociedad y como cultura'.

50 Her words, https://www.youtube.com/watch?v=dJU1DfUWo3c

51 '[L]a experiencia vivida internalizada reconstituida diariamente, fluida, de alteridades que están en plena colision'.

52 'Mi intención es la de rescatar enseñanzas y utopías de las luchas indígenas para el diseño de una utopía más amplia y compartida, en la que quizás, las mujeres de este continente, en toda nuestra diversidad cultural, podamos encontrar espejos interiores que nos permitan mirarnos en nuestras múltiples dimensiones y construir así la trinchera donde todas/os – mujeres, indios, clases subalternas – podamos dejar por fin de ser extranjeras/os en nuestra propia tierra.'

53 'A rapist in your way', https://www.bbc.com/mundo/noticias-50735010. And https://www.theguardian.com/society/2020/feb/03/the-rapist-is-you-chilean-protest-song-chanted-around-the-world-un-iolador-en-tu-camino

54 'Motley' connotes a chaotic, artless assemblage, whereas both *abigarrado* and 'mottled' have an aesthetically positive connotation. *Abigarrado* passed into common usage after being coined by René Zavaleta, with whom Rivera 'maintained an intense political and intellectual exchange', but his writing is more concerned with the political superstructure, and he did not develop it in a reflection on the country's ethnic and cultural heterogeneity. Followers,

NOTES TO PP. 62–74

however, are careful sometimes to distinguish the term from *heterogéneo* (Gago 2020: xx; Zavaleta Mercado 1986).

55 '... las élites mestizas letradas que se subieron al carro del "proceso de cambio" para envolver en discursos intelectuales de alto fuste lo que es un hecho por demás triste y redundante: la reedición de los estilos políticos del viejo MNR, desde la ch'ampa guerra hasta la división de las organizaciones sociales y el prebendas'.

56 In an interview in *Los Tiempos* on 12 August 2019, she says: 'lo mío es un indianismo anarco feminista.'

57 Most recently, at that time, in her bestselling and prizewinning *Olhos d'água* (2015).

58 'I am not saying that a Maori anthropologist has epistemic privileges over a New Zealand anthropologist of Anglo descent (or a British or US anthropologist). I am saying that a New Zealand anthropologist of Anglo descent has no right to guide the "locals" in what is good or bad for the Maori population. The decolonial and the anthropological are two distinct options. The former puts disciplinary tools at the service of the problem being addressed. The latter tends to put the problem at the service of the discipline' (Mignolo 2011: 137–8).

59 See the website of the Vaccine Confidence Project at the London School of Hygiene and Tropical Medicine, https://www.vaccineconfidence.org

60 The survey used *Understanding Society*, 'the UK's largest household survey'.

61 https://www.pewresearch.org/fact-tank/2016/11/09/how-the-faithful-voted-a-preliminary-2016-analysis/ft16-11-09religexitpollreligrace/

62 As an analogy, consider the ultra-Orthodox Jewish women who, in the face of incredulity when they tell people that they abstain from bodily contact with their husbands or any other man for two weeks every month throughout their menstrual cycle, explain that it makes the sex better. Maybe, but that is not the reason for the taboo.

Chapter 2 Indigeneity, Gender and Law

1 As well as a distinguished scholar, Stavenhagen was an indefatigable defender of indigenous causes worldwide, holding the position of UN Rapporteur on Indigenous Peoples between 2001 and 2008. He died in 2016.

2 For him, the religion and magical practices prevalent in indigenous communities were a cover for economic and political manipulation through labour contributions and fiesta obligations: 'la cultura mágico-religiosa y manipulación económica (que es la realidad del tequio y de la economía de prestigio) y, también . . . manipulación política' (González Casanova 1965: 107).

3 Funded in 1939, the INAH is responsible for 162 museums and 52,000 'zonas arqueológicas' and employs 400 academic staff plus the thousands of administrative and support staff required to manage and operate archaeological sites and its higher education branch, the Escuela Nacional de Antropología e Historia; cf. Luis Vázquez: *El Leviatán Arqueológico* (Vázquez León 2003). It must be among the largest institutions of its kind in the world.

4 Centro de Investigaciones y Estudios Superiores en Antropología Social. Today CIESAS employs some 180 research staff, not only anthropologists.

193

NOTES TO PP. 75–84

5 Echeverría somehow distracted attention from his human rights crimes by adopting a vociferous Third Worldist rhetoric in international affairs while president as well as continuing the PRI's time-honoured practice of co-opting left-wing intellectuals by for example arranging the election of the Gonzalez Casanova as Rector of the gargantuan UNAM (National Autonomous University) whose student numbers passed 100,000 as he took office. Many years later, aged 96, Casanova would provide further evidence of his reptilian political abilities, when the EZLN conferred on him a new name and an honour as 'Comandante Pablo Contreras del CCRI-Comandancia General del Ejército Zapatista de Liberación Nacional' in recognition of his 'critical and independent thought and work'. La Jornada, 22 April 2018 (found in Wikipedia).

6 President Fox (2001–2007) renamed the INI as the CDI (Comisión de Desarrollo para el Desarrollo de los Pueblos Indígenas) and later Andrés Manuel Lopez Obrador (elected in 2018) renamed it again as the Instituto Nacional de Pueblos Indígenas (INPI).

7 Despite much fanfare to flatter the US president, the new treaty was largely unchanged from NAFTA.

8 'Although it seems that Marcos does not speak an Indian language, he began to speak like the Indians. Or rather, he began to speak in a way that the urban population imagines that Indians speak: a strange mixture of expressions in archaic, Chiapanecan Spanish, the syntax of Indians in western movies and motifs from the European romantic, pastoral genre' (Pitarch 2004: 298).

9 In Chile, you are entitled to a benefit targeted for indigenous beneficiaries, including land allocation, if you have one grandparent who lived in a comunidad indígena (see below, p. 115).

10 Notably the highly contentious case arising from the death of the elderly couple Werner Luchsinger and Vivianne Mackay in a fire at their farm in January 2013. The case dragged on and on and was highly politicized with prolonged imprisonment of the equally elderly machi Francisca Linconao, in the Temuco jail where she was still held in late 2017.

11 I use the Spanish word in preference to 'colonist' which might lead to some confusion.

12 Tello's book, published barely a year after the 1994 uprising, was suspected of being written with the help of privileged access to police archives. Indeed, the abundance of names and aliases, and the lack of sources apart from newspapers, lend some credence to those suspicions. But the information is nevertheless useful and the tone is not tendentious.

13 'Les doy a vds. la tierra y todo lo que he hecho. Les doy un buen pensamiento en su corazón para que gobiernen toda la tierra y sean Vds. los dueños,' cf. Genesis 13:15.

14 '. . . la resurrección no del indígena sino de nuestra sociedad, está en el indígena'.

15 Zapatismo enjoys a faithful following among anthropologists and other academics, like Harvey, a political scientist. Their writings are not written in a propagandistic way, yet the undertone of sympathy and, in some publications like this one, the lack of detail or evidence of a systematic approach to the evidence, prevents me from being fully convinced. The material presented always seems to fit the 'official line'. The contrast between the deference of the literature on the Zapatistas and the treatment of Evo Morales is striking,

NOTES TO PP. 84–94

cf. the books reviewed by Alderman or Nancy Postero's 2017 book (Alderman 2020; Postero 2017)

16 In Brazil, the term does not work because the main ethnic-racial issue of racial exclusion is not a cultural one in any strong sense, while the indigenous peoples are set aside, in the official system, in separate institutional and territorial compartments, as we shall see below, and the policy (pre-2018) has aimed to preserve their integrity rather than encourage mutual interchange like *interculturalidad*.

17 See the website of Science-Based Medicine, https://sciencebasedmedicine. org/?s=measles&categoryname=&submit=Search

18 '[T]he last thing one wants at this stage from Eurocentered intellectuals is positive judgments of the worth of cultures that they have not intensively studied. For real judgments of worth suppose a fused horizon of standards, as we have seen; they suppose that we have been transformed by the study of the other, so that we are not simply judging by our original familiar standards. A favorable judgment made prematurely would be not only condescending but ethnocentric. It would praise the other for being like us' (Taylor 1992: 70–1).

19 'En vez de reificar "los saberes" como tales, una mirada procesual y "migratoria" logra descifrar cómo los diversos actores-emisores de discursos no son simples "portadores" de saberes, sino que los generan nutriéndose de muy heterogéneas fuentes discursivas como las aquí analizadas.'

20 Thus the 'diálogo de saberes' (dialogue of knowledges) formula is foregrounded, but immediately qualified by the observation that those 'saberes' draw on heterogeneous sources ('nutriéndose de muy heterogéneas fuentes') (Dietz and Mateos Cortés 2011: 169). 'La tensión bipolar entre indigenismo y normalismo, entre particularismo étnico y universalismo nacionalista, la superan estos actores [i.e. the academics – DL] mediante la importación de un discurso desesencializado, constructivista y transversalizador de la interculturalidad. Como sinónimo de "diversidad de diversidades", sus respectivas pantallas reflejan una noción abierta y dinámica de lo intercultural, que se mantiene de forma dialógica, reflexiva y autocrítica más allá de la dicotomía identitaria indígena-mestizo. Por último, los actores que promueven proyectos alternativos y/o 'autónomos' de educación intercultural ... [A]caban generando discursos alternativos, mucho más críticos con la interculturalidad exógena y más enfocados hacia el empoderamiento de los sujetos subalternos, de las comunidades con las que colaboran' (pp. 161–2).

21 '... la interculturalidad se concibe más como una vía adecuada a la realidad social heterogénea, abriendo la posibilidad de enraizar la educación en y a partir de la propia cultura, que promueva un diálogo crítico y creativo entre tradiciones diferentes'.

22 A new Article 4 was introduced as follows: 'La Nación tiene una composición pluricultural sustentada originalmente en sus pueblos indígenas que son aquellos que descienden de poblaciones que habitaban en el territorio actual del país al iniciarse la colonización y que conservan sus propias instituciones sociales, económicas, culturales y políticas, o parte de ellas.'

23 I observed this at first hand when Emilio Rabasa – occupant of this position – took part in an event in Cambridge to defend the government's policy in his capacity as secretary of COCOPA, the body nominally charged with applying the accords.

NOTES TO PP. 98–115

24 The series is entitled 'Cuaderno de Texto de primer grado del curso de la Escuelita "La Libertad segun l@s Zapatistas"', and the booklets are: *Gobierno Autónomo I, Gobierno Autónomo II, Participación de las Mujeres en el Gobierno Autónomo, Resistencia Autónoma.* Published by Ediciones Autónomas, Chiapas, 2013.

25 An ancient Sanskrit epic which was serialized with phenomenal success on Indian television in the late 1980s.

26 The Census question in 2018 asked 'De acuerdo con su cultura, pueblo o rasgos físicos, Vd. se reconoce como . . .?' There followed six possibilities, of which one was 'indígena' and another was 'negro, mulato, afrodescendiente', all bundled together.

27 See also the book produced by CRIC intellectuals and published by the country's Centro de Memoria Histórica (Bolaños et al. 2012).

28 Colombia's 1992 Constitution includes the following provisions: 'Indigenous office-holders may exercise judicial functions within their territorial areas in accordance with their own rules and procedures, so long as they are not contrary to the Constitution and laws of the Republic. The law shall establish the forms whereby coordination of this special jurisdiction will conform to the national judicial system (Article 246).' And 'In accordance with the Constitution and laws of the country, indigenous territories shall be governed by councils whose membership and procedures will be established in accordance with the customs and traditions of the communities (Article 330)' (official translation).

29 This term refers to the idea of a superior system of norms and values and therefore of Law (*derecho mayor*).

30 Originally legislation was intended to define *quilombos* in these terms, but slave descent is very difficult to establish, and over time the official definition has changed to denote a community in a broad sense. This has facilitated land redistribution, but the process remains complex and lengthy (Lehmann 2016c).

31 It should be added that since the advent of Bolsonaro, officials in these institutions have been stopped from fulfilling their mission and senior management positions have been left unfilled.

32 '. . . suas autodeclarações como negros foram fruto da construção de referenciais sociais relevantes e indicativos de um comportamento pautado pela boa-fé'. The report was posted on the UFMG website on 26 February 2021. https://ufmg.br/comunicacao/noticias/ufmg-decide-por-desligamento-de-22-estudantes-que-fraudaram-sistema-de-cotas?fbclid=IwAR0FlyPJFqwIqsgNF83IhQeF6kX_Y8UeFWzicwSXdLvii9-wmnJVg59dzAM

33 From a video produced by the university and reproduced by local newspaper *BHAZ* on 4 June 2020. https://bhaz.com.br/2020/06/04/fraude-cota-racial/#gref

34 The Planning Ministry's Personnel Management Secretariat (Secretaria de Gestão de Pessoas e Relações do Trabalho no Serviço Público do Ministério do Planejamento, Desenvolvimento e Gestão) issued 'Orientação Normativa no. 3, on 1 August 2016, governing commissions to check on declarations of 'racial identity' (not, note, of 'skin colour') which stipulated that only a candidate's 'phenotypical features' should be taken into account and that they should be checked in the presence of the candidate (Guimarães 2018).

35 The Decree is headed as follows: 'Aprueba reglamento que regula la

196

NOTES TO PP. 117–133

acreditacion de calidad de indigena, para la constitucion de comunidades indigenas y para la proteccion del patrimonio historico de las culturas indigenas' (Ministry of Planning and Cooperation).

36 A study by Adison Altamirano y Alejandro Miranda, of the Laboratorio de Ecología del Paisaje del Departamento de Ciencias Forestales of the Universidad de la Frontera, found that 19% of Chile's virgin forest (bosque bosque nativo) had been lost in the last 40 years, equivalent to 780,000 hectares. Sebastián Balcazar and Yasna Mussa: 'Chile: ¿un modelo forestal peligroso?', *Mongabay* LATAM, 14 February 2017. https://es.mongabay.com/2017/02/chile-modelo-forestal-peligroso/

Chapter 3 Religion and Culture: Popular, Indigenous and Hegemonic

1 The uprising's shock troops (armed with little more than their faith) were called the 'doze pares de França' – the 'twelve peers of France' celebrated in medieval legend and later mythology as Charlemagne's 'paladins'. The term 'literature de cordel', translated as chapbooks, derives from the string on which the pamphlets are hung in market stalls.

2 Because their eyes are surrounded by dark circles.

3 See the earlier discussion of Silvia Rivera's account of Andean kinship.

4 Still in 2019, a president at war with anything he could label left-wing lost no opportunity to denigrate Chico Buarque, now in his seventies but still an emblem of cultural and political dissidence.

5 'Asi como no funciona la oposición abrupta entre lo tradicional y lo moderno, tampoco lo culto, lo popular y lo masivo están donde nos habituamos a encontrarlos. Es necesario desconstruir esa división en tres pisos, esa concepción hojaldrada del mundo de la cultura, y averiguar si su *hibridación* puede leerse con las herramientas de las disciplinas que los estudian por separado: la historia del arte y la literatura, que se ocupan de lo "culto"; el folclor y la antropología, consagrados a lo popular; los trabajos sobre comunicación, especializados en la cultura masiva. Necesitamos ciencias sociales nómadas, capaces de circular por las escaleras que comunican esos pisos. O mejor: que rediseñen los planos y comuniquen horizontalmente los niveles.'

6 Here is the original Spanish: 'Cuando se define a una identidad mediante un proceso de abstracción de rasgos ... se tiende a menudo a desprender esas prácticas de la historia de mezclas en que se formaron. Como consecuencia se absolutiza un modo de entender la identidad y se rechazan maneras heterodoxos de hablar la lengua, hacer música ... Se acaba, en suma, obturando la posibilidad de modificar la cultura y la política ... La historia de los movimientos identitarios revela una serie de operaciones de selección de elementos de épocas distintas articulados por los grupos hegemónicos en un relato que les da coherencia, dramaticidad y elocuencia.'

7 That is to say, Indians assigned to townships (*reducciones*) in the sixteenth to eighteenth centuries, whose *caciques* were employed to provide the *mita*, forced labour in mines.

8 '[E]se pozo de gas "es un regalo de nuestra Pachamama para todas y todos los bolivianos"', in an article published by SERVINDI on 6 January 2021

197

NOTES TO PP. 135–148

https://www.servindi.org/actualidad-opinion/05/01/2021/pachamama-pacha
mamistas-y-otras-etiquetas-unas-notas-de-cautela

9 As described for Cuzco by Marisol de la Cadena (de la Cadena 2000, 2004).

10 Albó's precise words are as follows: 'En concreto, los grupos vinculados con clase media ascendiente y los potentes "residentes" (=inmigrantes urbanos) de los pueblos mestizos (no de las comunidades) bailan morenada, . . . Lo que más realza la sofisticación y costo de la coreografía (paradójicamente inspirada al principio en ·esclavos negros encadenados) es el mayor prestigio logrado; algo que, con todo, siempre se dice en un contexto simbólico andino: estos grupos emergentes no se visten de terno ni bailan rock o valses.'

11 The Peruvian military seized power in 1968, immediately nationalized the International Petroleum Company and soon afterwards decreed a radical land reform, seizing the then most advanced sector of agriculture, the sugar plantations, in an overnight raid. At the same time they announced the abandonment of the term *indio* and its replacement by *campesino* (peasant) while also decreeing that indigenous languages could be used on official business, such as in judicial proceedings, and making the figure of Tupac Amaru the symbol of the land reform.

12 The brainchild of General Barrientos, an ally of the United States, which during that period was very active in clandestine operations in Bolivia, not least the murder of Che Guevara in 1967. He died in a helicopter crash in 1969.

13 The leader of that interlude, General Juan José Torres, was murdered in Buenos Aires in 1976.

14 'Covering the Andean parts of Bolivia, the southern parts of Peru, northern Chile, and northern Argentina, Qullasuyu was one of the four *suyus* of Tawantinsuyu, the Inca territory' (Burman 2014: 268).

15 In an interview in *Los Tiempos* (La Paz) published on 12 August 2019, before Morales's last election, Rivera says of the origins of THOA, in a throwaway phrase that reflects the relationship between social movements and the international NGO community: 'Luego vino un gringo de Oxfam y le encantó nuestro plan [Then along came a gringo from Oxfam and he just loved our plan].' Richard Chase-Smith of OXFAM America has confirmed to me that he was the 'gringo'. In his words 'I wasn't any old gringo, I had lived for almost 15 years among the Yanesha people in the upper Amazon of Peru and had played a role in the founding of the indigenous peoples movement in Peru and in the whole Amazon. And I had a PhD in Anthropology as a student of John Murra at Cornell . . . My relationship with Silvia and THOA began in 1985 and went on for 15 years or more' (email, October 2020).

16 A stimulating and varied collection of writings from the period is freely available from the CLACSO website (Rivera Cusicanqui and Aillón Soria 2015).

17 According to Gutiérrez in 1999, Morales's allies persuaded the Christian NGO 'Pan para el Mundo' to cut off support for the CSUTCB because Quispe was opposing him (Gutiérrez Aguilar 2008: 123).

18 '[L]a alternancia de contrarios' or 'la vuelta o inversion del tiempo y del espacio'.

19 An 'explicitación del horizonte interior anidado contradictoriamente en el tejido comunitario'.

20 The source quoted is Raquel Gutiérrez in a personal communication.

21 I am aware that the validity of the 2019 presidential election is a matter of

NOTES TO PP. 148–159

dispute, so I have refrained from mentioning it since it is only marginally relevant to this discussion.

22 World Bank Database: https://data.worldbank.org/indicator/NY.GDP.PCAP. CD?end=2018&locations=BO&start=1961

23 'On May 7, 2011, the Depatriarchalization Unit of Bolivia's Vice Ministry of Decolonization brought together 355 indigenous couples to be married in a big public coliseum, the Coliseo Cerrado, in El Alto, a mostly Aymara city perched on the high plateau above Bolivia's capital, La Paz. There, in a grand spectacle of 'indigenous' religious and ethnic pride, the couples were wedded in a ceremony officiated by Andean religious experts called amautas. President Evo Morales played the role of padrino, or godfather, to all the couples' (Postero 2017: 64).

Chapter 4 From Popular Culture to the Cultures of the People: Evangelical Christianity as a Challenge to the Decolonial

1 On the difference between charismatic and fundamentalist variants, see Martin 2001; Lehmann 2011.

2 Consejo Latinoamericano de Ciencias Sociales (Latin American Social Sciences Council). A social science centre founded in 1967 which runs courses and publishes books and other materials. CLACSO adopts a strongly left-wing posture but remains a platform for the social sciences in general. CLACSO played an invaluable part in rescuing academics in the wake of the 1973 coup in Chile.

3 https://www.youtube.com/watch?v=e b7TC1Jbto

4 This is an imitation of the Catholic Eucharist, but normally without the doctrine of transubstantiation, which Pentecostals reject as 'pagan'.

5 https://www1.folha.uol.com.br/poder/2019/08/igreja-universal-expande-acoes-sociais-e-ocupa-espacos-ignorados-pelo-poder-publico.shtml

6 https://recordtv.r7.com/balanco-geral/videos/tratamento-para-vicio-das-drogas-cura-tres-milhoes-de-pessoas-21102018

7 Unlike the majority of Pentecostal political figures, Macedo did in the past publicly take up a pro-abortion stance on the grounds that people should not have more children than they can responsibly bring up (Moraes Teixeira 2012: 90–120; Teixeira 2014). However, perhaps due to the toxicity of the subject among evangelical preachers and their public, he has not mentioned it more recently.

8 'Faculdade' is a status below that of Universidade although this institution aims to become a fully-fledged university and is already offering courses in various branches of management. The Faculdade is funded by 20 per cent of the state funding accorded to the PRB (i.e. state funding of political parties) which has been its legal sponsor since November 2018, the person named as rector on an interim basis was also the leader/coordinator of the Party's youth department and is involved in IURD's youth movement (Força Jovem Universal), *Estado de São Paulo*, 11 November 2018. https://faculda-derepublicana.org.br/

9 https://oglobo.globo.com/brasil/bolsonaro-vai-ao-templo-de-salomao-e-aben coado-por-edir-macedo-23920121

10 Report by Vitória Régia da Silva from the project 'Religião e Poder' of the

199

NOTES TO PP. 159–183

Instituto Superior de Estudos da Religião (ISER). http://religiaoepolitica.com.br/eleitos-nomes-religiosos-14-2020/

11 *Censo Demográfico 2010* – Table 1.4.13: Pessoas de 10 anos ou mais de idade, residentes em domicílios particulares, por grandes grupos de religião, segundo o sexo e as classes de rendimento nominal mensal domiciliar per capita.

12 https://g1.globo.com/politica/noticia/2020/01/13/50percent-dos-brasileiros-sao-catolicos-31percent-evangelicos-e-10percent-nao--datafolha.ghtml

13 '. . . entre o que crê, o que aceita e o que abomina, transita pelo mundo da religião popular de acordo com as circunstâncias da vida profana e com os convites dos agentes de culto.'

14 Pesquisa Datafolha (Datafolha Survey), 25 October 2018.

15 San Cristobal has since become a much bigger city and the former outlying neighbourhoods have merged into its urban sprawl. http://www.scielo.org.mx/scielo.php?script=sci arttext&pid=S0188-77422012000200008

16 On 28 November 2019, the Swiss Federal Supreme Court (FSC) upheld Erwin Sperisen's sentence to 15 years in prison. In April 2018, the Geneva Court of Justice had found the former head of the Guatemalan police (PNC) guilty of being an accomplice to the murder of seven detainees of the Pavón prison in 2006, *Le Temps* (Geneva), 28 November 2019.

Conclusion

1 https://www.nodal.am/2021/03/carta-abierta-a-dos-jovenes-indigenas-ecuatorianos-por-boaventura-de-sousa-santos/.

2 Sen studied the catastrophic famine wartime colonial Bengal, transforming the basis for the modern study of the subject by showing that they were not caused by shortfalls in food production but by actions of the colonial government that raised prices by diverting supplies to the war effort in Burma. He then compared post-Independence India and China and reached the uncomfortable conclusion that whereas India, as a democracy needing to avoid instability, had avoided famine by massive reserve stockpiles, the Chinese system had achieved far greater success in poverty reduction, even under Mao, yet that same system had also created conditions for appalling famine during the industrialization and collectivization drives in the 1950s. Later, he developed a concept of capabilities as part of his conceptualization of freedom and justice (Alkire 2002; Sen 1981, 1988, 2001).

3 Since it is assumed that anyone who can afford to would send their children to a private school, the state school criterion is a rough proxy for 'low-income'. The assumption has not been systematically tested.

4 https://ufmg.br/comunicacao/noticias/ufmg-decide-por-desligamento-de-22-est udantes-que-fraudaram-sistema-de-cotas?fbclid=IwAR0FlyPJFqwIqsgNF83Ih QeF6kX_Y8UeFWzicwSXdLvii9-wmnJVg59dzAM

5 https://www.youtube.com/watch?v=e_b7TC1Jbto

6 The article in *Critical Times* is a translation of the Introduction to *La Guerra Contra las Mujeres*. Both are available as open access.

7 https://blogs.opovo.com.br/ancoradouro/2010/08/20/vou-abrir-minha-igreja-e-ja-volto/
The original article appeared in the *Folha de São Paulo*, c. 10 February 2011.

200

NOTES TO PP. 184–186

8 Statements by the Executive Secretary of CEPAL, the UN Economic Commission for Latin America and the Caribbean, *El Mostrador* (Chile), 4 March 2021.
9 'Theology with your feet on the ground': title of a 1984 book by Clodovis Boff (Boff 1984).

References

Abercrombie, Thomas. 1991. 'To be Indian, to be Bolivian: "ethnic" and "national" discourses of identity', in G. Urban and J. Sherzer (eds), *Nation-States and Indians in Latin America*, Austin: University of Texas Press, pp. 95–130.

Abercrombie, Thomas. 1992. 'La fiesta del carnaval postcolonial en Oruro: Clase, etnicidad y nacionalismo en la danza folklórica'. *Revista Andina* 20: 279–325.

Abercrombie, Thomas. 2003. 'Mothers and mistresses of the urban Bolivian public sphere: postcolonial predicament and national imaginary in Oruro's carnival', in Mark Thurner and Andrés Guerrero (eds), *After Spanish Rule: Postcolonial Predicaments of the Americas*. Durham, NC: Duke University Press, pp. 176–220.

Adorno, Rolena. 2001. *Guaman Poma and His Illustrated Chronicle of Colonial Peru: From a Century of Scholarship to a New Era of Reading [Guaman Poma y su crónica ilustrada del Perú colonial: un siglo de investigaciones hacia una nueva era de lectura]*. Bilingual edn in English and Spanish: Museum Tusculanum Press, University of Copenhagen and the Royal Library. http://wayback-01.kb.dk/wayback/20101126102603/http:/www2.kb.dk/elib/mss/poma/presentation/pres.htm.

Agier, Michel. 2000. *Anthropologie du carnaval: la ville, la fête et l'Afrique à Bahia*. Marseilles: Parenthèses.

Aguado, Teresa and Malik, Beatriz. 2009. 'Intercultural education in higher education: challenges and opportunities'. *Intercultural Education* 20(3): 201–2.

Aimé, Charles-Nicolas. 2006. 'L'actualité de Frantz Fanon, psychiatre martiniquais'. *VST – Vie sociale et traitements* 89(1): 37–42. https://dx.doi.org/10.3917/vst.089.42.

Alabrese, Eleonora, Becker, Sascha O., Fetzer, Thiemo and Novy, Dennis. 2019. 'Who voted for Brexit? Individual and regional data combined'. *European Journal of Political Economy* 56 (2019/01/01/): 132–50. https://dx.doi.org/https://doi.org/10.1016/j.ejpoleco.2018.08.002.

Albó, Xavier. 1992. 'Comentario sobre Abercrombie'. *Revista Andina* 20: 326–31.

Alderman, Jonathan. 2020. 'Unpacking disavowals of indigeneity in Bolivia'. *Latin American and Caribbean Ethnic Studies* 15(4): 430–8. https://dx.doi.org/10.1080/17442222.2020.1799492.

REFERENCES

Algranti, Joaquín. 2018. 'The making of an evangelical prison: study on neo-Pentecostalism and its leadership processes in the Argentine penitentiary system'. *Social Compass* 65(5): 1–17. https://dx.doi.org/doi.org/10.1177/0037768618800417

Alkire, Sabina. 2002. *Valuing Freedoms: Sen's Capability Approach and Poverty Reduction.* Oxford: Oxford University Press.

Andolina, Robert, Laurie, Nina and Radcliffe, Sarah A. 2009. *Indigenous Development in the Andes: Culture, Power, and Transnationalism.* Durham, NC and London: Duke University Press.

Andrade, Susana. 2004. *Protestantismo Indígena: procesos de conversión religiosa en la provincia de Chimborazo, Ecuador.* Quito: FLACSO, Abya Yala, Institut Français d'Etudes Andines.

Andreucci, Diego and Radhuber, Isabella M. 2017. 'Limits to "counter-neoliberal" reform: Mining expansion and the marginalisation of post-extractivist forces in Evo Morales's Bolivia'. *Geoforum* 84: 280–91. https://dx.doi.org/https://doi.org/10.1016/j.geoforum.2015.09.002.

Aragón Andrade, Orlando. 2013. 'El derecho en insurrección. El uso contrahegemónico del derecho en el movimiento purépecha de cherán.' *Revista de Estudos e Pesquisas sobre as Américas* (University of Brasilia) 7(2): 37–69.

Araujo, Victor Augusto. 2019. 'A religião distrai os pobres? Pentecostalismo e voto redistributivo no Brasil'. University of São Paulo.

Arteaga Böhrt, Ana Cecilia. 2017. '"Caminemos juntos": complementariedad *chacha-warmi* y autonomías indígenas en Bolivia', in Rachel Sieder (ed.), *Exigiendo justicia y seguridad: Mujeres indígenas y pluralidades legales en América Latina.* México, DF: CIESAS, pp. 159–85.

Artigas, Edda Gavida. 1997. 'Introducción: el VII Encuentro Feminista de Latinoamérica y el Caribe, Chile '96', in Ximena Bedregal (ed.), *Permanencia Voluntaria en la Utopía: la autonomía en el VII Encuentro Feminista Latinoamericano y del Caribe.* Centro de Investigación y Capacitación de la Mujer, pp. 11–25.

Atran, Scott. 2003. *In Gods We Trust: The Evolutionary Landscape of Religion.* New York: Oxford University Press.

Bacigalupo, Ana Mariella. 2004. 'Shamans' pragmatic gendered negotiations with Mapuche resistance movements and Chilean political authorities'. *Identities* 11(4): 501–41. https://dx.doi.org/10.1080/10702890490883849.

Baronnet, Bruno. 2011. 'La question de l'interculturalité dans les expériences d'éducation en terres zapatistes', in Christian Gros and David Dumoulin Kervran (ed.), *Le multiculturalisme au concret: un modèle latinoaméricain?* Paris: Presses Sorbonne Nouvelle.

Baronnet, Bruno. 2015. 'Derecho a la educación y autonomía zapatista en Chiapas, México'. *Convergencia Revista de Ciencias Sociales* 67: 85–110. http://www.scielo.org.mx/pdf/conver/v22n67/v22n67a4.pdf.

Bayer, Osvaldo. 1972. *Los vengadores de la Patagonia trágica.* Buenos Aires: Editorial Galerna.

Bedregal, Ximena (ed.). 1997. *Permanencia Voluntaria en la Utopía: la autonomía en el VII Encuentro Feminista Latinoamericano y del Caribe.* Colección Feminismos Cómplices: Centro de Investigación y Capacitación de la Mujer. https://fr.scribd.com/doc/42673016/permanencia-de-La-Utopia.

Bello, Alvaro. 2011. *Nampülkafe: el viaje de los mapuches de la Araucanía a*

203

REFERENCES

las pampas argentinas: territorio, política y cultura en los siglos XIX y XX. Temuco: Ediciones Universidad Católica de Temuco.

Bengoa, José. 1985. *Historia del Pueblo Mapuche (Siglo XIX y XX).* Santiago: Ediciones Sur.

Bengoa, José. 2014. *Mapuche, colonos y estado nacional.* Santiago: Catalonia.

Berger, Peter L. 1999. *The Desecularization of the World: Resurgent Religion and World Politics.* Grand Rapids, MI.: W. B. Eerdmans.

Biderman, Ciro and Guimarães, Nadya Araujo. 2004. 'Na ante-sala da discriminação: o preço dos atributos de sexo e cor no Brasil (1989–1999)'. *Estudos Feministas (Florianópolis)* 12(2): 177–200.

Birman, Patricia. 1996. 'Cultos de possessão e pentecostalismo no Brasil; Passagens'. *Religião e Sociedade* 17(1–2): 90–108.

Birman, Patricia. 1998. 'Cultes de Possession et Pentecôtisme au Brésil: Passages'. *Cahiers du Brésil Contemporain* 35–6: 185–208.

Birman, Patricia and Lehmann, David. 1999. 'Religion and the media in a battle for ideological hegemony'. *Bulletin of Latin American Research* 18(2): 145–64.

Bloch, Maurice. 2004. 'Ritual and deference', in James Laidlaw and Harvey Whitehouse (eds), *Ritual and Memory: Toward a Comparative Anthropology of Religion.* Lanham: Altamira Press/Rowman and Littlefield.

Bloch, Maurice. 2007. 'Durkheimian anthropology and religion: going in and out of each other's bodies', in Harvey Whitehouse and James Laidlaw (eds), *Religion, Anthropology and Cognitive Science.* Durham, NC: Carolina Academic Press.

Boccara, Guillaume and Ayala, Patricia. 2011. 'Patrimonializar al indígena. Imaginación del multiculturalismo neoliberal en Chile'. *Cahiers des Amériques Latines* 67. https://dx.doi.org/10.4000/cal.361.

Boccara, Guillaume and Seguel-Boccara, Ingrid. 1999. 'Políticas indígenas en Chile (siglos XIX y XX): de la asimilación al pluralismo – el caso Mapuche'. *Revista de Indias* 59(217): 741–74. http://journals.openedition.org/nuevo-mundo/594.

Boff, Clodovis. 1984. *Teologia Pé-no-chão.* Petropolis: Editora Vozes.

Bolaños, Graciela, Bonilla, Víctor Daniel, Fula, Jorge Caballero, et al. 2012. *Nuestra Vida ha Sido Nuestra Lucha: Resistencia y Memoria en el Cauca Indígena.* Bogota: Centro de Memoria Histórica.

Bolaños, Graciela, Tattay, Libia and Pancho, Avelina. 2009. 'Universidad Autónoma, Indígena e Intercultural (UAIIN): un proceso para fortalecer la educación propia y comunitaria en el marco de la interculturalidad [Colombia]', in Daniel Mato (ed.), *Instituciones Interculturales de Educación Superior en América Latina: procesos de construcción, logros, innovaciones y desafíos.* Caracas: IESALC-UNESCO (IES/2009/ED/PI/87), pp. 155–90.

Bonfil Batalla, Guillermo. 1987. *México Profundo: Una Civilización Negada.* México: Grijalbo.

Bourdieu, Pierre. 1984. *Homo academicus.* Paris: Minuit.

Bourdieu, Pierre. 1990. *Homo academicus,* trans. Peter Collier. Cambridge: Polity Press.

Boyer, Pascal. 2001. *Religion Explained: The Human Instincts that Fashion Gods, Spirits and Ancestors.* London: Heinemann.

Boyer, Véronique. 1996. 'Possession et exorcisme dans une Église pentecôtiste au Brésil'. *Cahiers des Sciences Humaines* 32(2) (01/01): 243–64.

REFERENCES

Boyer, Véronique. 2014. 'Misnaming social conflict: "identity", land and family histories in a Quilombola community in the Brazilian Amazon'. *Journal of Latin American Studies* 46(3): 527–55.

Boyer, Véronique. 2016. 'The demand for recognition and access to citizenship: ethnic labelling as a driver of territorial restructuring in Brazil', in David Lehmann (ed.), *The Crisis of Multiculturalism in Latin America*. New York: Palgrave Macmillan.

Boyer, Véronique. Forthcoming. 'Le choix en vertu du "mélange": mobilisations sociales, revendications politiques et positionnements identitaires en Amazonie brésilienne'.

Brablec, Dana. 2019. 'Relational goods and endurance of voluntary associational participation: the case of the indigenous mapuche in Santiago de Chile'. *Bulletin of Latin American Research* 38(2): 222–36. https://dx.doi.org/10.1111/blar.12837.

Brading, D. A. 2001. *Mexican Phoenix: Our Lady of Guadalupe: Image and Tradition across Five Centuries*. Cambridge: Cambridge University Press.

Braga, Maria Lúcia de Santana and da Silveira, Maria Helena Vargas (eds). 2007. *O Programa Diversidade na Universidade e a Construção de uma Política Educacional Anti-Racista*. Brasilia: UNESCO/MEC/BIDÙ. http://unesdoc.unesco.org/images/0015/001545/154582por.pdf.

Brandão, Carlos Rodrigues. 2007 (1980). *Os Deuses do Povo: um estudo sobre a religião popular* (new and unabridged edn). Uberlândia: Editora da Universidade Federal de Uberlândia.

Brennan, Timothy. 2021. *Places of Mind: A Life of Edward Said*. New York: Farrar Strauss.

Brenneman, Robert E. 2012. *Homies and Hermanos: God and the Gangs in Central America*. New York: Oxford University Press.

Brubaker, Rogers. 2016. *Trans: Gender and Race in an Age of Unsettled Identities*: Princeton, NJ: Princeton University Press. http://www.jstor.org/stable/j.ctt1wf4ckd.

Brunegger, Sandra. 2011. 'Legal imaginaries: recognizing indigenous law in Colombia'. *Studies in Law, Politics and Society* 55: 77–100.

Burke, Peter. 1978. *Popular Culture in Early Modern Europe*. New York and London: Harper & Row.

Burke, Peter. 1997. 'Carnival in the Old World and the New', in *Varieties of Cultural History*. Cambridge: Polity Press.

Burman, Anders. 2011. 'Chachawarmi: silence and rival voices on decolonisation and Gender politics in Andean Bolivia'. *Journal of Latin American Studies* 43(1): 65–91. https://dx.doi.org/10.1017/S0022216X10001793.

Burman, Anders. 2014. '"Now we are Indígenas": hegemony and indigeneity in the Bolivian Andes'. *Latin American and Caribbean Ethnic Studies* 9(3): 247–71. https://dx.doi.org/10.1080/17442222.2014.959775.

Calderón, Fernando and Castells, Manuel. 2020. *The New Latin America*. Cambridge: Polity Press.

Cândido, Antônio. 1970. 'Dialética da Malandragem'. *Revista Do Instituto De Estudos Brasileiros* 8: 67–89. https://dx.doi.org/https://doi.org/10.11606/issn.2316-901X.v0i8p67-89.

Canessa, Andrew. 2010. 'Dreaming of fathers: Fausto Reinaga and indigenous masculinism'. *Latin American and Caribbean Ethnic Studies* 5(2): 175–87. https://dx.doi.org/10.1080/17442221003787100.

REFERENCES

Canessa, Andrew. 2016. 'Paradoxes of multiculturalism in Bolivia', in David Lehmann (ed.), *The Crisis of Multiculturalism in Latin America*. New York: Palgrave Macmillan.

Carranza, Brenda and Vital Da Cunha, Christina. 2018. 'Conservative religious activism in the Brazilian Congress: Sexual agendas in focus'. *Social Compass* 65(4): 486–502. https://dx.doi.org/10.1177/0037768618792810.

Cerda, Rodrigo. 2017. 'Situación socioeconómica reciente de los mapuches: 2009–2015', in Isabel Aninat, Verónica Figueroa and Ricardo González (eds), *El pueblo mapuche en el siglo XXI: propuestas para un nuevo entendimiento entre culturas en Chile*. Santiago: Centro de Estudios Públicos.

Cervone, Emma, and Cucurí M., Cristina. 2017. 'Desigualdad de género, justicia indígena y Estado intercultural en Chimborazo, Ecuador', in Rachel Sieder (ed.), *Exigiendo justicia y seguridad: Mujeres indígenas y pluralidades legales en América Latina*. Mexico, DF: CIESAS, pp. 126–58.

Crenshaw, Kimberle. 1989. 'Demarginalizing the intersection of race and sex: a black feminist critique of antidiscrimination doctrine, feminist theory and antiracist policies'. *University of Chicago Legal Forum* 1: 139–67.

Crenshaw, Kimberle. 1991. 'Mapping the margins: intersectionality, identity politics, and violence against women of color'. *Stanford Law Review* 43(6): 1241–99.

Curiel Pichardo, Ochy. 2014. 'Hacia la construcción de un feminismo descolonizado', in Yuderkys Espinosa Miñoso, Diana Gómez Correal and Karina Ochoa Muñoz (eds), *Tejiendo de otro modo: feminismo, epistemología y apuestas coloniales en Abya Yala*. Popayán: Editorial Universidad del Cauca, pp. 325–34.

Cuyul Soto, Andrés. 2013. 'Salud intercultural y la patrimonialización de la salud Mapuche en Chile', in Hector Nahuelpan Moreno et al. (eds), *Historia, Colonialismo y Resistencia desde el país Mapuche (Ta iñ fijke xipa rakizualmeluwün)*. Temuco: Ediciones Comunidad de Historia Mapuche.

da Costa, Alexandre Emboaba. 2014. *Reimagining Black Difference and Politics in Brazil: from Racial Democracy to Multiculturalism*. New York: Palgrave Macmillan.

da Cunha, Euclides. 1995 [1902]. *Rebellion in the Backlands (Os sertões)*. London: Picador.

da Matta, Roberto. 1983. *Carnavais, Malandros e Heróis: para uma sociologia do dilema brasileiro*. Rio de Janeiro: Zahar.

da Matta, Roberto. 1992. *Carnivals, Rogues and Heroes: Interpretation of the Brazilian Dilemma*. Indiana: University of Notre Dame Press.

Dangl, Benjamin. 2019. *The Five Hundred Year Rebellion: Indigenous Movements and the Decolonization of History in Bolivia*. Chico, CA and Edinburgh: AK Press.

Dary, Claudia. 2018. 'Guatemala: entre la Biblia y la constitución', in José Luis Pérez Guadalupe and Sebastian Grundberger (eds), *Evangélicos y Poder en América Latina*. Konrad Adenauer Stiftung and Instituto de Estudios Social Cristianos, pp. 317–55.

Davis, Colin. 1996. *Levinas: An Introduction*. Cambridge: Polity Press.

de Freitas, Jefferson, Portela, Poema Eurístenes, Feres Jr, João, Nascimento, Vivian and Bessa, Águida. 2020. *Políticas de Ação Afirmativa nas Universidades Federais e Estaduais (2013–2018)*. Grupo de Estudos Multidisciplinaresgda Ação Afirmativa, UERJ/IESP. https://gemaa.iesp.uerj.br.

REFERENCES

de la Cadena, Marisol. 2000. *Indigenous Mestizos: The Politics of Race and Culture in Cuzco, 1919–1991*. Durham, NC: Duke University Press.

de la Cadena, Marisol. 2004. *Indígenas mestizos. Raza y cultura en el Cusco*. Lima: IEP.

de la Maza, Francisca and Bolomey Córdova, Carlos. 2020. 'Persistence and changes in state dependence in a Mapuche indigenous territory, Chile'. *Critique of Anthropology* 40: 146–68. https://dx.doi.org/ https://doi.org/10.1177/0308275X18821178.

de la Maza, Francisca, Bolomey, Carlos and Ahues, Dalma. 2018. 'Políticas públicas y políticas indígenas desde la Araucanía: el eso del "conflicto" en la construcción de políticas', in Francisca de la Maza, Maite de Cea and Gabriela Rubilar (eds), *Políticas indígenas y construcción del estado desde lo local*. Santiago: Pehuén Editores.

de la Peña, Guillermo. 2005. 'Social and cultural policies toward indigenous peoples: perspectives from Latin America'. *Annual Review of Anthropology* 34: 717–39.

de la Peña, Guillermo. 2006. 'A new Mexican nationalism? Indigenous rights, constitutional reform and the conflicting meanings of multiculturalism'. *Nations and Nationalism* 12(2): 279–302.

de Sousa Santos, Boaventura. 1983. 'Os Conflitos Urbanos no Recife: o caso do "Skylab"'. *Revista Critica de Ciencias Sociais (Coimbra)* 11.

de Sousa Santos, Boaventura. 1987. 'Law: A Map of Misreading. Toward a Postmodern Conception of Law'. *Journal of Law and Society* 14(3): 279–302.

de Sousa Santos, Boaventura. 1995. *Toward a New Common Sense: Law, Science and Politics in the Paradigmatic Transition*. New York: Routledge.

de Sousa Santos, Boaventura. 2010. *Descolonizar el Saber. Reinventar el Poder*. Montevideo: Ediciones Trilce.

della Cava, Ralph. 1970. *Miracle at Juaseiro*. New York: Columbia University Press.

Diacon, Todd A. 1991. *Millenarian Vision, Capitalist Reality: Brazil's Contestado Rebellion, 1912–1916*. Durham, NC: Duke University Press.

Dias, Camila Caldeira Nunes. 2006. 'Conversão evangélica na prisão: sobre ambigüidade, estigma e poder'. *Plural – Revista do Curso de Pós-graduação em Sociologia da USP* 13(2): 85–110. http://www.espen.pr.gov.br/arquivos/File/ArtigoPlural_CamilaCaldeiraNunesDias_1_.pdf.

Dietz, Gunther. 2009. 'Intercultural universities in Mexico: empowering indigenous peoples or mainstreaming multiculturalism?' *Intercultural Education* 20(1): 1–4.

Dietz, Gunther. 2012. 'Diversity regimes beyond multiculturalism? A reflexive ethnography of intercultural higher education in Veracruz, Mexico'. *Latin American and Caribbean Ethnic Studies* 7(2): 173–200.

Dietz, Gunther and Mateos Cortés, Laura Selene. 2011. *Interculturalidad y educación Intercultural en México: un análisis de los discursos nacionales e internacionales en su impacto en los modelos educativos mexicanos*. Mexico City: SEP, CGEIB.

Dussel, Enrique. 1973. *Caminos de liberación latinoamericana II: teología de la liberación y ética*. Buenos Aires: Latinoamérica Libros. http://bibliotecavirtual.clacso.org.ar/clacso/otros/20120131101011/TEOLOGIA.pdf.

Dussel, Enrique D. 1974. *Historia de la Iglesia en América Latina: coloniaje y liberación (1492–1973)*, 3rd edn. Barcelona: Nova Terra.

REFERENCES

Dussel, Enrique (ed.). 1983–1994. *Historia General de la Iglesia en América Latina* (11 vols). Salamanca: CEHILA, Ediciones Sígueme.

Dussel, Enrique. 1985. *Philosophy of Liberation*. Maryknoll, NY: Orbis Books.

Dussel, Enrique. 2013. *Filosofía de la Liberación*, new edn. Buenos Aires: Editorial Docencia.

Egan, Patrick J. and Mullin, Megan. 2017. 'Climate change: US public opinion'. *Annual Review of Political Science* 20: 209–27. https://dx.doi.org/10.1146/annurev-polisci-051215-022857.

Espinosa Miñoso, Yuderkys. 2014. 'Etnocentrismo y colonialidad en los feminismos latinoamericanos: complicidades y consolidación de las hegemonías feministas en el espacio transnacional', in Yuderkys Espinosa Miñoso, Diana Gómez Correal and Karina Ochoa Muñoz (eds), *Tejiendo de otro modo: feminismo, epistemología y apuestas coloniales en Abya Yala*. Popayán: Editorial Universidad del Cauca, pp. 309–24.

Espinosa Miñoso, Yuderkys, Gómez Correal, Diana and Ochoa Muñoz, Karina. 2014a. 'Introducción', in Yuderkys Espinosa Miñoso, Diana Gómez Correal and Karina Ochoa Muñoz (eds), *Tejiendo de otro modo: feminismo, epistemología y apuestas coloniales en Abya Yala*. Popayán: Editorial Universidad del Cauca.

Espinosa Miñoso, Yuderkys, Gómez Correal, Diana and Ochoa Muñoz, Karina (eds). 2014b. *Tejiendo de otro modo: feminismo, epistemología y apuestas coloniales en Abya Yala*. Popayán: Editorial Universidad del Cauca.

Evans-Pritchard, E. E. 1965 [1937]. *Witchcraft, Oracles and Magic among the Azande*. Oxford: Clarendon Press.

Evaristo, Conceição. 2015. *Olhos d'água*. Rio de Janeiro: Pallas.

Fanon, Frantz. 1952. *Peau Noire, Masques Blancs*. Paris: Editions du Seuil.

Fanon, Frantz. 1986. *Black Skin, White Masks*, trans. Charles Lam Markman. London: Pluto Press.

Fanon, Frantz. 2002. *Les Damnés de la Terre*. Paris: La Découverte.

Fanon, Frantz. 2004. *The Wretched of the Earth*, trans. Richard Philcox. New York: Grove Press.

Fanon, Frantz. 2011. *Oeuvres (Peau Noire Masques Blancs; l'An V de la révolution algérienne; Les Damnés de la Terre; Pour la revolution africaine)*. Paris: Editions La Découverte.

Fanon, Frantz. 2014. *Oeuvres vol. II: écrits sur l'aliénation et la liberte, textes réunis*, intro. and ed. Jean Khalfa and Robert Young. Paris, Algiers: La Découverte, Hibr Editions.

Fernandes, Rubem Cesar, Sanchis, Pierre, Velho, Otávio Guilherme et al. 1998. *Novo Nascimento: os Evangélicos em casa, na Igreja e na Política*. Rio de Janeiro: Mauad.

Fernández Tapia, Joselito, Torres, Robles Daniel and Hernández Ríos, María Esther. 2018. 'Participación y representación política de las mujeres en Oaxaca, 2000–2016', in Maria Del Rosario Varela Zuñiga (ed.), *Género y política desde la diversidad regional*. Saltillo, Mexico: Universidad Autónoma de Coahuila, pp. 145–80.

Figueiredo Netto, Gabriela and Speck, Bruno Wilhelm. 2017. 'O dinheiro importa menos para os candidatos evangélicos?' *Opinião Pública* 23(30): 809–36.

Fontana, Lorenza. 2014. 'Indigenous peasant "otherness": rural identities and political processes in Bolivia'. *Bulletin of Latin American Research* 33(4): 436–51.

REFERENCES

Fontana, Lorenza B. and Grugel, Jean. 2016. 'The politics of indigenous participation through "free prior informed consent": reflections from the Bolivian case'. *World Development* 77: 249–61. https://dx.doi.org/https://doi.org/10.1016/j.worlddev.2015.08.023.

Franks, Bradley, Bangerter, Adrian and Bauer, Martin. 2013. 'Conspiracy theories as quasi-religious mentality: an integrated account from cognitive science, social representations theory, and frame theory'. *Frontiers in Psychology* 4(424) (July): 1–12. https://dx.doi.org/10.3389/fpsyg.2013.00424.

French, Jan Hoffman. 2009. *Legalizing Identities: Becoming Black or Indian in Brazil's Northeast*. Durham, NC: University of North Carolina Press.

Fry, Peter. 2000. 'Politics, nationality and the meanings of "race" in Brazil'. *Daedalus* 129(2): 82–113.

Fry, Peter. 2009. 'The politics of "racial" classification in Brazil'. *Journal de la Société des Américanistes* 95(2): 261–82.

Gago, Verónica. 2020. 'Introduction: the Silvia Rivera Cusicanqui principle: the rebellion of thought', in Silvia Rivera Cusicanqui (ed.), *Ch'ixinakax utxiwa: On Practices and Discourses of Decolonization*. Cambridge: Polity Press.

Galindo, María. 2013. *A despatriarcalizar*. Buenos Aires: Lavaca.

Galindo, María. 2020. 'No se puede descolonizar sin despatriarcalizar', in Gaya Makaran and Pierre Gaussens (eds), *Piel blanca, máscaras negras: Crítica de la razón decolonial*, México DF: México: Bajo Tierra A.C.; Centro de Investigaciones sobre América Latina y el Caribe-UNAM, pp. 289–314.

Galvão, Walnice Nogueira. 1974. *No calor da hora: a guerra de Canudos nos jornais, 4a expedição*. São Paulo: Ática.

García, María Elena. 2003. 'The politics of community: education, indigenous rights and ethnic mobilization in Peru'. *Latin American Perspectives* 30(1): 70–94.

García, María Elena. 2005. *Making Indigenous Citizens: Identities, Education and Multicultural Development in Peru*. Stanford, CA: Stanford University Press.

García Canclini, Néstor. 1989. *Culturas híbridas: estrategias para entrar y salir de la modernidad*. Mexico, DF: Grijalbo.

García Canclini, Néstor. 1995. *Hybrid Cultures: Strategies for Entering and Leaving Modernity*. Minneapolis, MN: University of Minnesota Press.

García Canclini, Néstor. 2001. *Culturas híbridas: estrategias para entrar y salir de la modernidad* (new edn). Buenos Aires: Paidos.

García Canclini, Néstor. 2002. *Culturas populares en el capitalismo*, 6th edn. Mexico, DF: Grijalbo.

García Canclini, Néstor. 2005. *Hybrid cultures: strategies for entering and leaving modernity*, 2nd edn. Minneapolis, MN: University of Minnesota Press.

Garrard, Virginia. 2010. *Terror in the Land of the Holy Spirit: Guatemala Under General Efraín Ríos Montt, 1982–1983*. New York: Oxford University Press.

Garrard, Virginia. 2020. *New Faces of God in Latin America: Emerging Forms of Vernacular Christianity*. New York: Oxford University Press.

Gledhill, John. 2012. 'Limits of indigenous autonomy and self-defence: Mexican experiences'. *Mana – Estudos De Antropologia Social* 18(3): 449–70.

Gledhill, John. 2015. *The New War on the Poor: The Production of Insecurity in Latin America*. London: Zed Books.

Gomes, Edlaine de Campos. 2011. *A Era das Catedrais: a autenticidade em exibição*. Rio de Janeiro: Garamond.

REFERENCES

Gonzalez Apodaca, Erika. 2009. 'The ethnic and the intercultural in conceptual and pedagogical discourses within higher education in Oaxaca, Mexico'. *Intercultural Education* 20(1): 19–25.

González Casanova, Pablo. 1965. *La Democracia en México*. México, DF: Edicions Era.

Goodale, Mark. 2019. *A Revolution in Fragments: Traversing Scales of Justice, Ideology, and Practice in Bolivia*. Durham, NC: Duke University Press.

Grisaffi, Thomas. 2019. *Coca Yes, Cocaine No: How Bolivia's Coca Growers Reshaped Democracy*. Durham, NC and London: Duke University Press.

Gros, Christian. 1991. *Colombia Indígena: Identidad cultural y cambio social*. CEREC.

Gros, Christian. 1999. 'Evangelical protestantism and indigenous populations'. *Bulletin of Latin American Research* 18(2): 175–98.

Gros, Christian. 2010. *Nación, Identidad y Violencia: el desafío latinaamericano*. Bogotá: Universidad Nacional de Colombia, Universidad de los Andes, Institut Français d'Etudes Andines.

Gross, Toomas. 2003. 'Protestantism and modernity: the implications of religious change in rural Oaxaca'. *Sociology of Religion* 64(4): 479–98.

Gruzinski, Serge. 1988. *La colonisation de l'imaginaire: sociétés indigènes et occidentalisation dans le Mexique espagnol, XVIe–XVIIIe siècle*. Paris: Editions Gallimard.

Guimaräes, Antonio Sérgio. 2018. 'Recriando fronteiras raciais'. *Sinais Sociais* 11(34): 21–43.

Guimaräes, Antonio Sérgio. 2019. 'Racialisation and racial formation in urban spaces'. *Social Identities* 25(1): 76–90. https://dx.doi.org/10.1080/13504630.2017.1418600.

Guimaräes, Antonio Sérgio, Rios, Flavia and Sotero, Edilza. 2020. 'Coletivos negros e Novas Ixdentidades Racais'. *Novos Estudos CEBRAP* 39: 309–27. https://dx.doi.org/org/10.25091/s01013300202000020004.

Gustafson, Bret. 2009. *New Languages of the State: Indigenous Resurgence and the Politics of Knowledge in Bolivia*. Durham, NC: Duke University Press.

Gutiérrez, Gustavo. 1993 [1992]. *Las Casas: In Search of the Poor of Jesus Christ*. Maryknoll, NY: Orbis Books.

Gutiérrez Aguilar, Raquel. 2008. *Los Ritmos del Pachakuti: Movilización y Levantamiento Popular-Indígena en Bolivia (2000–2005)*. Buenos Aires: Tinta Limón.

Gutiérrez Aguila, Raquel. 2014. *Rhythms of the Pachakuti: Indigenous Uprising and State Power in Bolivia*. Durham, NC: Duke University Press.

Hale, Charles. 2002. 'Does multiculturalism menace? Governance, cultural rights and the politics of identity in Guatemala'. *Journal of Latin American Studies* 34: 485–524.

Hale, Charles. 2006. 'Activist research v. cultural critique: Indigenous land rights and the contradictions of politically engaged anthropology'. *Cultural Anthropology* 21(1): 96–120. https://dx.doi.org/10.1525/can.2006.21.1.96.

Hansen, Helena. 2017. *Addicted to Christ: Remaking Men in Puerto Rican Pentecostal Drug Ministries*. Oakland, CA: University of California Press.

Harris, Mark. 2013. 'The werewolf in between Indians and Whites: imaginative frontiers and mobile identities in eighteenth century Amazonia'. *Tipití: Journal of the Society for the Anthropology of Lowland South America* 11(1): 87–104.

REFERENCES

Harris, Olivia. 2000. 'The mythological figure of the Earth Mother', in *To Make the Earth Bear Fruit: Essays on Fertility, Work and Gender in Highland Bolivia*. London: Institute of Latin American Studies.

Harvey, Neil. 2016. 'Practicing autonomy: Zapatismo and decolonial liberation'. *Latin American and Caribbean Ethnic Studies* 11(1): 1–24. https://dx.doi.org/10.1080/17442222.2015.1094872.

Henriques, Ricardo. 2001. *Desigualdades raciaias no Brasil: evolução das condições de vida na década de 90*. Brasilia: IPEA, Texto para Discussão 807.

Hernández Castillo, Rosalva Aída. 2003. 'Between civil disobedience and silent rejection: differing responses by Mam peasants to the Zapatista rebellion', in Jan Rus, Rosalva Aída Hernández, and Shannan Mattiace (eds), *Mayan Lives, Mayan Utopias: The Indigenous Peoples of Chiapas and the Zapatista Rebellion*. Lanham, MD: Rowman and Littlefield.

Hernández Castillo, Rosalva Aída. 2006. 'Between feminist ethnocentricity and ethnic essentialism: the Zapatistas' demands and the National Indigenous Women's Movement', in Shannon Speed, Rosalva Aída Hernández Castillo and Lynn Stephen (eds), *Dissident Women: Gender and Cultural Politics in Chiapas*, Austin, TX: University of Texas Press, pp. 57–75.

Hernández Castillo, Rosalva Aída. 2008a. 'On feminisms and colonialisms: Reflections south of the Rio Grande', in Mabel Moraña and Carlos Jáuregui (eds), *Revisiting the Colonial Question in Latin America*. Berlin: Iberoamericana, pp. 257–80.

Hernández Castillo, Rosalva Aída. 2008b. 'Feminismos poscoloniales: reflexiones desde el sur del Río Bravo', in Liliana Suárez Navas and Rosalva Aída Hernández Castillo (eds), *Descolonizando el feminismo. Teorías y prácticas desde las márgenes*. Madrid: Cátedra, pp. 75–113.

Hernández Castillo, Rosalva Aída. 2014. 'Entre el etnocentrismo feminista y el esencialismo étnico: Las mujeres indígenas y sus demandas de género', in Yuderkys Espinosa Miñoso, Diana Gómez Correal and Karina Ochoa Muñoz (eds), *Tejiendo de otro modo: feminismo, epistemología y apuestas coloniales en Abya Yala*. Popayán: Editorial Universidad del Cauca, pp. 279–94.

Hernández Castillo, Rosalva Aída. 2016. 'Indigenous injustices: new spaces for struggle for women', in Rosalva Aída Hernandez Castillo (ed.), *Multiple Injustices: Indigenous Women, Law and Political Struggle in Latin America*. Tucson, AZ: Arizona University Press, pp. 123–62.

Hernández Castillo, Rosalva Aída, Paz, Sarela and Sierra, María Teresa (eds). 2004. *El Estado y los indígenas en tiempos del PAN: neoindigenismo, legalidad e identidad*. Mexico, DF: CIESAS, Porrúa.

Hernández Castillo, Rosalva Aída and Terven, Adriana. 2017. 'Rutas metodológicas: hacia una antropología jurídica crítica y colaborativa'. in Rachel Sieder (ed.), *Exigiendo justicia y seguridad: Mujeres indígenas y pluralidades legales en América Latina*. Mexico, DF: CIESAS, pp. 294–319.

Hochschild, Arlie Russell. 2016. *Strangers in Their Own Land: Anger and Mourning on the American Right*. New York: The New Press.

Hooker, Juliet. 2005. 'Indigenous inclusion/black exclusion: race, ethnicity and multicultural citizenship in Latin America'. *Journal of Latin American Studies* 37(2): 285–310.

Hudis, Peter. 2015. *Frantz Fanon: Philosopher of the Barricades*. London: Pluto Books.

Huenchuñir, Sigrid. 2015. 'Exilio interior: ser mapuche en Santiago', in Angela

REFERENCES

Boitano and Alejandra Ramm (eds), *Rupturas e identidades: Cuestionando la Nación y la Academia desde la etnia y el género*. Santiago: RIL Editores.

ILO (International Labour Organisation). 2017. *2017 Labour Overview of Latin America and the Caribbean*. Geneva: International Labour Office.

Irvine, Andrew B. 2011. 'An ontological critique of the trans-ontology of Enrique Dussel'. *Sophia* 50(4): 603–24. https://dx.doi.org/10.1007/s11841-010-0210-8.

Jimeno, Myriam and Klatt, Andy. 2014. 'Juan Gregorio Palechor: between the community and the nation', in *Juan Gregorio Palechor: The Story of My Life*: Durham, NC: Duke University Press.

Khalfa, Jean. 2006. 'Fanon, Corps perdu'. *Les Temps Modernes* 635–6: 97–117. https://dx.doi.org/10.3917/ltm.635.0097.

Khalfa, Jean. 2011. 'Fanon, psychiatre révolutionnaire,' in Jean Khalfa and Robert Young (eds), *Frantz Fanon: Oeuvres, vol. II: écrits sur l'aliénation et la liberté*, vol. II, pp. 137–67.

Kotler, Rubén Isidoro. 2008. 'Mujeres militantes en el movimiento de Derechos Humanos de Argentina. El caso Tucumán'. *Amnis* 8. https://dx.doi.org/https://doi.org/10.4000/amnis.573.

Krauze, Enrique. 1999 (December 16). 'Chiapas: the Indians' prophet'. *New York Review of Books*. http://www.enriquekrauze.com.mx/joomla/index.php/krauze-in-english/83-chiapas-the-indians-prophet.html.

Larson, Brooke. 2019. 'Revisiting Bolivian studies: reflections on theory, scholarship, and activism since 1980'. *Latin American Research Review* 54: 294–309. https://dx.doi.org/http://doi.org/10.25222/larr.352.

Lavinas Picq, Manuela. 2016. 'Inventing rights of our own: women transcending the opposition between the indigenous and the universal', in David Lehmann (ed.), *The Crisis of Multiculturalism in Latin America*. New York: Palgrave Macmillan, pp. 133–54.

Lazar, Sian. 2008. *El Alto, Rebel City: Self and Citizenship in Andean Bolivia* (Latin America Otherwise). Durham, NC: Duke University Press.

Lehmann, David (ed.) 1982. *Ecology and Exchange in the Andes*. Cambridge: Cambridge University Press.

Lehmann, David. 1990. *Democracy and Development in Latin America: Economics, Politics and Religion in the Post-War Period*. Cambridge: Polity Press.

Lehmann, David. 1996. *Struggle for the Spirit: Religious Transformation and Popular Culture in Brazil and Latin America*. Cambridge: Polity Press.

Lehmann, David. 2011. 'Charismatic and conversion movements', in David Lehmann and Humeira Iqtidar (eds), *Fundamentalism and Charismatic Movements*, vol. 3. London: Routledge.

Lehmann, David. 2013. 'Intercultural universities in Mexico: identity and inclusion'. *Journal of Latin American Studies* 45(4): 779–811.

Lehmann, David. 2015. 'Convergencias y divergencias en la educación superior intercultural en México.' *Revista Mexicana de Ciencias Políticas y Sociales* 60(223): 133–70.

Lehmann, David (ed.). 2016a. *The Crisis of Multiculturalism in Latin America*. New York: Palgrave Macmillan.

Lehmann, David. 2016b. 'Introduction', in David Lehmann (ed.), *The Crisis of Multiculturalism in Latin America*. New York: Palgrave Macmillan.

Lehmann, David. 2016c. 'The politics of naming', in David Lehmann (ed.),

REFERENCES

The Crisis of Multiculturalism in Latin America. New York: Palgrave Macmillan.

Lehmann, David. 2018. *The Prism of Race: The Politics and Ideology of Affirmative Action in Brazil.* Ann Arbor, MI: Michigan University Press.

Lehmann, David. 2021. 'The evangelical mindset and political polarization', in Katerina Hatzikidi (ed.), *A Horizon of (Im)possibilities: A Chronicle of Brazil's Conservative Turn.* London: Institute of Latin American Studies.

Lennon, Kathleen and Alsop, Rachel. 2020. *Gender Theory in Troubled Times.* Cambridge: Polity Press.

Levinas, Emmanuel. 1961. *Totalité et infini: Essai sur l'Extériorité.* Paris: Kluwer Academic.

Levinas, Emmanuel. 1982. *Ethique et infini: Dialogues avec Philippe Nemo.* Paris: Fayard/France Culture.

Levinas, Emmanuel. 1984. *Ethics and Infinity: Conversations with Philippe Nemo*, trans. Richard A. Cohen. Pittsburgh, PA: Duquesne University Press.

Levinas, Emmanuel. 1994a. *In Times of the Nations.* London: Athlone Press.

Levinas, Emmanuel 1994b. *Nine Talmudic Readings*, trans. and intro. Annette Aronow, 1st Midland Book edn. Bloomington: Indiana University Press.

Levine, Daniel (ed.) 1980. *Churches and Politics in Latin America.* Beverly Hills, CA: Sage.

Levine, Robert M. 1992. *Vale of Tears: Revisiting the Canudos Massacre in Northeastern Brazil, 1893–1897.* Berkeley, CA: University of California Press.

Levitt, Peggy and Merry, Sally Engle. 2009. 'Vernacularization on the ground: local uses of global women's rights in Peru, China, India and the United States'. *Global Networks* 9(4): 441–61.

Leyva Solano, Xóchitl. 2001. 'Regional, communal, and organizational transformations in Las Cañadas'. *Latin American Perspectives* 28(2): 20–44. https://dx.doi.org/10.1177/0094582x0102800203.

Leyva Solano, Xochitl and Franco, Gabriel Ascensio. 1996. *Lacandonia al filo del agua.* Mexico, DF: CIESAS, UNAM, Fondo de Cultura Económica.

Lima, Deborah. 1999. 'A construção histórica do termo caboclo sobre estruturas e Representações sociais no meio rural amazônico'. *Novos Cadernos NAEA* 2 (2): 5–32.

Longa, Francisco. 2017. 'Del antipatriarcado al feminismo: derivas del ethos militante en un movimiento social de la Argentina (2004–2015)'. *Estudios de Género de El Colegio de México* 3: 57–89. https://estudiosdegenero.colmex.mx/index.php/eg/article/view/96/58.

Lopes, Maria Auxiliadora and Braga, Maria Lúcia de Santana (eds). 2007. *Acesso e Permanência da população negra no ensino superior.* Brasilia: Ministério da Educação, SECAD: UNESCO.

López, Luis Enrique. 2005. *De resquicios a boquerones: la Educación intercultural bilingüe en Bolivia.* La Paz: PROEIB-Andes/Plural.

López, Luis Enrique and Sichra, Inge. 2004. 'La educación en áreas indígenas de América Latina: balances y perspectivas', in Ignacio Hernaíz (ed.), *Educación en la diversidad: experiencias y desafíos en la educación intercultural bilingüe.* Buenos Aires: IIPE-UNESCO.

Lugones, María. 2014. 'Colonialidad y género', in Yuderkys Espinosa Miñoso, Diana Gómez Correal and Karina Ochoa Muñoz (eds), *Tejiendo de otro modo: feminismo, epistemología y apuestas coloniales en Abya Yala.* Popayán: Editorial Universidad del Cauca, pp. 57–74.

REFERENCES

Macey, David. 2000. *Franz Fanon: A Biography*. London: Verso.

Mahmood, Saba. 2005. *Politics of Piety: The Islamic Revival and the Feminist Subject*. Princeton, NJ: Princeton University Press.

Mahmood, Saba. 2006. 'Secularism, hermeneutics and empire: the politics of Islamic reformation'. *Public Culture* 18(2): 323–47.

Makaran, Gaya and Gaussens, Pierre. 2020. 'Autopsia de una impostura intelectual', in Gaya Makaran and Pierre Gaussens (eds), *Piel blanca, máscaras negras: Crítica de la razón decolonial*. Mexico, DF: Mexico: Bajo Tierra A.C.; Centro de Investigaciones sobre América Latina y el Caribe-UNAM, pp. 9–44.

Maldonado-Torres, Nelson. 2007. 'Sobre la colonialidad del ser: contribuciones al desarrollo de un concepto', in Sergio Castro-Gomez and Ramón Grosfoguel (eds), *El Giro Decolonial: reflexiones para una diversidad espistémica más allá del capitalismo global*. Bogota: Siglo del Hombre Editores, pp. 127–68.

Mallon, Florencia E. 2005. *Courage Tastes of Blood: The Mapuche Community of Nicolás Ailío and the Chilean State, 1906–2001*. Durham, NC: Duke University Press.

Mariz, Cecilia Loreto. 1993. *Coping with Poverty: Pentecostals and Christian Base Communities in Brazil*. Philadelphia, PA: Temple University Press.

Martin, David. 1990. *Tongues of Fire: The Pentecostal Revolution in Latin America*. Oxford: Blackwell.

Martin, David. 2001. *Pentecostalism: The World Their Parish*. Oxford: Blackwell.

Martinez Novo, Carmen. 2018a. 'Discriminación y colonialidad en el Ecuador de Rafael Correa, 2007–2017'. *Alteridades* 28(55): 49–60.

Martinez Novo, Carmen. 2018b. 'Ventriloquism, racism and the politics of decoloniality in Ecuador'. *Cultural Studies* 32: 389–413.

McCulloch, J. 1983. *Black Soul, White Artifact: Fanon's Clinical Psychology and Social Theory*. Cambridge: Cambridge University Press.

Merry, Sally Engle. 1988. 'Legal pluralism'. *Law and Society Review* 22: 869–96.

Merry, Sally Engle. 2006. *Human Rights and Gender Violence: Translating International Law into Local Justice*. Chicago: Chicago University Press.

Merry, Sally Engle. 2012. 'Legal pluralism and legal culture', in B. Tamanaha, C. Sage and M. Woolcock (eds), *Legal Pluralism and Development: Scholars and Practitioners in Dialogue*. Cambridge: Cambridge University Press, pp. 66–82.

Meyer, Jean. 1973–4. *La Cristiada* (3 vols). Mexico, DF: Siglo XXI.

Mignolo, Walter. 2007. 'Introduction: coloniality of power and decolonial thinking'. *Cultural Studies* 21(2–3): 155–67. https://dx.doi.org/10.1080/09502380601162498.

Mignolo, Walter. 2010. *Desobediencia Epistémica: Retórica de la Modernidad, Lógica de la Colonialidad, y Gramática de la Descolonialidad*. Buenos Aires: Ediciones del Signo.

Mignolo, Walter. 2011. *The Darker Side of Western Modernity*. Durham, NC: Duke University Press.

Mignolo, Walter and Escobar, Arturo. 2013. *Globalization and the Decolonial Option*. Abingdon: Routledge.

Molano, Alfredo. 1992. 'Violence and land colonization', in Charles Bergquist and Ricardo Peñaranda (eds), *Violence in Colombia: The Contemporary Crisis in Historical Perspective*. Wilmington: Scholarly Resources.

Molano, Alfredo. 1994. *Trochas y fusiles*. Bogotá: Instituto de Estudios Políticos y Relaciones Internacionales; El Áncora Editores.

Molinié, Antoinette. 2005. 'La transfiguración eucarística de un glaciar: una con-

REFERENCES

strucción andina del Corpus Christi', in *Etnografías de Cuzco*. Lima: Institut français d'Etudes Andines, pp. 69–87.

Molyneux, Maxine, Adrija Dey, Gatto, Malu A. C. and Rowden, Holly. 2020. 'Feminist activism 25 years after Beijing'. *Gender & Development* 28(2): 315–36. https://dx.doi.org/10.1080/13552074.2020.1750140.

Molyneux, Maxine and Osborne, Thomas. 2017. 'Populism: a deflationary view'. *Economy and Society* 46(1): 1–19. https://dx.doi.org/10.1080/030851 47.2017.1308059.

Moraes Teixeira, Jacqueline. 2012. 'Da controversia às práticas: conjugalidade, corpo e prosperidade na Igreja Universal'. University of São Paulo.

Morales Bermúdez, Jesús. 2005. *Entre Asperos Caminos Llanos: la Diócesis de San Cristóbal de las Casas 1950–1995*. México, DF and San Cristóbal: UNICACH, COSICH, COCYTECH, Casa Juan Pablos.

Muratorio, Blanca. 1980. 'Protestantism and capitalism revisited, in the rural highlands of Ecuador'. *Journal of Peasant Studies* 8(1): 37–60. https://dx.doi. org/10.1080/03066158008438125.

Murra, John V. 1972. 'El control vertical de un máximo de pisos ecológicos en la economía de las sociedades andinas', in *Formaciones económicas y políticas del mundo andino*. Lima: Instituto de Estudios Peruanos, pp. 59–115.

Murra, John V. 1975. *Formaciones económicas y políticas del mundo andino*, 1st edn. Historia andina. vol. 3. Lima: Instituto de Estudios Peruanos.

Murra, John V. 1980. *The Economic Organization of the Inka State*. Research in Economic Anthropology Supplement. Greenwich, CT: JAI Press.

Murra, John V., Wachtel, Nathan and Revel, Jacques. 1986. *Anthropological History of Andean Polities*. Cambridge and Paris: Cambridge University Press and Editions de la Maison des Sciences de l'Homme.

Nair, Stella. 2007. 'Witnessing the in-visibility of Inca architecture in colonial Peru'. *Buildings & Landscapes: Journal of the Vernacular Architecture Forum* 14: 50–65. https://dx.doi.org/10.1353/bdl.2007.0006.

Nussbaum, Martha. 2000. *Women and Human Development: The Capabilities Approach (The Seeley Lectures)*. Cambridge: Cambridge University Press.

O'Donnell, Guillermo. 1993. 'On the state, democratization and some conceptual problems: a Latin American view with glances at some post-communist countries'. *World Development* XXI(8).

O'Donnell, Guillermo. 1996. 'Delegative democracy', in Larry Jay Diamond and Marc F. Plattner (eds), *The Global Resurgence of Democracy*, Baltimore, MD: Johns Hopkins University Press, pp. xxxiii, 393.

O'Donnell, Guillermo. 1999. *Counterpoints: Selected Essays on Authoritarianism and Democracy*. Notre Dame: University of Notre Dame Press.

Omi, Michael and Winant, Howard. 2015. *Racial Formation in the United States*, 3rd edn. New York: Routledge.

O'Neill, Kevin Lewis. 2019. *Hunted: Predation and Pentecostalism in Guatemala*. Chicago and London: University of Chicago Press.

O'Neill, Onora. 1993. 'Justice, gender, and international boundaries', in Martha Nussbaum and Amartya Sen (eds), *The Quality of Life*. Oxford: Oxford University Press.

Oosterbaan, Martijn. 2017. *Transmitting the Spirit: Religious Conversion, Media and Urban Violence in Brazil*. University Park, PA: Penn State University Press.

Oro, Ari Pedro and Seman, Pablo. 2001. 'Brazilian Pentecostalism crosses national

215

REFERENCES

borders', in André Corten and Ruth Marshall-Fratani (eds), *Between Babel and Pentecost: Transnational Pentecostalism in Africa and Latin America*. London: Hurst and Company.

Oro, Ari Pedro and Tadvald, Marcelo. 2015. 'A Igreja Universal do Reino de Deus e a reconfiguração do espaço público religioso brasileiro'. *Ciencias Sociales y Religón/ Ciências Sociais e Religião* 17(23): 76–113.

Pairícan Padilla, Fernando. 2014. *Malón: la Rebelión del Movimiento Mapuche 1990–2013*. Santiago: Pehuén Editores.

Paschel, Tianna. 2016. *Becoming Black Political Subjects: Movements and Ethnoracial Rights in Colombia and Brazil*. Princeton, NJ: Princeton University Press.

Péreira de Queiroz, Maria Isaura. 1976. *O Messianismo no Brasil e no Mundo*. Sao Paulo: Alfa-Omega.

Péreira de Queiroz, Maria Isaura. 1985. 'The samba schools of Rio de Janeiro'. *Diogenes* 33(129).

Péreira de Queiroz, Maria Isaura. 1992a. *Carnaval brasileiro: o vívido e o mito*. São Paulo: Brasiliense.

Péreira de Queiroz, Maria Isaura. 1992b. *Carnaval brésilien. Le vécu et le mythe*. Paris: Gallimard.

Phillips, James. 2005. *Heidegger's Volk: Between National Socialism and Poetry*. Stanford, CA: Stanford University Press.

Pitarch, Pedro. 2004. 'The Zapatistas and the art of ventriloquism'. *Journal of Human Rights* 3(3): 291–312. https://dx.doi.org/10.1080/1475483042000224851.

Pitarch, Pedro. 2010. *The Jaguar and the Priest: An Ethnography of Tzeltal Souls*. Austin, TX: University of Texas Press.

Platt, Tristan. 1982a. *Estado Boliviano y Ayllu Andino: Tierra y Tributo en el Norte de Potosí*. Lima: Instituto de Estudios Peruanos.

Platt, Tristan. 1982b. 'The role of the Andean Ayllu in the reproduction of the petty-commodity regime in Northern Potosí', in D. Lehmann (ed.), *Ecology and Exchange in the Andes*. Cambridge: Cambridge University Press.

Platt, Tristan. 1984. 'Liberalism and ethnocide in the Southern Andes'. *History Workshop Journal* 17: 3–18.

Polgovsky Ezcurra, Mara. 2019. *Touched Bodies: The Performative Turn in Latin American Art*. London: Routledge.

Poole, Stafford. 1995. *Our Lady of Guadalupe: The Origins and Sources of a Mexican National Symbol, 1531–1797*. Tuscon, AZ: University of Arizona Press.

Postero, Nancy. 2015. '"El Pueblo Boliviano, de Composición Plural": a look at plurinationalism in Bolivia', in Carlos de la Torre (ed.), *Power to the People?* Lexington, KY: University Press of Kentucky, pp. 398–430.

Postero, Nancy. 2017. *The Indigenous State: Race, Politics, and Performance in Plurinational Bolivia*. Berkeley, CA: University of Calfornia Press.

Programa de las Naciones Unidas para el Desarrollo (PNUD). 2009. *Innovar para incluir: jóvenes y desarrollo humano: informe sobre desarrollo humano para Mercosur*. Buenos Aires: Libros del Zorzal.

Quijano, Aníbal. 1992. 'Colonialidad y Modernidad/Racionalidad'. *Perú Indígena* 13(29): 11–20.

Quijano, Aníbal. 2007. 'Coloniality and modernity/rationality'. *Cultural Studies* 21(2–3): 168–78. https://dx.doi.org/10.1080/09502380601164353.

REFERENCES

Radcliffe, Sarah. 2015. *Dilemmas of Difference: Indigenous Women and the Limits of Postcolonial Development Policy*. Durham, NC: Duke University Press.

Rappaport, Joanne. 1990. *The Politics of Memory: Native Historical Interpretation in the Colombian Andes*. Cambridge: Cambridge University Press.

Rappaport, Joanne. 2005. *Intercultural Utopias: Public Intellectuals, Cultural Experimentation, and Ethnic Pluralism in Colombia*. Durham, NC: Duke University Press.

Rappaport, Joanne. 2008. *Utopías interculturales: intelectuales públicos, experimentos con la cultura y pluralismo étnico en Colombia*. Bogota: Universidad del Rosario.

Recondo, David. 2007. *La Política del Gatopardo. Multiculturalismo y democracia en Oaxaca*. Mexico, DF: CIESAS – Casa Chata.

Reinaga, Fausto. 2007 [1970]. *La Revolución India*. La Paz: Fausto and Hilda Reinaga.

Ribeiro, Djamila. 2017. *O que é lugar de fala?* Belo Horizonte: Letramento.

Richards, Patricia. 2013. *Race and the Chilean Miracle: Neoliberalism, Democracy, and Indigenous Rights*. Pittsburgh, PA: Pittsburgh University Press.

Rivera Cusicanqui, Silvia. 1986. *Oprimidos pero no Vencidos: Luchas del campesinado Aymara y quechwa de Bolivia, 1900–1980*. Geneva: UNRISD (United Nations Research Institute for Social Development).

Rivera Cusicanqui, Silvia. 1990. 'Liberal democracy and *ayllu* democracy in Bolivia: the case of Northern Potosí'. *Journal of Development Studies* 26(4): 97–121.

Rivera Cusicanqui, Silvia. 2010a. *Ch'ixinakax utxiwa: una reflexión sobre prácticas y discursos descolonizadores*. Buenos Aires: Tinta Limón. www.tintalimonediciones.com.ar.

Rivera Cusicanqui, Silvia. 2010b. *Violencias (re)encubiertas en Bolivia*. La Paz: La Mirada Salvaje; Editorial Piedra Rota.

Rivera Cusicanqui, Silvia. 2010 [1997]. 'Mujeres y estructuras de poder en los Andes: de la etnnohistoria a la política', in *Violencias (re)encubiertas en Bolivia*. La Paz: La Mirada Salvaje; Editorial Piedra Rota.

Rivera Cusicanqui, Silvia. 2015. *Mito y Desarrollo en Bolivia: el giro colonial del gobierno del MAS*. La Paz: Plural, Piedra Rota.

Rivera Cusicanqui, Silvia. 2020. *Ch'ixinakax Utxiwa: On Practices and Discourses of Colonisation*, trans. Molly Geidel, intro. Veronica Gago. Cambridge: Polity Press.

Rivera Cusicanqui, Silvia and Aillón Soria, Virginia (eds). 2015. *Antología del pensamiento crítico boliviano contemporáneo*. Buenos Aires: CLACSO.

Rivera Farfán, Carolina et al. 2005. *Diversidad religiosa y conflicto en Chiapas: Intereses, utopías y realidades*. Mexico, DF and Tuxtla Gutierrez: UNAM, CIESAS, Estado de Chiapas.

Rochabrun, Guillermo (ed.). 2011. *¿He vivido en vano? La mesa redonda sobre 'Todas las sangres'*. Lima: IEP.

Rodrigues-Silveira, Rodrigo and Urizzi Cervi, Emerson. 2019. 'Evangélicos e voto legislativo: Diversidade confessional e voto em deputados da bancada evangélica no Brasil'. *Latin American Research Review* 54(3): 560–73. https://dx.doi.org/http://doi.org/10.25222/larr.449.

REFERENCES

Rodríguez-Labajos, Beatriz and Özkaynak, Begüm. 2017. 'Editorial: environmental justice through the lens of mining conflicts'. *Geoforum* 84: 245–50. https://dx.doi.org/https://doi.org/10.1016/j.geoforum.2017.06.021.

Román Burgos, Denisse. 2019. '"We are indigenous of the Purhépecha people": hegemony, multiculturalism and neoliberal reforms in Mexico'. *Dialectical Anthropology* 43: 259–77. https://dx.doi.org/https://doi.org/10.1007/s10624-019-9542-0.

Rosemberg, Fúlvia and Madsen, Nina. 2011. 'Educação formal, mulheres e género no Brasil contemporâneo', in Leila Linhares Barsted and Jacqueline Pitanguy (eds), *O Progresso das Mulheres no Brasil 2003–2010*. Rio de Janeiro: ONU Mulheres.

Rousseau, Stéphanie. 2011. 'Indigenous and feminist movements at the Constituent Assembly in Bolivia: locating the representation of indigenous women'. *Latin American Research Review* 46(2): 5–28. www.jstor.org/stable/41261455.

Rousseau, Stéphanie and Hudon, Anahi Morales. 2018. *Movimientos de Mujeres Indígenas en Latinoamérica: género y etnicidad en el Perú, México y Bolivia*. Lima: Fondo Editorial PUCP.

Rowe, William and von Schelling, Vivian. 1991. *Memory and Modernity: Popular Culture in Latin America*. London: Verso.

Rus, Jan. 1995. 'La comunidad revolucionaria institucional: la subversión del gobierno indígena en los Altos de Chiapas, 1936–1968', in Juan Pedro Viqueira and Mario Humberto Ruz (eds), *Chiapas: Los Rumbos de Otra Historia*. Mexico City: UNAM-CIESAS-CEMCA-UDG.

Said, Edward. 1978. *Orientalism*. New York: Vintage Books.

Said, Edward. 1983. *The World, the Text, the Critic*. Cambridge, MA: Harvard University Press.

Said, Edward. 1994. *Culture and Imperialism*. New York: Vintage.

Said, Edward. 2003. 'Preface' in *Orientalism*. New York: Vintage Books.

Saldívar Moreno, Antonio, Micalco Mendez, Miriam Moramay, Santos Baca, Elizabeth and Avila Naranjo, Rocío. 2004. 'Los retos en la formación de maestros en la educación intercultural'. *Revista Mexicana de Investigación Educativa* 9(20) (January–March): 109–28.

Salomon, Frank. 1999. 'Testimonies: the making and reading of native South American historical sources', in Frank Salomon and Stuart Schwartz (eds), *The Cambridge History of the Native Peoples of the Americas*. Cambridge: Cambridge University Press.

Sánchez-Sibony, Omar. 2021. 'Competitive authoritarianism in Morales's Bolivia: skewing arenas of competition'. *Latin American Politics and Society* 63(1): 118–44. https://dx.doi.org/10.1017/lap.2020.35.

Sartre, Jean-Paul. 1946. *Reflexions sur la Question Juive*. Paris: Paul Morihien.

Sartre, Jean-Paul. 1948a. *Portrait of the Anti-Semite*, trans. Erik de Mauny. London: Secker & Warburg.

Sartre, Jean-Paul. 1948b. *Anti-Semite and Jew*, trans. George Becker. New York: Schocken.

Schmelkes, Sylvia. 2009. 'Intercultural universities in Mexico: progress and difficulties'. *Intercultural Education* 20(1): 5–17.

Schwartzman, Luisa Farah. 2009. 'Does money whiten? Intergenerational changes in racial classification in Brazil'. *American Sociological Review* 72: 940–63.

REFERENCES

Schwarz, Roberto. 1992a. 'Ideias fora do lugar', in *Ao vencedor as batatas*. São Paulo: Duas Cidades.

Schwarz, Roberto. 1992b. *Misplaced Ideas: Essays on Brazilian Culture*, ed. John Gledson. London: Verso.

Segato, Rita. 2014. 'Colonialidad y patriarcado moderno: expansión del frente estatal, modernización, y la vida de las mujeres', in Yuderkys Espinosa Miñoso, Diana Gómez Correal and Karina Ochoa Muñoz (eds), *Tejiendo de otro modo: feminismo, epistemología y apuestas coloniales en Abya Yala*. Popayán: Editorial Universidad del Cauca, pp. 75–90.

Segato, Rita. 2016. *La Guerra Contra las Mujeres*. Madrid: Traficantes de Sueños.

Segato, Rita. 2018. 'A manifesto in four themes', trans. Ramsey McGlazer. *Critical Times* 1(1): 198–211. https://dx.doi.org/10.1215/26410478-1.1.198.

Sen, Amartya. 1981. *Poverty and Famines: An Essay on Entitlement and Deprivation*, ed. Programme World Employment. Oxford: Oxford University Press.

Sen, Amartya. 1988. *The Standard of Living*. Cambridge: Cambridge University Press.

Sen, Amartya. 2001. *Development as Freedom*. Oxford: Oxford University Press.

Sen, Amartya. 2006. *The Argumentative Indian: Writings on Indian Culture, History and Identity*. London: Penguin

Sieder, Rachel (ed.). 2017. *Exigiendo justicia y seguridad: Mujeres indígenas y pluralidades legales en América Latina*. México, DF: CIESAS.

Sierra, María Teresa. 2002. 'Derecho indígena: herencias, construcciones y rupturas', in Guillermo de la Peña and Luis Vazquez (eds), *La antropología sociocultural en el México del Milenio: Búsquedas, encuentros y transiciones*. México, DF: INI, pp. 247–88.

Sierra, María Teresa. 2009. 'Las mujeres indígenas ante la justicia comunitaria: perspectivas desde la interculturalidad y los derechos'. *Desacatos* 31: 73–88.

Sierra, María Teresa. 2013. 'Seguridad y justicia bajo acoso en tiempos de violencia neoliberal: las respuestas de la policía comunitaria de Guerrero'. *Revista de Estudos e Pesquisas sobre as Américas* 7(2): 11–36. http://periodicos.unb.br/index.php/repam/article/view/10021/7335.

Simmons, William. 2011. 'Derrida, Levinas, and the rights of the other', in William Simmons (ed.), *Human Rights Law and the Marginalized Other*. Cambridge: Cambridge University Press, pp. 85–106.

Slater, Candace. 1982. *Stories on a String: The Brazilian* literatura de Cordel. Berkeley, CA: University of California Press.

Smith, Amy Erica. 2019. *Religion and Brazilian Democracy: Mobilizing the People of God*. Cambridge Studies in Social Theory, Religion and Politics. Cambridge: Cambridge University Press. https://www.cambridge.org/core/books/religion-and-brazilian-democracy/D9B7921525E8C676CFE11AEDC5C4102D.

Sommer, Barbara A. 2006. 'Cracking down on the Cunhamenas: renegade Amazonian traders under Pombaline reform'. *Journal of Latin American Studies* 38(4): 767–91. https://dx.doi.org/10.1017/S0022216X0600160X.

Sommer, Barbara A. 2014. 'The Amazonian native nobility in late-colonial Para', in Hal Langfur (ed.), *Native Brazil: Beyond the Convert and the Cannibal, 1500–1900*. Tucson. AZ: University of New Mexico Press, pp. 108–31.

Speed, Shannon, Hernández Castillo, Rosalva Aída and Stephen, Lynn (eds).

REFERENCES

2006. *Dissident Women: Gender and Cultural Politics in Chiapas.* Austin, TX: University of Texas Press.

Sperber, Dan. 1996. *Explaining Culture: A Naturalistic Approach.* Oxford: Blackwell.

Spivak, Gayatri. 1988. 'Can the subaltern speak?' in Cary Nelson and Lawrence Grossberg (eds), *Marxism and the Interpretation of Culture.* Chicago: University of Illinois Press, pp. 271–313.

Stavenhagen, Rodolfo. 1981 [1965]. 'Siete tesis equivocadas sobre América Latina', in *Sociología y Subdesarrollo.* Mexico: Nuestro Tiempo.

Stephen, Lynn. 2006. 'Indigenous women's activism in Oaxaca and Chiapas', in Shannon Speed, Rosalva Aída Hernández Castillo and Lynn Stephen (eds), *Dissident Women: Gender and Cultural Politics in Chiapas.* Austin, TX: University of Texas Press, pp. 157–75.

Stephenson, Marcia. 2002. 'Forging an indigenous counterpublic sphere: the taller de Historia Oral Andina in Bolivia'. *Latin American Research Review* 37(2): 99–118. www.jstor.org/stable/2692150.

Tabbush, C. and Caminotti, M. 2015. 'Igualdad de género y movimientos sociales en la Argentina posneoliberal: la Organización Barrial Tupac Amaru'. *Perfiles Latinoamericanos (Flacso México)* 23: 147–71.

Taylor, Charles. 1992. *The Politics of Recognition.* Princeton, NJ: Princeton University Press.

Teixeira, Jacqueline Moraes. 2014. 'Mídia e performances de género na Igreja Universal: O desafio Godllywood'. *Religião & Sociedade* 34: 232–56. http://www.scielo.br/scielo.php?script=sci_arttext&pid=S0100-85872014000 200232&nrm=iso.

Teixeira Monteiro, Duglas. 2011 [1974]. *Os Errantes do Novo Século: um Estudo sobre o Surto Milenarista do Contestado.* Sao Paulo: Edusp.

Telles, Edward. 2004. *Race in Another America: The Significance of Skin Color in Brazil.* Princeton, NJ: Princeton University Press.

Telles, Edward (ed.). 2014. *Pigmentocracies: Ethnicity, Race and Color in Latin America.* Durham, NC: University of North Carolina Press.

Tello Díaz, Carlos. 1995. *La Rebelión de las Cañadas.* Mexico, DF: León y Cal Editores.

Theije, Marjo de. 1998. 'Charismatic renewal and base communities: the religious participation of women in a Brazilian parish', in B. Boudewijnse, A. Droogers and F. Kamsteeg (eds), *More Than Opium: An Anthropological Approach to Latin American and Caribbean Pentecostal Praxis.* Lanham, MD: The Scarecrow Press, pp. 225–48.

Uribe Cortez, Jaime and Martínez Velasco, Germán. 2012. 'Cambio religioso, expulsiones indígenas y conformación de organizaciones evangélicas en Los Altos de Chiapas'. *Política y cultura* 38 (Mexico): 141–61. http://www.scielo.org.mx/ scielo.php?script=sci_arttext&pid=S0188-77422012000200008&nrm=iso.

Valentin, Thierry. 2001. 'L'Amazonie métisse: narrations et définitions des figures de soi et d'autrui au sein de villages ruraux du Nord du Brésil – État du Pará'. Université de Lyon 2/Universidade Federal do Ceará.

Van Cott, Donna Lee. 2000. *The Friendly Liquidation of the Past: The Politics of Diversity in Latin America.* Pittsburgh, PA: University of Pittsburgh Press.

van Wyck, Ilana. 2008. *A Church of Strangers: The Case of the Universal Church of the Kingdom of God in South Africa.* New York: Cambridge University Press.

REFERENCES

Varga, István van Deursen. 2019. 'A cabeça branca da hidra, e seus pântanos: subsídios para novas pesquisas sobre comunidades indígenas, quilombolas e camponesas na Amazônia maranhense'. *Revista de História (São Paulo)* 178. https://dx.doi.org/http://dx.doi.org/10.11606/issn.2316-9141.rh.2019.138543.

Vázquez León, Luis. 2003. *El Leviatán Arqueológico: antropología de una tradición científica en México*. Mexico: CIESAS.

Vázquez León, Luis. 2010. 'El multiculturalismo como arma jurídica: el uso del concepto "pueblo originario" en los conflictos agrario-territoriales en Michoacán', in Luis Vázquez León (ed.), *Multitud y distopía: ensayos sobre la nueva condición étnica de Michoacán*. Mexico, DF: UNAM; Colección La Pluralidad de México.

Vázquez León, Luis. 2016. 'Multiculturalism as a juridical weapon: the use and abuse of the concept of "pueblo originario" in agrarian conflicts in Michoacán, Mexico', in David Lehmann (ed.), *The Crisis of Mulculturalism in Latin America*. New York: Palgrave Macmillan.

Venugopal, Rajesh. 2015. 'Neoliberalism as concept'. *Economy and Society* 44(2): 165–87.

Vieira, Marco. 2019. 'The decolonial subject and the problem of non-western authenticity'. *Postcolonial Studies* 22(2): 150–67. https://dx.doi.org/10.1080/13688790.2019.1608795.

Vilaça, Aparecida. 2002. '"Missions et conversions chez les Wari": entre protestantisme et catholicisme'. *L'Homme* 164: 57–79. www.jstor.org/stable/25133614.

Vinhas de Queiroz, Mauricio. 1981. *Messianismo e conflito social: a guerra sertaneja do Contestado: 1912–1916*. São Paulo: Atica.

Vital da Cunha, Christina. 2015. *Oração de Traficante: uma etnografia*. Rio de Janeiro: Garamond.

Vital da Cunha, Christina, Lopes, Paulo Victor Leite and Lui, Janayna. 2017. *Religião e Política: medos sociais, extremismo religioso e as eleições 2014*. Rio de Janeiro: Fundação Heinrich Böll, Instituto de Estudos da Religião.

Wachtel, Nathan. 1971. *La vision des vaincus: les Indiens du Pérou devant la conquête espagnole, 1530–1570*. Bibliothèque des histoires. Paris: Gallimard.

Wachtel, Nathan. 1977. *The Vision of the Vanquished: The Spanish Conquest of Peru through Indian Eyes, 1530–1570*. Brighton: Harvester Press.

Wachtel, Nathan. 2014. *Des archives aux terrains: essais d'anthropologie historique*. Paris: EHESS/Gallimard/Seuil.

Walsh, Catherine. 2009. 'Interculturalidad crítica y pedagogía de-colonial: in-surgir, re-existir y re-vivir'. *Revista "Entre palabras"* 3 (Facultad de Humanidades y Ciencias de la Educación, Universidad Mayor de San Andrés): 129–56.

Walsh, Catherine. 2012. 'The politics of naming: (inter)cultural studies in de-colonial code'. *Cultural Studies* 26(1): 108–25. https://dx.doi.org/10.1080/09502386.2012.642598.

Walsh, Peter and Lehmann, David. 2021. 'Academic celebrity'. *International Journal of Politics, Culture, and Society* 34: 21–46. https://dx.doi.org/https://doi.org/10.1007/s10767-019-09340-9.

Warman, Arturo, Nolasco, Margarita, Bonfil, Guidlermo, Olivera, Mercedes and Valencia, Enrique. 1970. *De eso que llaman la antropología mexicana*. Mexico, DF: Nuestro Tiempo.

Warren, Austin and Wellek, René. 1949. *Theory of Literature*. New York: Harcourt, Brace. https://doi.org/10.1080/19306962.1949.11786442.

REFERENCES

Wolford, Wendy. 2016a. 'The *casa* and the *causa*: institutional histories and cultural politics in Brazilian land reform'. *Latin American Research Review* 51(4): 24–42.

Wolford, Wendy. 2016b. 'State–society dynamics in contemporary Brazilian land reform'. *Latin American Perspectives* 43(2): 77–95.

Womack, John (ed.). 1999. *Rebellion in Chiapas: An Historical Reader*. New York: New Press.

Zamorano Villarreal, Gabriela. 2020. 'Indigeneity, race, and the media from the perspective of the 2019 political crisis in Bolivia'. *Journal of Latin American Cultural Studies* 29(1): 151–74. https://dx.doi.org/10.1080/13569325.2020.1 785406.

Zavaleta Mercado, René. 1986. *Lo Nacional-Popular en Bolivia*. Mexico, DF: Siglo XXI.

Žižek, Slavoj. 1997. 'Multiculturalism, or, the cultural logic of multinational capitalism'. *New Left Review* 225: 28–51.

Index

Abercrombie, Thomas 130–7
academia
  politics of, in Latin America and
    United States 4–5
affirmative action in Brazil 11, 22
  extends into new fields 68
  and racial classification 113–15,
    179–80
anthropology
  of indigenous society 72–6
  as Mexico's official indigenism
    and multiculturalism 73–4,
    95–6
  Mexican anthropologists adopt
    anti-capitalist and feminist stance
    95
  activist 78
authenticity 10, 91, 130
  absent from Fanon 32
  in Canclini 128–30, 150
  in Dussel 49
  in Heidegger and Levinas 41
  in the Oruro carnival 131
  in the recognition of indigenous
    practices 71
  in Said 24
  in Sartre 30
autonomous feminism, 53–5
  criticism of NGOs and bourgeois
    feminism 53

theoretical turn 55
  see also Segato, Rita

Bolivia 109–10, 130–50
  burguesía criolla 10
  cocaleros 45, 141
  convulsions in 2000–5 141
  democracy of the grass roots 143
  irridentist indigenism 146
  1952 Revolution 62, 132, 137–9
  Oruro carnival 130–7
  see also gender; legal pluralism;
    MAS; Morales, Evo; Rivera
    Cusicanqui, Silvia
Bonfil Batalla, Guillermo 74–6
Brazil
  Pentecostalism and neo-
    Pentecostalism 15
  see also affirmative action
    in Brazil; *caboclos*; racial
    classification

caboclos
  a population in search of a
    classification 112–13
Chiapas Diocese
  role in developing Zapatista
    organization 80–3
Chile 115
  see also Mapuche people

223

INDEX

cholas, cholos
  issues of definition 136, 187 n.2
  and social mobility 174
  as socio-racial category 61, 132–4
clientelism
  encouraged by multicultural policies 21
cocaleros (coca growers) *see* Bolivia
colonialism
  see internal colonialism
coloniality
  defined 42
  and modernity 36
  see also Mignolo, Walter; de Sousa Santos, Boaventura; Radcliffe, Sarah
Crenshaw, Kimberle 21, 41, 64–5, 174, 181–2
CRIC (Consejo Regional Indígena del Valle del Cauca, Colombia) 11, 92–3, 105–9
cultural relativism
  ethnic differences unreliable as explanations of trust in science 69, 86–8

de Sousa Santos, Boaventura
  accepts necessity of a western outlook 39
  concept of the 'abyss' 7, 36–7, 174–5
  concept of human rights 39–40
  and the philosophy of science 37
  critic of 'Eurocentric' theory 45
  see also epistemicide
decolonialism, Latin American variant of 44–5
  academicism and political quietism 1, 176
  challenge to science 5
  denigration of western culture 24
  denunciation of Descartes 7, 48
  deprecates universalist values 173
  grand theory 45
  and indigenous belief systems 9–10

interpretation of Levinas 48–52
  main bases for critique of 6
  and Marxism 5
  and modernity 5
  risk of co-optation by governments 78
  on science and folk wisdom 9
  weaknesses in thought of its three leading figures 7
  see also cultural relativism; popular religion; postcolonial hierarchies
Descartes, René
  decolonial interpretation 48
Dietz, Gunther
  non-essentialist approach to *interculturalidad* 91
Dussel, Enrique
  biography 6
  denounces ontology and classic philosophy 49
  erudition 6
  on Levinas and Heidegger 49

epistemicide 37
epistemology
  distinguished from culture 20, 37, 39, 86–90
  see also cultural relativism; science
ethnicity
  its predominance in scholarship 1
  see also race and ethnicity
evangelical churches 13–15
  and the 'abyss' 7
  as challenge to the decolonial 14
  and gender 14
extractive industries
  prior consent by communities affected by mining 109–10

Fanon, Frantz
  the abolition of racial categories 29
  on an 'African culture' 29
  on the Algerian family 34
  and the Black Man's inner self 31–2

224

INDEX

cultural sensitivity 28, 34
as innovative psychiatrist 28
misinterpreted by decolonials 33–4
personality 26–7
pleads for all people to be freed of colour 32
style compared to the decolonials
universalism 6
white and black imprisoned by their situation 32
Second World War experience 26
see also Sartre, Jean-Paul
feminism
in Argentina 185
the Bartolinas of Bolivia 145
black feminism as aesthetic 67
fourth wave 184
in indigenous and Afro-descendant leadership 180–2
in Mexican anthropology 8
see also autonomous feminism; gender; indigenous movements; Segato, Rita

García Canclini, Nestor 127–30
calls for end to division between high art and popular art 127
hybridity defined 127–9
Tijuana as simulacrum 128
gender
in Andean kinship 60–1
and Bolivia's *burguesía criolla* 149
chachawarmi as intermediate Andean category 58
gender parity in Bolivian elections and Bolivian Plurinational Assembly 145, 177
intersection with race in education 65
in Pentecostalism 156–7, 163
women leaders in social movements 65–6, 145, 177, 181, 185
see autonomous feminism; feminism; Segato, Rita; Zapatistas

Gonzalez Casanova, Pablo 73, 194 n.5
Guatemala
human rights 17
see also evangelical churches

Heidegger, Martin 48
Hernandez Castillo, Aida 58, 59, 96, 119
human rights 100–2

identity politics
meaning 3–4
official indigenism 78–9
India
women and the law 100–1
indigenous culture
as constructed by the state 95, 127–8
indigenous identity
reshaped by Morales 140–1
indigenous knowledge 69–71
indigenous law
compatibility with universal rights 3
see also MAS; *usos y costumbres*
indigenous medicine
misunderstood by the decolonial 71
not a matter of knowledge 71
not only for indigenous people 69
see also Mapuche people
indigenous movements 12
and knowledge of climate change 70–1
and other social movements 13
women's protagonism in 8, 12
see also CRIC; Zapatistas
intercultural education 37
in the CRIC 92
as seedbed of community leaders 91
serving as a claim to citizenship 91
its several purposes 84–5
in Zapatista communities 92
intercultural universities 22, 85, 91–2
interculturalidad 84–5
Canclini's interpretation 129

225

INDEX

consciousness-raising role 92–4
definitions 85
as 'intimate estrangement' 23
see also intersectionality
internal colonialism 8, 73–6
intersectionality 3, 20–1, 63–71, 174
'from below' 67
of gender and race 65–6
of gender, race and citizenship 66
illustrated by Fanon 68
in *interculturalidad* 93

judicialization
of race and ethnicity 11–12, 179

land restitution
in Brazil 112–13, 178
in Chile 115–17
Latin American Studies, field of
its polarization 7
legal pluralism 99
in Colombia 105–9
Merry, Sally Engle on 99
in Mexico 103–4
relevance of procedural norms 102
unsuccessful implementation in
Bolivia 102–3
vernacularization and *métissage* 99
see also universalism
Levinas, Emmanuel 46–52
interpreted by decolonials 6, 47–51
liberation theology
in Chiapas 81

Macedo, Edir, leader of the Universal
Church of the Kingdom of God
156–8
anoints Bolsonaro 158
media interests 157
Maldonado-Torres, Nelson
critic of Descartes, Heidegger 48
makes use of Levinas 49
Mapuche people 12, 79
emblems of national struggle for
greater democracy 117

land restitution 116
Mapuche medicine and shamans
69, 71, 136–7
MAS (Movimiento al Socialismo –
Bolivia) 141–50
contemptuous attitudes to lowland
Indians 146–7
plurinational constitution 144
see also Bolivia; Morales, Evo
mestizaje 21
and the 1952 Bolivian Revolution
138–9
Rivera Cusicanqui on the *mestizo*
condition 59–60
in culture *see* García Canclini,
Nestor
Mexico 73–84
official indigenism 73–4
pluricultural amendment to
Constitution 94
repression and co-optation 73–5
San Andrés accords 94
see also anthropology; Zapatistas
Mignolo, Walter
coloniality 36
deprecates freedom 172
'quasi-racial' notion of intellectual
legitimacy 38–9
substitutes sarcasm and innuendo
for argument 172
see also epistemicide
Morales, Evo 137–44, 179
abuses of power and his populism
147–50
and coca growers' demands 10
development strategy 13
pan-ethnic indigenism 10, 13,
146
political skills 13, 140–4
promotion of women 145
regime compared to 1952
revolution 62
MST (Movimento dos Trabalhadores
Rurais sem Terra – Brazil) 45
multiculturalism 78–9, 180

226

INDEX

and bureaucracy 79
neo-liberal 77, 93–4, 139

neo-liberalism
origins and loss of precise meaning
172

Orientalism 22–6
foreshadows multiculturalism 23
see also Said, Edward

Pachamama
an all-purpose indigenist emblem
133
Pentecostalism and neo-Pentecostalism
152–61
and the 'abyss' 169
and Amazonian Indians 164–5
boycott of village fiestas 166
in Brazil's 2018 election 162
and drugs traffickers 168
and Ecuadorian highland Indians
165–6
electoral strategies 158–9
and entrepreneurship 165–6
and gender 183
and Guatemalan Indians 165
main features 152–5
neo-Pentecostalism breaks the rules
of decorum 162
Pentecostal members of Brazilian
Congress 158
in, or as, prisons 167, 169
and social hierarchy 163
and spirit possession 164
voting influenced by moral 'wedge'
issues 159–60, 162
see also gender; Guatemala; popular
culture; Universal Church of the
Kingdom of God (IURD)
phenomenology
appeal to decolonials 48
Poma de Ayala, Guaman
mistakenly described as early
advocate of delinking 38

popular art
should not be consigned to the
category of crafts 128
popular culture
dialectic of the erudite and the
popular 125–7, 163, 173
dissident character of 126–7
the dissolution of the dialectic by
Pentecostalism 164
rescued from museum and market
129
see also popular religion
popular religion 9, 121–5
absence from decolonial theory 121
in the Andes 123–4
in Brazil 123, 161
as product of colonial and
indigenous, elite and popular
influences 122
postcolonial hierarchies
defined 22

Quijano, Aníbal 22, 38
intellectual trajectory 35

race and ethnicity
ambiguities in Latin American race
relations 24
Bolivia's changing racial and socio-
economic hierarchy 148–9
contrasting remedies against racism
177–8
limitations of in explaining
inequality 20–1
limitations of in explaining trust in
and distrust of modern science
70–1, 86–8
see also affirmative action in Brazil;
mestizaje; racial classification;
social movements
racial classification
in Brazil, 16, 111–15
involvement of the state 113–14
by self-assignment 11–12
verification committees 115

INDEX

racial classification (*cont.*)
  see also affirmative action; Chile
Radcliffe, Sarah 42–4
  criticizes discourse of indigeneity 43
  defines coloniality 42
Rappaport, Joanne 92–3, 106–9, 181
Rivera Cusicanqui, Silvia 8, 58–63, 137–8
  attacks Morales 148
  on Bolivia's modernity 62
  a decolonized utopia 60
  interpretations of the *mestizo* 59–60
  polemics against decolonial 'gurus' 41
  summarizes Andean kinship history 60–1
  see also mestizaje
Ruiz, Monseñor Samuel *see* Chiapas Diocese

Said, Edward 19, 22–6
  aversion to authenticity and essentialism 24–5
  dislike of 'third-worldism' and its binary oppositions 24
  on Fanon 29
  as politician 41
  and postmodernism 24–5
  sources of Orientalism 22
Sartre, Jean-Paul
  influence on Fanon 30–1
  on the Jewish question 30–1
science 86–8
  and folk knowledge 86
Segato, Rita 182
  'El Violador Eres Tú' 61
  on women in precolonial society 56

social mobility
  and gender and race in Bolivian history 61, 174
social movements
  in decolonial theory and changing social base 45
  expanding scope of black activism in Brazil 67–8
Spivak, Gayatri
  criticizes discourses of victimization 43

Universal Church of the Kingdom of God (IURD) 155–8
  and Africa-originating *cultos* 164
  in politics 158–9
  social service 156
  its women's movements 156–7
  see also Macedo, Edir
universalism 2–3, 176–80
  in feminist anthropology 8
  Martha Nussbaum's defence 101
  Onora O'Neill's defence 102
usos y costumbres 11–12
  in Colombia 105, 107
  institutionalization in municipal government in Mexico 103–4
  tension with rational-legal procedures 119

Zapatistas 11
  feminism and women's rights 8, 84, 181
  ideological shifts 77
  and local democracy 84
  origins 13, 79–84
  universalism 13, 84
  women's rights and democratic procedure vs. indigenous tradition 98